Net 600

W9-CSD-150

VON STROHEIM

VON STROHEIM

Thomas Quinn Curtiss

NEW YORK

FARRAR, STRAUS AND GIROUX

COPYRIGHT © 1971 BY THOMAS QUINN CURTISS
All rights reserved
Library of Congress catalog card number: 78-143300
SBN 374.2.8520.9
Published simultaneously in Canada by Doubleday Canada Ltd.
Toronto
First printing, 1971
Printed in the United States of America

Contents

CONTENTS

Illustrations

BLIND HUSBANDS

THE DEVIL'S PASSKEY

FOOLISH WIVES

THE MERRY WIDOW

THE WEDDING MARCH

x

MISCELLANEOUS

Foreword *by René Clair*

OF THE FRENCH ACADEMY

W E are gathered here* to render homage to the memory of a man whose work is major, and whose life is symbolic.

To measure fully the importance of this work, it is necessary to go back into history and put oneself in the period when it first appeared. It is among the most authentic work of our profession. The passage of time may have lessened its shock; the physical changes all around us may have disfigured it; the films that it influenced and the imitations it inspired have tended to blur its originality. But this work of Erich von Stroheim, even though mutilated by others, shines with a power and newness that a quarter of a century cannot diminish.

---

* René Clair's address was delivered at a retrospective showing of von Stroheim films at the Venice Film Festival in 1958.

A quarter of a century! That is the time that has passed since the pitiless Hollywood system crushed an artist who, with Chaplin, is the greatest of those who have left their unique mark on the screen.

It is in the light of this fact that the life of Erich von Stroheim is symbolic, because man's fight against the machine is never-ending. The career of this artist lasted only twelve years. Later he was only allowed to be a performer and, however good an actor he was, we cannot help thinking of the work, which we will never see, that he might have created and directed himself. His early films had an enormous success; their author reigned, like the *seigneur* he was, in an industry that resented his rule. But the game he played was dangerous. In order to go on, he had to follow every success with an even greater success. The slightest faltering meant failure, and revenge at the hands of mediocrity.

The day on which a young man at Universal, whose name was Irving Thalberg, took it on himself to stop the filming of *Merry-Go-Round*, and assign it to a director of his own choice, marked the start of a new era. The age of the great pioneers, who brought the American cinema to flower, became that of half-anonymous producers, businessmen, bankers. They created, in Hollywood, an organization so perfect that it could thenceforth shield itself against the slightest intrusion of genius.

Genius! In talking of films, what meaning can we give this word so devalued by hypocrisy and confused standards? An artist of genius is one who creates without imitating, and who draws out of the depths of his own being the least predictable part of his work. How many in the history of the cinema fit this definition? Whatever their number, Erich von Stroheim is at their head. He owed nothing to anyone. Yet it is to this man, who died in poverty, that every one of us is in debt.

Introduction

F AME has been defined by Rainer Maria Rilke as the sum
 total of the misconceptions gathered about a name.

Since Erich von Stroheim's death in 1957, there have been
speculations about various aspects of his personality and
career, including his origins. One published account gives his
birthplace as Brooklyn. Another claims that he was the son of
a Jewish father, who was born in Prussia and engaged in the
hat trade in Vienna. (An alleged Austrian birth certificate
containing such information has been published. It remains
inexplicable, however, that this should have escaped the
scrutiny of the Nazis, whose attacks on von Stroheim are
recounted elsewhere in this book; and it is also acknowledged
that the Nazis were capable of forging such documents.) If
von Stroheim was the son of Jewish parents and affixed a

"von" to his name—as de Balzac and other artists added
a "de" to theirs—I consider both details minor ones that do
not contradict his own story of his youth. Jewish birth, though
at that time it set up certain social barriers, did not exclude
subjects from either army commissions or titles in the empire
of Franz-Josef. As for those who insist that von Stroheim
had no military background, how do they account for a great
deal of his early career, including his superb horsemanship?
Then too they have to explain the existence of his youthful
photographs, including one as a cadet, reproduced in this
book. I can also attest from personal knowledge to the fact
that von Stroheim was a practicing Catholic most of his life.

Another legend about von Stroheim that has gained cred-
ence since his death is that he was a mythomaniac. The theory
goes this way: von Stroheim, ostracized in Austria, found
consolation by re-creating on the screen the world from which
he had been excluded, and played a role not only in motion
pictures but in real life—for almost half a century. All this
may add a piquant and Pirandello-like quality to his biography, but those who hold to this theory can have had little
first-hand knowledge of the character of the man.

I was privileged to be his close friend for many years, and
his utter honesty about himself and everything else was constant, one of his most striking traits. During our long friendship he often recounted the incidents of his life. He was a
splendid raconteur, and though he might polish up or expand
some anecdote in retelling it, I can recall no instance of his
altering it basically or of contradicting himself, as certainly
a mythomaniac would. There is a consistency to his own story
that I find entirely convincing.

Apropos of his consistency, I remember a revealing incident.
One June day in 1954 my old friend, Clarence Brown, arrived
in Paris and asked me to lunch with Louis B. Mayer, with

whom he was traveling. Mayer, knowing that I was an intimate of von Stroheim, launched into an account of the days when Metro and Goldwyn became Metro-Goldwyn-Mayer. He spoke about his troubles with that gifted Anglo-Irish director, Rex Ingram, of the tantrums of temperamental Mae Murray, and of his clash with von Stroheim over the release of *Greed*, which had just been completed before Mayer was placed in charge of the studio. Mayer became increasingly excited as he talked and, rising from the table in the Plaza-Athénée garden, he acted out the scene of striking von Stroheim in a fit of uncontrolled fury.

That evening I happened to be dining with von Stroheim and he asked me to repeat what Mayer had said about their famous row. I did so and he listened intently, nodding his head in agreement. When I finished, he sat back. "That's entirely accurate," he said and then he retold the scene himself, as it appears on page 179.

A remark that Mayer also made about von Stroheim that day is so characteristic that it might be termed a "Mayerism." It expressed all the admiration and resentment he harbored for his old enemy. "Von Stroheim," he said, "was the greatest director in the world. That's a fact, and no one who knows pictures would dispute it. But he was impossible, a crazy artist. If he had only been ten percent less himself and ten percent more reasonable, we would still be making pictures together." It is probable that some may succeed in pretending to be ten percent less themselves—this was doubtlessly the practice of the movie "yes-men"—but it was never possible for von Stroheim. He was always one hundred percent himself, come what might.

My interest in von Stroheim and his work began when I first saw his films and was fascinated by them. That was in my boyhood, back in the twenties. There were always long waits for the next von Stroheim film. One read about the mounting costs of the film-in-progress, the threats of the censors to scissor out reportedly daring and erotic scenes. Von Stroheim's interminable disputes with his producers were almost daily in the theatrical news. Even that great organ of the American home, *National Geographic*, published an illustrated article about an Alpine village that von Stroheim had built in the Sierras for the mountain scenes of the second half of *The Wedding March* (later to be released, in Europe only, as *The Honeymoon*). But despite such overwhelming publicity, no von Stroheim film proved disappointing. He inevitably announced, prior to release, that the new film was not in the form he had intended. Yet each film was unusual, intensely personal, the indisputable work of a fine and conscientious artist.

Whenever I encountered any of his associates or people who knew him well—which was frequently, when I became a theatrical journalist—I would question them. By the time I first interviewed him, in New York in 1940, he was amazed at my knowledge of so many aspects of his life. I had studied in Vienna at one time, and there, too, I had heard gossip about him. The Viennese did not conceal their resentment over the sardonic nostalgia with which he viewed his native city in his films.

At the time of our first meeting, von Stroheim was anxious to try the stage. He had left Paris for Hollywood, just before France fell to the Nazis, to appear in *I Was an Adventuress*. He had made a second film in California, *So Ends Our Night*, and had hoped to play the German officer in *Escape*, a bestselling novel about German refugees that was about to be filmed. Conrad Veidt was given the role instead, and now von Stroheim was in New York, unable to return to France, looking into the possibilities of acting in the theater.

We liked each other at once and took to dining together, attending first-nights, and making the rounds of the fashionable bars where the theatrical elite gathered. Fortunately, I was able to be of some service in the matter of his stage ambitions. One night in "21" he told me that he had just read that an actor was being sought to play the Boris Karloff role in the touring company of *Arsenic and Old Lace*, which had just opened on Broadway and was a smash hit. Did I know anyone who might arrange an interview with the play's producers? Both its producers—Howard Lindsay and Russel Crouse—happened to be friends of mine, and as Lindsay was playing Father Day in *Life with Father* at the Empire, I telephoned the theater immediately, and he came to the phone. Lindsay was enthusiastic about the suggestion of von Stroheim for the part and the next day they met and signed a contract. The moment this news was published, von Stroheim received many other offers. Franz Werfel wanted him for the colonel in his play, *Jacobowsky and the Colonel*, and Lillian Hellman proposed that he play the "good" German in her new play, *Watch on the Rhine*. The arrangement with Lindsay and Crouse, however, promised long-range financial security, calling for von Stroheim to tour for a season and then to replace Karloff in the New York production; and the salary was a handsome one.

During these last months of 1940 I made a happy discovery. Pat Powers, who maintained offices in New York, had a print of *The Wedding March* that had been invisible since 1928. Von Stroheim and I called on Powers, who was delighted by this surprise visit and with genial humor recalled the stormy days when the film was being made. When Powers granted me permission to show *The Wedding March* privately, I invited many celebrities of the literary, theater, and film worlds, in the hope that it might bring von Stroheim another directorial assignment. The guests included Thomas Mann and his family; Franz

Werfel and his wife, Alma, widow of Gustav Mahler; Max Reinhardt, Erwin Piscator, Rudolf Kommer, and Berr-Hofmann. There were also Karen Michaelis, the Danish novelist, a favorite writer of von Stroheim; Ernest Boyd, Ferenc Molnár, Lili Darvas, and Raiumund von Hofmannsthal, son of the Austrian poet. Among the American guests were Muriel Draper, Gifford Cochran, Howard Dietz, Clare Boothe Luce, and Albert Lewin. Hans Eisler, the composer, volunteered to play an accompanying score, but the records of the sound track—synchronized music and dialogue were not on the film itself in early sound films—were discovered in Powers's office. Everyone was amazed at the originality and style of *The Wedding March*, but this special performance did not, alas, lead—as we had hoped—to the financing of another von Stroheim film. When Powers died many years later, I purchased the *Wedding March* print from the estate and gave it to von Stroheim as a birthday present. At the Cinémathèque Française, he supervised the placing of the sound-track records on the film.

In February 1941 von Stroheim embarked on the tour of *Arsenic and Old Lace* and I, enlisted as a member of the National Guard, was mobilized for active service. Von Stroheim would wire me (at the Georgia camp where I was then stationed) the news of the play's reception in various cities across the land. He wrote that he enjoyed acting in the theater: it required only a few hours' work each evening—though each evening he suffered stage fright before the performance—and allowed him the day and the night for his writing. He had begun a play about Paris under a German air raid, but the course of the war quickly made this situation obsolete. We had a reunion in 1942, when I was stationed temporarily at Governors Island before going overseas, and he came to Broadway to replace Karloff in *Arsenic and Old Lace*. It was then that Billy

Wilder wired him, offering him the role of Rommel in *Five Graves to Cairo*, and he was off to Hollywood.

We were in New York again in 1945, just after I had been demobilized, and he was en route to France. He passed through Manhattan again in 1949 on his way to Hollywood for *Sunset Boulevard*. On his return journey to France, he saw New York for the last time. He had hated the city in the days of his early struggles, having lived there in poverty when he first came to the United States, and later having had an unhappy and insecure period working there as John Emerson's assistant during World War I. He seldom visited New York during the twenties, but now late in life he enjoyed its bustle and glitter. I remember his enthusiasm for *South Pacific*, and an amusing cocktail session with George Jean Nathan at "21."

In the spring of 1950 he invited me to come and spend the summer with him in France. I had lived and studied in Europe before the war, but from my observations in the army there during the war, I felt that the world I knew had been destroyed and I was reluctant to go back. However, I did want to see von Stroheim and I finally decided to go over on a six-week holiday. Denise Vernac and he were at the boat train to meet me, and we drove directly out to Mlle Vernac's charming château at Maurepas, where he lived. I spent several weeks there and it became my country residence after I had settled in Paris, for I was unexpectedly offered the post of drama and film critic of the Paris *Herald Tribune* and have stayed on ever since. From then until his death in 1957, I was constantly in his company, seeing him almost daily—or rather nightly—for he would motor into town to attend theater and film openings and to supper in the cabarets. I was at Maurepas every weekend my schedule allowed, and we often undertook travels together in vacation time.

I made it a habit to keep records of our conversations from

our first meeting, for the table talk of von Stroheim was always brilliant. Often I would draw on my notes for articles about him. In 1952 he began talking about writing his autobiography and discussed the project with me. He envisioned it as a four-volume work, and he would relate what it would contain, going over again and again the experiences he wanted to include. He talked so well that I suggested that he make recordings, for the labor of writing quickly tired him. The difficult summer he had spent finishing his two-volume novel, *Fires of St. Jean,* had weakened him; he also believed it had caused a decline in his health. Unfortunately, he had not adopted the recording idea and now, anxious for a publisher's advance on his autobiography, he sat down to start it. He only succeeded in jotting down in rough draft some experiences of his early life, which he intended to rewrite later in full detail as he often described them.

These notes were submitted to the representatives of several American publishers, whom he asked me to see. None could be found who would sign a contract for the book with only his jottings as outline, so he became discouraged with the idea and abandoned it. Instead he wrote a novel, *Poto-Poto,* drawn from one of his unrealized scenarios.

During the last months of his life, he was confined to his bed. As I sat beside him, he sometimes said that when he recovered —*if* he recovered—he must set about writing his autobiography. A week or two before his death, he brought up the subject again. "But I'm too tired, so tired," he said wearily. Then, mustering his energy, he spoke in a firm voice and delivered this command: "*You* tell them who I was."

That is why I have written this book.

PART ONE

1

Vienna

Eighty years ago the Austro-Hungarian Empire ruled over thirty-five million subjects and, with the Imperial Royal Army as its guardian, the Habsburg domain extended from Trieste to Lemberg, from Prague to Budapest, and from Lake Garda to the Carpathians. Vienna, the capital, was enjoying a newfound prosperity. Its ancient walls, outmoded as a military defense, were demolished at last and the dreamy rococo city, in which an eighteenth-century grace lingered, was drawn into the modern world by a sudden building boom. The political slogan of the day was "Peace and Progress."

The Ringstrasse was the central feature of the wide-flung reconstruction. Its horseshoe design encircled the heart of Vienna, where the Gothic cathedral, St. Stefan's, had stood as a symbol of the capital's invincibility since the thirteenth century. Within the Ringstrasse were the Hofburg, the Imperial residence with its gardens and renowned Spanish riding school; and the Kapuzinerkirche, in whose crypt the Habsburg dead slept in stony austerity. There were also the fashionable shopping areas—the Kärntnerstrasse, the Kohlmarkt, and the Graben, sprinkled with smart restaurants and coffeehouses. The Ringstrasse, beginning and ending on the Danube Canal, encompassed a new town hall, the Rathaus, a pseudo-medieval pile; a new opera house; and a rebuilt state theater, the Burgtheater. Luxurious hotels and the palaces of the aristocracy and parvenu millionaires dotted its sections.

Vienna's boulevards were patterned after the plan of Haussmann and suggested, in the late seventies and early eighties, that the city had inherited the frivolity and opulence of Second Empire Paris. Indeed it had, and it was to suffer a similar debacle. But in the last decades of the nineteenth century and until the fatal August of 1914, it seemed utterly impossible that such a fate awaited this new Babylon. Here, as the popular air of the period proclaimed, was the city of golden dreams. Voluptuous music and dazzling uniforms set its characteristic tone. Exquisitely dressed ladies and gentlemen danced and flirted to the waltzes of Lanner and Strauss. Even the humble had a share in the carnival, sporting themselves in the Prater's Luna Park, or making excursions to the Vienna Woods.

It was in this Vienna that Erich von Stroheim was born on September 22, 1885. He asserted that his full name was Erich Oswald Hans Carl Stroheim von Nordenwald and that his father was Frederick von Nordenwald, then serving as a major in the sixth regiment of Dragoons. His mother, née Johanna Bondy, whose brother was an Imperial Counsellor, was of Czech origin; though subject to melancholia and hypochondria, she was of strong constitution and survived into her eighties (she died in Vienna in 1941).

A second son, Bruno, was born in 1887. The two little boys were close companions during their childhood. Like small boys everywhere and particularly those in Franz-Josef's Austria, they appointed themselves commanding generals of opposing forces and plotted to conquer each other's armies of tin soldiers. They had mastered the details of the innumerable uniforms, grades, and rituals of the Imperial Army years before they graduated into long trousers.

When Erich was twelve, he was dispatched to a preparatory boarding school for cadets. Though lonely, and missing the company of his brother, he had no regrets about being parted from his parents. Life at home was oppressively overcast as he grew up. Erich's father retired from active service in the nineties to try his luck at moneymaking. He quickly squandered his wife's fortune in disastrous business speculations, which she never forgave him or ceased to remind him of. Erich's mother was always on the verge of hysterics, and his father, in self-defense, feigned cold indifference to her weeping fits and bitter recriminations. The chilly superiority he maintained in the face of his wife's outbursts was extended to his relations with his sons.

After the first open quarrels, the father adopted a policy of frozen silence, refusing to reply to his wife's abuse or to speak to her at all except when visitors were present or when some household emergency forced him to do so. At the family table, a strained hush prevailed. After the meal, the husband would hastily leave the apartment to take his coffee at his club or in some café. His sons were aware that their father, in escaping from the resentment displayed at home, was now consoling himself with other women.

The perpetual battle between his parents did not daunt the

natural high spirits of the elder son, though it may have over-shadowed them at times and helped to form his belief that the marital state was usually unhappy. There were compensations for and escapes from the family gloom. Erich as a boy delighted in the sight of Vienna of the nineties with its sartorial elegance, its beautiful avenues and spacious parks—where military bands gave concerts on holidays—and the picturesque public ceremonies of the Imperial city. On Maundy Thursday the Emperor and the Empress observed an elaborate ritual of feeding twelve old beggars and washing their feet as a token of Christian humility. Each Corpus Christi Day saw a spectacle that Erich was never to forget and that he later re-created in his film *The Wedding March*. Aristocrats on horseback led the procession to the cathedral, followed by a long retinue of carriages. The vehicles of the archducal couples were drawn by milk-white Lippizaners from the Imperial stables. Escorted by cavalrymen, the Emperor appeared in the uniform of a field marshal, rolling by in the golden Habsburg coronation coach. In the wake of hundreds of priests and candle-bearing monks came Vienna's old cardinal, Prince Dr. Grusha, holding the Host aloft. All down the Kärntnerstrasse the crowds sank to their knees and the men uncovered at the sight of the Eucharist.

At cadet school Erich emerged as a bright student, if not one of model behavior, and a promising army career was predicted for him. Physically robust, he won honors for horsemanship and fencing and excelled as a crack shot. Extremely precocious, he was initiated into the mysteries of sex by a buxom chambermaid before he left home. He remembered that his amorous instincts were first aroused even earlier, as a child, when his brother's wet-nurse accidentally touched his genitals.

Unlike most youths of his class, he was a voracious reader. At cadet school he developed a system of absorbing the contents of a book in a few hours of concentration. At the Mariahilfe

Academy, from which he graduated as a second lieutenant in 1902, he devoured novels and the literary reviews, while his classmates idled over cards or fluttered the leaves of naughty magazines like *La Vie Parisienne*. At this time a new group of Austrian authors was gaining recognition. The avant-garde literary movement—known as "Young Vienna"—included Hermann Bahr, Arthur Schnitzler, Hugo von Hofmannsthal, and Peter Altenberg. Altenberg's impressionistic *feuilletons* left their mark on von Stroheim, and he imitated their rapid evocation of moods in writing the subtitles for his films.

The theater was another of Erich's passions and he retained many memories of the Viennese stage. In those years the Vienna-born Max Reinhardt, who had established himself as the most venturesome director in Berlin, brought his company to his native city. His naturalistic staging of Gorki's *The Lower Depths* was a revelation, and realism seemed to have reached its limits when he had an automobile driven onstage and then run out of gas in his production of Shaw's *Man and Superman*. In addition to staging the classics—Shakespeare, Schiller, Goethe, and Goldoni—Reinhardt introduced to the German-speaking public many new German and Austrian playwrights who were creating a revolution in drama: Wedekind, Schnitzler, von Hofmannsthal, Max Dreyer, and the Swedish giant, Strindberg. Among the renowned performers Erich saw during these years were Eleonora Duse, who visited Vienna in 1900 to play before the Austrian court at the Burgtheater, and Yvette Guilbert, who appeared for an engagement at the Ronacher music hall.

There was also Meyer-Förster's *Old Heidelberg*, a wistful tale of the prince who must sacrifice his student romance with a waitress when he is called to reign. This sentimental comedy of the fast-fleeting charms of life's springtime—the days of wine and roses—caused even cynics to shed a few tears. Erich loved this play, and its theme is the basic leitmotiv of more than one of his films. In later years Erich remembered another theatrical event he witnessed at the Burgtheater on the evening that the star, Josef Kainz, played Goethe's *Götz von Berlichingen* before the Emperor. At one point in this classic drama the royal warrior hero utters a line known to every German-speaking schoolboy, but one usually omitted at command performances. The saucy line is: "Tell him he may lick my behind!" Kainz, about to utter the insult, bowed low to the Emperor in his box and said: "Begging your Majesty's permission—tell him he may lick my behind!"

After receiving his commission as second lieutenant at the Mariahilfe Academy, Erich spent most of his time—save when on maneuvers or on vacation leave—in Vienna from 1902 to 1909. The family was dealt a shocking blow shortly after Erich's graduation. While on a hunting expedition in Innichen in the Tyrol, his brother Bruno accidently shot his camping companion. In an unsuccessful attempt to save the life of the wounded boy, Frederick spent nearly every penny he had. Specialists and surgeons were sent from Vienna in this endeavor, but all in vain. When the boy died, Bruno was faced with a manslaughter charge, and a battery of high-priced lawyers was engaged in his defense. He was found innocent—thus escaping a prison term of a year—and was granted full pardon by the Emperor on Christmas Eve. Not only this expensive tragedy but the serious heart condition that Bruno subsequently developed became a further financial drain, and the family was in difficulties. They were now dependent on their rich relatives—especially on the wife's brother, Emil Bondy, the Imperial Counsellor. Such money as they were advanced was always accompanied by much advice. The futures of Erich and Bruno were now controlled not by their parents but by their affluent uncles and aunts.

In that period, the code that governed the army officer was not only strict but expensive. An officer was forbidden to carry even the smallest package in the street. He was not allowed to use the plebeian omnibus or even to drive in a one-horse *droschke*—only in a *fiaker*. He had to buy box seats or at least orchestra seats when attending a theater and could not sit farther back than the tenth row. He was compelled to frequent only the most expensive cafés and restaurants and to wear white gloves even off-duty. The image of the superman in uniform had to be maintained at all costs.

Hot-blooded young Erich, always the outward figure of military elegance, was given to additional extravagances. He insisted on having a private carriage and his own coachman. His boon companion was a fellow cavalry lieutenant, the son of an opera ballerina who had married a colonel and after his death opened an exclusive dancing school. There were drinking bouts, visits to Madame Rosa's brothel, gambling parties, and amorous intrigues—the faithless Mizzi whom the two young blades taught a cruel lesson; the lovely hospital nurse with forget-me-not eyes; the charming Irish governess of the children of the German ambassador; and a selection of the lights-o'-love of Vienna. It was impossible to live in this spendthrift fashion on Erich's small allowance and he soon was hopelessly in debt and borrowing money left and right. One summer when his parents were away, he obtained the keys to their apartment from the concierge and pawned not only the living-room piano but the Persian rug. He had intended, with an expected birthday gift from one of his aunts, to restore the piano and rug before his parents' return. But his mother cut her vacation short, and there was a lamentable family scene.

On another occasion, financially pressed, Erich came to a Sunday luncheon at his parents' home. In hopes of inducing sympathy, he sucked blood from his gums and feigned a coughing fit during the meal. When his mother saw blood on his napkin, she was certain he had contracted tuberculosis and ordered him to bed. His father arranged for the payment of his son's urgent debts and obtained a lung specialist. The doctor diagnosed the case as an incurable one, and Erich's silverware was tied with tiny red bands so that it could be washed separately to spare the other members of the family from possible contagion. The doctor, tricked by Erich's recital of his imaginary symptoms, was surprised at his patient's miraculous recovery.

On October 5, 1908, the Emperor Franz-Josef proclaimed the annexation of Bosnia and Herzegovina to the Dual Monarchy. Due to this highhanded action, there arose an imminent danger of war with Serbia and Montenegro, with perhaps Russia and Italy as their protecting allies. Turkey, the country most concerned, was too weak at the time to remonstrate. The Chief of General Staff, Field Marshal Baron Konrad von Hötzendorf, had foreseen such an eventuality and had long urged strong reinforcement in Bosnia and Herzegovina. On March 15, 1909, an order for the "preconceived and essential reinforcements and movement of troops" was issued—a diplomatic term for partial mobilization. Mobilized army corps were sent to various possible "fronts," and the Second Army Corps (Vienna), consisting of the 4th, the 25th, and the 47th Infantry Divisions and one cavalry division composed of Hussars, Dragoons, and Uhlans— to which von Stroheim's regiment belonged—were put on a war footing and dispatched to the river Save, which forms the natural border of Bosnia.

Erich remained three months in the field, his regiment being deployed along the north bank of the Save, opposite the point where the Bosnia River enters it between Brod and Županje with Samac as the center. Once he came under machine-gun fire from the Serbian irregulars who harassed the enemy whenever the opportunity arose. This occurred when the young lieutenant was leading a patrol of twelve along the riverbank in columns of twos with two machine guns and ammunition mules. He thought the patrol was hidden from sight of the other shore by the high foliage, but their bright-red riding trousers gave them away. There was a burst of machine-gun fire and he ordered his men to dismount and, using every cover possible, to open fire. Needing at least two riders to hold eleven horses, he had a fire force of only eight carbines at his disposal as two men were dismounting the machine gun from the bucking mule. They sprayed the opposite shore and silenced the insurgents' guns. A corporal, one of the advance guard, came staggering back, leading his horse with a badly wounded comrade in its saddle. One horse had received the full blast of bullets and, mortally wounded, had to be given the *coup de grâce*. It was miraculous that, exposed to a stream of fire, the patrol had but one casualty and one horse dead. When Erich proudly reported the encounter at headquarters, he was severely reprimanded for having risked a possible border incident. However, that evening in the mess tent over a few drinks, the commanding officer confessed that he would have acted exactly as the lieutenant had.

That night—as he was to be off-duty the following day— the elated lieutenant bribed an ambulance driver to take him and two fellow officers to a nearby gypsy encampment to listen to the tzigane fiddles and to indulge in a bit of gypsy love. The first excursion was repeated almost nightly, and these summer evenings amid the gypsy caravans along the shores of the Save were later drawn upon by Erich for his novel, *Paprika*. A gypsy crone read the lieutenant's palm one evening by the light of the campfire. She predicted that he would soon leave Austria, cross the ocean, and find great fame in a foreign land. The lieutenant was puzzled by this strange prophecy. Why should he ever leave his homeland? What could he ever do that would make him world renowned?

On his return to Vienna, the specter of financial ruin loomed more imposingly than ever. He was determined to wipe out his old debts and to restrict his pleasure to his means. He advertised in the newspapers for a professional moneylender who would lend a lieutenant on active duty 5,000 crowns on a simple promissory note. In response he received a dozen letters with all sorts of propositions, only one of which seemed worth investigating. He made an appointment by telephone to meet a certain Herr Pollock at the Café Wormser in the Leopoldstadt, the second district of Vienna and a ghetto without walls.

The proposition of Herr Pollock was odd and complicated, and a shrewder man than Erich would have been on his guard. The lieutenant would receive the desired 5,000 crowns if he would sign a paper certifying that he had purchased twenty-five high-grade coffins! At the end of ninety days he would repay the loan at four-percent interest, and the cargo of coffins would become the property of a merchant named in the contract. The lieutenant signed the questionable document, snapped up the bank notes, gave a condescending salute, and fled to his carriage.

Next day the "reformed" lieutenant scurried about Vienna, paying off outstanding debts. When he returned to his barracks in the evening, he found a message to come in all urgency to his parents' home. Arriving at their apartment, he let himself in with his own key and stepped into the entrance hall, noticing that a light shone in the salon. Before he had time to take off his overcoat, his mother appeared in her night robe.

"What has happened?" he asked anxiously.

"Father will tell you," she replied.

He found his father, dressed in a black velvet lounging jacket, sitting dejectedly in a rocking chair by the fireside. He seemed to have aged suddenly and his face was haggard and drawn as though he had suffered a terrible shock. The paper he held was the "coffin" contract.

"Is that your signature?" he demanded, handing over the paper.

Erich froze as he took the document and examined it. "Yes, it is."

Before he could say another word, his father slapped his face with such force that his cap, which he had neglected to take off in the excitement of his arrival, went spinning across the room.

Erich now realized what must have happened. After he had signed the promissory note, the moneylender had predated it and was demanding immediate payment.

"How did you get this paper?" he inquired.

"Two men brought it here at eight o'clock this evening," his mother began to explain. "They said they couldn't find you, so they came to your father. In case of non-payment they threatened to present this bill to your colonel in the morning. I didn't have that much money here or anywhere, so I begged Uncle Emil to settle it and avoid a disgrace," his mother continued. "He sent the money over and everything is paid, but . . ."

"But what?" asked the son, his hands trembling.

"Uncle Emil helped only on the express condition that you leave the service at once and go to America," concluded the mother, sobbing.

The family decision had been made and Erich had no choice

in the matter. Next morning he tendered his resignation. To be impelled to abandon his army career was a shattering blow. He was suited and trained only for the soldier's life. What could an ex-officer do in civilian life? After a week of meditation he decided to accept his uncle's suggestion as the only way out. In America, if he had to start at the bottom of the social ladder— as a janitor or as a longshoreman—at least there would be no one to sneer at his fall.

His uncle paid for his second-class passage on the North German Lloyd liner *Prince Friedrich Wilhelm*, sailing from Bremen to New York on November 14, 1909. This officious relative also outfitted his wayward nephew with a wardrobe of hand-me-downs, presented him with a hundred marks in cash, and deposited a hundred dollars with the steamship company in New York on which his nephew might draw ten dollars a week.

Greatly depressed, the ex-lieutenant spent his last night in Vienna carousing at Madame Rosa's. Arriving in Bremen on the eve of his departure, he dissipated another night in waterfront cabarets. On a foggy, drizzly November morn the *Friedrich Wilhelm* slowly made for the open sea. Von Stroheim (as he had decided to call himself in his new existence) stood on the deck watching the port disappearing even as his youthful dream had faded away. For the twenty-four-year-old Austrian, this was the end of the beginning.

Erich's mother, née Johanna Bondy

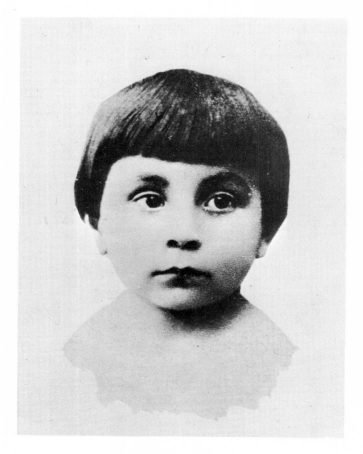

Erich's first photograph

Erich (left) and his younger brother, Bruno. Photo taken in 1896 at Hahn's studio, Vienna

Erich as a cadet at the Mariahilfe Academy

Emil Bondy, an Imperial Counsellor and Erich's uncle

2

New York and San Francisco

ERICH shared his cabin with a German baker who had emigrated to the United States some years before. Returning from a vacation in his native land, this unwanted companion, common and loudmouthed, explained the American way of life to the exiled Austrian and nursed him through attacks of homesickness, seasickness, and toothaches on the rough winter voyage. Though Erich sought to escape being seen with him in the dining hall and on the promenade deck, the young man knew he had found a good-natured and generous friend. When they reached New York, the baker invited him to share his room over a Brooklyn bakery. Having nowhere to stay, Erich accepted the kind offer.

It was the Christmas season and he at once secured a temporary job in New York, wrapping packages at the Simpson-

Crawford Department Store on Fifth Avenue, but an argument with a pompous floorwalker led to his dismissal. His discharge pay, however, enabled him to go it alone as his pride demanded. He moved from the bakery loft to a Brooklyn rooming house. He tried his talents as an "entertainer" in a second-class rathskeller before a German-speaking audience. Imitating the music-hall performers he had seen, he did some impersonations of theatrical stars. This proved a dismal failure, and he had to pay for his own supper, which left him without carfare.

One night, with only a two-cent stamp in his pocket, he was held up on the Bowery. When he tried to call for help in German, his attackers, being German, relented and, instead of stripping him of his fur-lined overcoat, invited him to join them for drinks at a low bar. He escaped their company and began the long trek home on foot. Crossing Brooklyn Bridge, he stumbled over the body of a woman. Alarmed, he hurried to the Fulton Street side at a run that attracted the attention of two policemen. They questioned him and in halting English he sought to explain. He was made to retrace his steps, but the fallen woman proved to be only dead drunk and he was given a free ride home in the patrol wagon.

At this time he wrote some short stories for the New York *Staats-Zeitung*, the German daily, and for the weekly magazine, *Austria*, whose editor, Dr. Karl Weiss, befriended him and invited him to the Austrian Ball. He donned his old uniform for the occasion and caused something of a sensation when he rode to the gala event on the subway.

The movies in the nickelodeons—"5 reels for 5 cents"—caught his interest. An announcement of the showing of new movies on a variety program drew him one evening to a vaudeville theater where Thurston, the magician, was starred. When he called for someone in the audience to be hypnotized, the ex-lieutenant volunteered. He proved such a comic "stooge" that Thurston proposed that he join his company. This offer was politely rejected.

Observing the mistreatment of a fallen horse on Fifth Avenue, von Stroheim intervened and before a gaping crowd made the horse rise. An army officer, Captain MacLean, happened to be among the bystanders and introduced himself. He was a member of Squadron "C" of the New York Cavalry and he invited Erich to enlist.

MacLean, learning the young man's background, promised him the rank of sergeant as a start, but von Stroheim's still faltering English prevented such an appointment. He enlisted, however, as a private for a two-year stretch and took out his first American citizenship papers. He soon discovered that, in the United States, peacetime soldiers were looked down upon. He, too, found them a poor lot and avoided their company preferring to improve his English by reading in the armory library.

When he had completed his service in the U.S. forces, his Uncle Emil wrote from Vienna, sending him a letter of recommendation to Max Grab, an ex-Austrian officer who had founded a fashion house in New York. Von Stroheim was put in charge of the traveling-salesman department and mapped out salesman tours and kept accounts of their sales. He now took a room in the house of an elderly, motherly Irish lady, Mrs. Jones, on 126th Street. Mrs. Jones had a daughter, May, who was beginning to show promise as a fashion designer. She was a pretty girl, too, and in the evenings he escorted her to Pabst-Harlem, a pre-Prohibition beer emporium where one could dance to the strains of a café orchestra. Its organist, Sigmund Romberg, was a young man from Vienna and the two Austrians were soon friends. Romberg was later to achieve

NEW YORK AND SAN FRANCISCO

renown as a composer, writing such operettas as *The Blue Paradise, Blossom Time,* and *The Student Prince.* (Ten years later Romberg also composed a special musical score to accompany von Stroheim's *Foolish Wives.*)

In due course, von Stroheim was appointed one of Max Grab's traveling salesmen, and was sent to San Francisco on his first assignment. He arrived there on New Year's Eve, 1912.

San Francisco, with which von Stroheim at once fell in love, was to be one of three cities that would play an important part in his artistic career, the other two being the Vienna of his youth and the Paris of his later years. Six years after the great earthquake and fire, San Francisco was celebrating its resurrection. Crowds danced in Market Street and from the Ferry Building on the Bay to the heights of Twin Peaks. The notorious Barbary Coast crib joints with their dollar Chinese girls were wide-open again, and the city's quaint Chinatown quarter with its bobbing paper lanterns flourished anew. One hardly ever saw paper money, everything being paid for in silver or gold coin.

Von Stroheim found his work distasteful. There was something silly and effeminate in representing a dress concern and being forced to discuss in ingratiating tones the styles of women's apparel. But his customers, mostly women, liked him. They were amused by his accent, and his manners struck them as "different" and "Continental." He had not made the slightest effort to become "a hundred percent American" in appearance. His bearing was stiffly military and he clicked his heels on being introduced. He continued to wear white gloves and twirled his cane as though it were a swagger stick. He kept his hair closely cropped, his neck shaved.

Trouble was brewing for him as he made the rounds of the

San Francisco dressmaking establishments. The man who had replaced him as head of the out-of-town department did not send him his salary and commissions regularly. He was also mailing cards to the Grab clients, falsely informing them that von Stroheim was no longer with the firm and that no payments should be made to him. By chance, von Stroheim came on one of these cards when calling on an Oakland customer who happened to be in conference with an old lady, a professional psychic. This helpful old woman advised him to inform the postal inspector and engage an attorney. The Grab company was profuse in apologies and even augmented the salary of its maligned representative in hopes of avoiding a libel action. But the attorney had neglected to put a time-stipulation into the conciliatory agreement, and a week later von Stroheim was discharged.

He then took such employment as he could find. For a time he worked as a fly-paper salesman, and though San Francisco is not fly-pestered, he managed by his convincing sales talk to eke out a living. He also worked as a telephone-company repairman and as a clerk in a travel agency, preparing tours for the projected San Francisco Exposition of 1914, which never took place.

Weary of peddling and office drudgery, he craved fresh air and the open spaces. An old Austrian acquaintance, Captain Masjon, owned a hotel—The West Point Inn—in the mountains across the Bay. Von Stroheim had spent several weekends at this resort and now decided to ask its proprietor for work. Packing his meager belongings, he quit his back-street rooming house and boarded the ferry for Sausalito.

He arrived in Mill Valley too late to catch the last train up the mountain and climbed the "thousand steps" trail along the railroad tracks. As he paused on his hike, he gazed at the panorama of San Francisco stretched out before him in the summer moonlight: the graceful bay, the Golden Gate opening to the Pacific, Oakland twinkling in the distance, the sinister prison island Alcatraz, and the faraway glow of the city lights brightening the sky.

Captain Masjon took him on as a general handy-man. He could pay him no salary, but von Stroheim would have free room and board and free wine and cigarettes and he might mingle with the guests. He was to feed the pigs and chickens, chop wood, and perform other such chores. At this time there was only one resident guest, but she was an interesting one. Her name was Margaret Knox and she was the daughter of a New England family that had come West and owned much property in Oakland. She was rich, independent, and intelligent. She was a practicing physician and a militant suffragette. "A bit emancipated," confided the captain, "but strikingly handsome." In any case, as the new Chinese boy had not arrived, would Erich serve her supper?

Erich had never served anyone supper, but he agreed. He took a plate of boiling soup into the dining room where this unusual young woman sat at table. Struck by her beauty, he fumbled in setting the plate before her and spilled the hot soup in her lap. She jumped up in anger and pain, cursed him, and rushed to her room. When she returned, she excused herself for losing her temper and he apologized for his shortcomings as a waiter.

They began to talk, and after Erich had served the rest of the meal without mishap, they took a long stroll along the mountain ridge to see the sun set over the Golden Gate. He told her his story and she told him hers. She had been engaged to a U.S. Navy lieutenant commander, but their engagement had been dissolved when President Theodore Roosevelt ordered the fleet to sail on a tour of the world. She had suffered a nervous breakdown and her mother had sent her on a trip to China and Japan. This had happened only a few years previously and she had recovered, though the emotional crisis had left her with weakened lungs and the threat of tuberculosis. Erich tried to laugh this away, relating how an eminent Viennese specialist had been taken in by his pretense of consumption and given him only a few months to live.

This encounter was a case of love at first sight. Miss Knox suggested that they become engaged, and that Erich give up his hotel job and come to stay with her at her bungalow halfway up the mountain from Mill Valley. Later she would break the news of their forthcoming marriage to her family. The suggestion was irresistible and they moved next day. It was Margaret Knox, von Stroheim believed, who gave him his basic American education. She made him read aloud to her and corrected his pronunciation. She introduced him to such books as Edgar Lee Masters's *Spoon River Anthology* and Stephen Crane's *The Red Badge of Courage*. She reawakened his interest in music and the drama. She encouraged him to write and bolstered his faith in himself, which had flickered low in the face of so many reverses. She also taught him one of the drinking habits of her country, how to down whiskey "neat."

In her bungalow he wrote—with her aid—his first film script, a sort of forerunner of the scenarios of *The Wedding March* and *Merry-Go-Round*. It was submitted by mail to G. M. (Broncho Billy) Anderson, the Western star, who headed the Essanay studios in Los Angeles. It must have caused the studio some merriment, for at that time they mainly produced "horse operas." Of course, it was immediately rejected. But a dramatic sketch upon which the engaged couple collaborated, *The Black Mask*, was purchased by Holbrook Blinn, who acted in it on the stage, in a program of one-act "horror" plays. And a von Stroheim short story was bought by the editor of *Smart Set* and was published that year.

This inactive existence in the hills, though pleasant and fruitful as far as his "American education" was concerned, made this young man, burning with undefined but spurring ambitions, restless. Other men of his age—he was twenty-eight—had already begun their careers. Life was passing him by, he felt. Out in the great world there must be a place for him. He obviously could not live on his literary efforts (he had received a check for only twenty-five dollars for his story in the *Smart Set*), and he was anxious to prove to his fiancée that he could earn his own living. He wrote to a man whom he had met once or twice in New York, a munitions dealer who supplied arms to the Latin American republics. Could he not find a former Austrian officer at least a lieutenancy in the Argentine or Mexican Army?

Next he called at the main office of the Southern Pacific Railroad in Oakland. Sending in his Austrian visiting card he requested an interview with a vice president. The interview was granted and his case heard. He evidently made an impression on the vice president with his show of spirit and his willingness to start at the bottom. Within three days he received a notice to report for a medical examination. The railroad's doctor found him hale and hearty and he was soon an assistant section foreman, the boss of a gang of Mexican laborers. As an officer he had learned to demolish train rails, but he was ignorant of the construction of a railroad line. He decided to learn the job and lent his hands and shoulders to the lifting of the steel spans and the heavy ties.

Miss Knox was delighted to be the future wife of a railroad worker and thought the time was ripe for Erich to be presented to her mother, also a lady physician, and her sister. He was invited to spend a Sunday at the Knox home in Oakland. Though the elder Dr. Knox was a formidable woman, ultra-conventional and hidebound, the initial impression he made on her was favorable. Dressed in his best clothes and with his heel-clicking and hand-kissing, he was accepted by Dr. Knox as a European gentleman. He was a good conversationalist and his breeding was obviously impeccable. When he succeeded in making this staid matron laugh, he knew he had won her daughter's hand. The mother informed him that henceforth he would always be welcome in her house. However, a few nights later, after a day on the railroad line, when he unthinkingly showed up in his overalls while she was entertaining some of her snobbish neighbors, he felt the chill of her disapproval.

Margaret Knox and von Stroheim were married at the Knox residence in Oakland some weeks later by a minister of the First Unitarian Church. Their honeymoon was spent in the Mill Valley bungalow. Shortly afterward, thanks to the recommendation of the New York munitions dealer, the bridegroom received a sealed and beribboned document in the mail. He had been appointed a captain in the Mexican Army by President Madero.

The prospect of continuing his military career elated him. After all, to attain a captaincy at twenty-nine was not so bad. So it was off with the overalls and on with the uniform. He would have to learn Spanish, of course, and the geography and history of Mexico; but he was a quick student. The newlyweds hurried to San Francisco, Margaret to search the bookshops for Spanish dictionaries and grammars and Erich to conduct research on Mexican uniforms in the public library before consulting his tailor.

Von Stroheim arranged passage to Mexatlano, this time traveling first-class. From there he intended to travel by rail to the capital and report for duty. On the very day his ship docked, the news came that President Madero had been assassinated. The country was in a turmoil and the telephone lines to Mexico City were down. The American consul, predicting that the new regime would not honor appointments made by the late president, advised von Stroheim to leave at once by the same ship that had brought him.

Back in San Francisco, von Stroheim was reluctant to return from braided uniform to humble overalls. He brooded about the Mill Valley bungalow and worried about what to do next.

One afternoon, as he sat in the local barbershop, a real-estate agent who also acted as notary public in the district came in and occupied the next chair. After commiserating with him about Madero's assassination, his neighbor inquired what he was doing at the moment.

"Looking for a job," Erich replied.

"I think I have just the thing," the man said. He went on to explain that the caretaker of the Muir Woods forest, the property of Congressman Kent, was too old to fulfill all his functions as supervisor of the territory. The Congressman had written from Washington that he wanted to find some young man who could be trusted to take over the duties of riding the range, guarding against fires, overseeing the cutting down of trees and the reforestation, and being on the lookout for poachers. The pay was not much—fifty dollars a month—but the saddle horse and its feed were free and it was an opportunity to learn forestry, with perhaps a chance to enter the U.S. Forest Service as an inspector later on. Would von Stroheim consider it?

After a few minutes' reflection, he agreed. Before taking up his duties as forest warden, he was sworn in as deputy sheriff. This transaction, recalling a scene in a Bret Harte story of the Old West, amused him. He solemnly took the oath and was presented with a sheriff's badge, a revolver, and a carbine and permitted to buy his own horse. He was pleased to be "mounted" again. There was actually very little to do, except marking dead trees with an ax and informing the woodmen to clear the footpaths of branches and fallen trees, checking the

forest telephones, and arresting poachers. He quickly made
friends with the forest workers, who staged his dramatization
of his short story *Brothers* at a Woodmen of the World benefit performance.

But his mother-in-law, when she learned that he was now a
forest warden, was greatly displeased. She insisted through her
daughter that he find a situation more in harmony with her
social standing. Why should he, a gentleman, endlessly take
menial employment? As a result, he resigned his post as a ranger
and took a job as secretary in the Sacramento Steamship Company in San Francisco and he and his wife moved into the Knox
mansion in Oakland.

The steamship company's president, a smooth-spoken swin-
dler, proposed that von Stroheim become a member of the firm.
For the small sum of $5,000 he could become part owner of
the *Santa Anita*, a lumber-carrying vessel, and participate in its
high profits. The young man repeated this tempting offer to his
mother-in-law and she, eager that he snatch up this opportunity
to rise in the business world, sat down at once and wrote out a
check for this amount.

On receipt of the check, the steamship company president
raised his secretary's salary, an action that seemed suspicious. A
week later, as the firm's new partner entered his employer's
office, he found him excitedly talking over the telephone. The
good ship *Santa Anita* had gone to the bottom of the Pacific, he
explained, and with it the secretary's investment. Dr. Knox
never forgave her son-in-law, probably believing that he had
simply stolen her money with a trumped-up tale. Her distrust
and scorn made it impossible for him to go on living in her
home.

The proprietors of the Zinkend Café in San Francisco offered
him a post as lifeguard in a hotel they managed on Lake Tahoe.
Erich accepted, though he was only a moderately good swim-

mer. At Lake Tahoe he discovered that, in addition to serving as lifeguard, he could make a few extra dollars by rowing the hotel guests about on the lake and accompanying them as a guide on fishing expeditions.

It was now the fatal summer of 1914, and on July 27 the news flashed that Austria had declared war on Serbia. Von Stroheim, still an Austrian citizen and a lieutenant in the reserves, wired the Austrian Consul General that he was prepared to return to Austria when and if called but that he was without sufficient funds to pay for his passage. He telephoned his wife at her mother's home. Dr. Knox answered the long-distance call: "Margaret isn't here. She is ill and she has started divorce proceedings against you based on non-support, desertion, and mental cruelty!" Before he could utter a word, she hung up.

The guests on the piazza of the Lake Tahoe hotel all had definite if differing opinions about the outbreak of war in Europe. One summer visitor, Mrs. Bissinger, delighted in taunting the Austrian lifeguard. Serbia, she told him teasingly, would soon wipe Austria off the map. Von Stroheim, his national pride wounded, flew into a rage. After his violent show of temper, his tormentor calmed him by saying she had only been joking. They became friends and he gave her some of his writings to read. The wife of a California millionaire, she offered to finance the production of his playlet *Brothers* on the vaudeville circuit in the autumn. Somewhat to his surprise, she later proved as good as her word.

When the summer season at Lake Tahoe ended, Bill Bergman who ran the hotel's riding stable and had observed the smart riding of the ex-cavalry lieutenant, proposed that von Stroheim take his twenty-four horses to his riding school in Pasadena. Once there, he could have the position of riding master and escort some of the wealthy and beautiful ladies on their daily bridle-path trots and canters. This alluring project changed rapidly into a nightmare. Von Stroheim and the twenty-four horses in his charge were tightly boxed into a freight car for the train transportation to Los Angeles. One blue-ribbon stallion became "water-foundered" and died during the journey, and there was great trouble in removing the cadaver. At the Bergman stables in Pasadena, instead of daily outings on the bridle paths with lovely ladies, von Stroheim was assigned to cleaning the stalls, taking care of saddles, and exercising the mounts. In lieu of a salary, he was given a meal ticket to the corner café and allotted a cot in the riding academy. This treatment inevitably led to a quarrel with Bergman, who was only too glad to be rid of his stable hand without having to pay him at all.

Left now with only a few dollars in his pocket, von Stroheim telegraphed Mrs. Bissinger, reminding her of her promise to finance his one-act play. He had grave doubts that he would receive a reply, but to his amazement he found a money order for five hundred dollars awaiting him when he called at the post office next day. His first expenditures were on a new shirt, a flashy polka-dot necktie, and a visit to the public baths after having spent a night on a park bench. He then purchased a huge box of chocolates and a dozen red roses to present to the girl, a non-actress, who would play the only feminine role in his dramatic sketch. She lived in Culver City and her brother, a real-estate agent, was full of advice. He recommended that von Stroheim place a want ad for actors in the *Los Angeles Examiner*. The next morning there was a mob scene in front of the Leonide Hotel on Main and Fifth Street. A police squad had to be summoned to maintain order.

From the milling army of Indians, Mexicans, and white derelicts, von Stroheim selected the only two intelligent men among the crowd of would-be actors—an ex-Marine captain, Benny Lewis, and an ex-automobile mechanic, John Hull. Both explained that they were motion-picture players, engaged as extras at the moment in *The Birth of a Nation*, which D. W. Griffith had begun shooting in Hollywood that summer.

Rehearsals of the play were held in von Stroheim's hotel room, but as it proved rather cramped, it was decided to hire the Lyceum Theater on Spring Street—by the week instead of by the hour—which caused a dent in the production funds. Carl Walker, the manager of the Pantages Theater, promised a tryout before Alexander Pantages, who controlled a wide circuit of vaudeville houses. But Pantages was away and the cast was threatening to desert. Walker, realizing the urgency, booked the sketch for a small theater, the Alhambra, but neglected to inform his clients that they would be performing on "amateur night." The rowdy youths in the audience soon made *Brothers* inaudible, and pelted its actors with vegetables and eggs. Von Stroheim was hit by two tomatoes before the curtain mercifully descended. In anger and despair, he ran from the theater back to his hotel without bidding his company goodbye. The five hundred dollars was now gone, and the following morning he began looking for employment along Main Street. On the street, he ran into Captain Lewis. They discussed the fiasco at the Alhambra, and the captain suggested that, instead of seeking a lowly job, von Stroheim come with him to the Griffith studios. They jumped aboard a streetcar, Hollywood-bound.

3

D. W. Griffith

Eᴿɪᴄʜ's first glimpse of the budding movieland was anything but glamorous. Hollywood at that time was only a
suburb of Los Angeles, a district of empty lots, overgown
with tall weeds, in some of which cows grazed. Amid these
desolate spaces drugstores, gas stations, and open markets were
cropping up out of proportion to the surrounding wilderness.
At a corner where the streetcar line ended was a children's
hospital, and beside it stood a series of large, weather-beaten
barns with a spacious, fenced-in yard. Over the entrance hung
a large sign, ʀᴇʟɪᴀɴᴄᴇ-ᴍᴀᴊᴇꜱᴛɪᴄ ꜱᴛᴜᴅɪᴏꜱ.

Von Stroheim, ever superstitious, made certain to enter the
wired enclosure with his right foot first. He was at last in the
antechamber of the movies, the "cattle yard," where a cross-
section of humanity milled about. There were down-and-

outers in rags; sprucely turned-out actors "at liberty," with boutonnieres in their lapels; Negroes from blackest ebony to lightest *café-au-lait*; Indians of the Sioux and Wabash tribes, in shabby but modern clothes, smoking cigarettes in long holders (this startled the Austrian newcomer, whose concepts of the noble red man had been formed by reading Fenimore Cooper.) Cowboys, authentic ones from Texas and Arizona, with tight blue jeans over their high-heeled boots, mingled with their effeminate "drugstore" imitators, who were also equipped with rattling spurs. There were former members of the Tsar's lifeguard, former bit players in stock companies that had been stranded, and vaudevillians from the lesser circuits. There was even a music-hall headliner, Toto, the famous clown of the New York Hippodrome. The women were equally diverse. There was a bearded lady from a traveling circus, a "stage" mother with her offspring, prostitutes who betrayed their profession by their vulgarity, and pretty maidens chaperoned by their grandmothers. All hoped for the big break—film stardom—or at least a day's work.

As a black Mercedes limousine drew up to the gate, a tall, middle-aged man stepped out and entered the yard. He walked with slow, measured step and his appearance and manner bespoke authority. He was elegantly dressed except for a white silk shirt with wide black stripes and a panama hat of gigantic dimensions which shaded his heavily lined but noble features.

"There's Griffith," some shouted, and the waiting crowd turned to greet him.

Looking at Griffith's face and trying to guess his profession, one might have thought him to be a Shakespearean tragedian of renown. In a white toga and with a laurel wreath about his forehead, he could have posed as a Roman emperor.

This first glimpse of the master was a fleeting one. Griffith, determined to avoid delay, reciprocated all greetings with a cool "Good day!" and, courteously raising his panama to the ladies, passed on to his office.

Now the stars of the Griffith company began to arrive, to be cheerfully welcomed by the hopeful extras as they passed through the cattle yard. Lillian and Dorothy Gish, then still in their teens, accompanied by their mother; Blanche Sweet, Mae Marsh, Norma and Constance Talmadge; handsome Wallace Reid; dark-haired Bobby Harron, and courtly Henry Walthall, who had the lead role in *The Birth of a Nation*, all arrived.

A short while later, George Siegman and Bert Sutch, Griffith's assistants, dressed in khaki breeches and puttees, came out to select types from the assembled mob. Siegman, a tall, bulky man with the face of a German butcher, looked about officiously and then pointed to various people in the crowd. "You, you . . . and you," he ordered, and the winners stepped aside while Sutch inscribed their names on a list and gave them pink slips.

Captain Lewis, taking von Stroheim by the elbow, introduced him to Siegman. "This is Erich von Stroheim, who served as a lieutenant in the Austrian Army and as a trooper in the U.S. Cavalry. Perhaps you have something for him. He needs a job, and so incidentally do I," said Lewis.

"Sorry, nothing," replied Siegman gruffly, while his second, Sutch, a shortened shadow of his master, deliberately turned his back.

This initial rebuff did not discourage Erich. His first peek at moviemaking had fascinated him and he was determined to find a place for himself in this novel theatrical medium. For several weeks he walked the eight-mile stretch from his Main Street hotel to the Reliance-Majestic Studios on Sunset Boulevard, to spend the day in vain waiting in the cattle yard. At nightfall he tramped home again. He was unable to move to quarters nearer the studio, as his rent was unpaid.

During the day, some of the directors who worked under Griffith's supervision on other films passed by with their assistants and some of their principal actors. Captain Lewis and Jack Hull told him their names: Christy Cabanne, with his tiny waxed mustache and a charming smile for everyone; Tod Browning, later to become the Edgar Allan Poe of the screen; Raoul Walsh, Jack Conway, and George Nichols. Nichols, a burly man in his fifties, had come from the New York stage. He had a whimsical expression and carried a pint flask of bourbon whiskey in his hip pocket. A generous, expansive fellow, he would urge his acquaintances to take a nip from his flask.

Captain Lewis introduced him to von Stroheim and thereafter he would greet the new arrival with a loud and hearty, "Hello, Von!" The middle-aged actor-director and the young foreigner became friends. He was to give von Stroheim his first "acting" role and many years later appeared prominently in his protégé's films—as the abused doorkeeper of the cabaret who assassinated the crown prince in *The Merry Widow* and as the corn-plaster king in *The Wedding March*.

The camaraderie of the cattle yard eased the burden of the young man's long wait to break into the movies. His lack of money had made him forswear a midday meal, but other would-be extras often shared their sandwiches and crackers with him.

One morning Siegman picked him along with a batch of extras to go before Griffith, who observed the group critically.

"That fellow with the pretty hairdo"—von Stroheim's hair was clipped short, in Austrian Army fashion. "You are to make up black and put on a Confederate uniform. You will climb up on that roof." Griffith pointed at the roof of a Southern mansion about eighteen feet high. "You fire your rifle and at the sound of the whistle you realize you are hit! Your hands fly to your breast. You turn around a little . . . like this." Griffith acted out the scene. "Then you let yourself fall to the ground."

Von Stroheim glanced uncertainly at the height of the roof.

"Don't worry," Griffith reassured him. "Mr. Siegman will have some mattresses put where you are to fall. Then you lie still until you hear the whistle again."

Von Stroheim, standing at attention, repeated the orders in military style and then, executing a smart about-face, hurried off to prepare. The makeup man blackened his face and hands and equipped him with a wool wig to cover his shaven head. He quickly donned the Confederate uniform and peaked cap that Sutch threw him and rushed to the set to climb a ladder to his perch. The realistic fall was filmed and then refilmed twice. It pleased Griffith, but it left von Stroheim with an aching back.

Next day he was ordered into uniform again—this time as a Union soldier, also black. Billy Bitzer, Griffith's chief camera-man, congratulated the novice on his resounding fall and joked about his "falling into the movies." As they talked, Griffith strolled over to explain the next scene.

It was to be a hand-to-hand bayonet fight between a North-ern Negro soldier and a Confederate private. By now Griffith had heard of von Stroheim's army service, and he intended to pair him with a British Army veteran. Von Stroheim was audacious enough to make a suggestion to the master: both participants were ex-soldiers, so why not have the encounter fought with real bayonets to give the thrill of authenticity? This advice was taken. The dangerous duel was acted before the cameras, with von Stroheim injecting a grisly battlefield touch by wiping his supposedly bloodstained bayonet on the uniform of his fallen enemy after pretending to run him through. At the end Griffith boomed out enthusiastically, "Very good, Von."

Unfortunately, this scene is not preserved in existing prints of *The Birth of a Nation*, though they contain the fall from the roof, the first appearance of von Stroheim on the screen.

Griffith's praise made the young man's head reel. He looked about to find that many members of Griffith's stock company had gathered to watch the scene, including the Gish girls, Blanche Sweet, and Wallace Reid. But his moment of glory was immediately darkened when he went to collect his wages from Siegman, who, among his other duties, acted as paymaster.

Siegman, who is remembered for his portrayals of villains in Griffith productions (he was the half-breed carpetbagger who attempted to violate the heroine in *The Birth of a Nation*, and the brutal Prussian commander in *Hearts of the World*), had taken an intense dislike to von Stroheim, in whom he sensed a rival. When von Stroheim asked for his pay checks, he snapped, "Don't bother me now."

Von Stroheim saw that Griffith was spending the lunch hour on the set reading in a camp chair. He went over to him and explained his predicament, as Siegman watched furtively.

"Siegman, make out the checks for Von at once," ordered Griffith, and the bully responded with a meek "Yes, sir!" Siegman quickly wrote out the pay slips, but as he handed them to von Stroheim, he hissed out of the corner of his mouth, "These are the last ones you'll get at this studio. You're through here!"

But von Stroheim's fortitude was to prove stronger than Siegman's malice. He had made up his mind to enter the motion pictures and he would hold fast to his resolution. As he waited daily in the cattle yard, he began to work out a story for the screen. It had an Alpine setting, and he called it *The*

Pinnacle. It was to serve as the scenario for his first directorial effort, *Blind Husbands*.

Another "stunt" assignment was not long in coming. One morning he was recruited by Emmet Flynn, the assistant of Jack Conway who had been selected to direct a film based on Richard Harding Davis's story, *Captain Maclean*. Flynn (who was later to become an important director himself—*A Connecticut Yankee at King Arthur's Court* is his best-remembered film) came to scan the cattle yard for possible cavalrymen.

"Who can ride?" he demanded, and virtually all the male extras rushed forward to volunteer. Had he inquired "Who can cook?" or "Who can play the accordion?" he would have been met with a similar response, and von Stroheim remained seated on a bench, not wishing to join in this ridiculous competition. Instead, he lit a cigarette with arrogant nonchalance. Flynn noticed him and approached.

"Aren't you the man who fell from the roof and did that bayonet stunt for Mr. Griffith?" he inquired.

"I am," answered von Stroheim, still seated.

"Don't you ride?"

"Yes, but I didn't want to compete with them. I *do* ride."

Baffled, Flynn asked the stubborn extra's name and then wrote it down.

"You're to go to Goldstein, the costumer," he said. "Get an officer's uniform and boots and report here tomorrow morning at seven."

"An officer's uniform? Of what army? Of what grade?" asked the exacting von Stroheim.

"Makes no difference," was the reply and the newcomer to motion pictures, amazed at such irresponsibility about details, set off to the costumer to dress himself as he saw fit.

Next morning at seven, von Stroheim in a blue Uhlan tunic

and khaki riding breeches arrived at the studio, to be met by his "soldiers," a motley lot of cowboys, Indians, and Mexican half-breeds. He kept apart from this awful riffraff, and after an hour's wait the detachment was loaded into buses and packed off to Griffith Park.

Griffith Park, which was not named after D. W. Griffith, was the site for most film exteriors in those days. There was a forest in the park, and if a forest scene occurred in any script—be the location Germany or China—it was inevitably shot in Griffith Park. The park was used so often that local audiences recognized the scenery at once.

Horses for the cavalry-charge scene in *Captain Maclean* were provided from a riding academy across from the park, and once the extras were mounted, Flynn inspected the troops and nodded his approval. Then he disappeared and soon returned carrying a long pole on the end of which was nailed a small pennant of nondescript color combination, supposedly a cavalry standard.

"You'll carry this," Flynn announced, handing the pole to von Stroheim, who was to head the detachment.

"But I'm an officer. Officers don't carry standards," protested the former lieutenant.

"I don't care what you are—or were. You'll carry this—or else," roared Flynn.

Von Stroheim decided to rehearse with the degrading, loathsome standard and then discard it when the cavalry-charge sequence was filmed, but Flynn maintained a hawklike watch and rudely reminded him to take it along just before Conway's cry, "Action," rang out.

As the mounted detail sat in their saddles awaiting zero hour, von Stroheim squeezed the end of the pole deep into his boot shaft and slipped his right arm through the loop so that the colors rested against his shoulder. To hold the saber aloft at the same time was difficult but possible.

"Gallop! Charge!" the order came, and they were off into a woodland clearing. Suddenly the detested pole caught in the hanging branches of a tree, and von Stroheim, brandishing his saber, fell backward from his horse, his mounted men approaching in full cry. He lay hugging the ground as the thumping of steel hoofs grew louder and the earth beneath him trembled. Then, as a hundred horses jumped over him, he tried to shield his face with his hands. After a few minutes the wild thunder of hoofs diminished and only a distant thud could be heard. Von Stroheim raised himself and opened his eyes as Flynn cantered up to inquire what had happened and to aid him in pulling the pole from his boot shaft.

"Them Austrian officers are sure some riders," kidded a cowboy in the rank of horsemen that had ridden back to discover what had happened to their commander. There was a roar of laughter, but the Sioux Indian chief of the company, who had remarked von Stroheim's horsemanship at rehearsals, silenced the derision with a gruff, "Oh, shut your damned traps. That guy can ride, all right!"

Flynn was of the same opinion as the Indian and a few days later requested von Stroheim for another stunt. This time he was to ride a horse down a pier and plunge into the ocean waves. The horse balked at the leap during rehearsals, but when the cameras began to click, a sly assistant blew pepper in the horse's eyes and the distracted animal jumped off the pier frantically, with its rider in the saddle.

There was a great struggle to get the crazed beast ashore. By this time the company had fled and von Stroheim, charged with cruelty to animals, was led off to a police station, followed by an indignant crowd. He was retained in a prison cell for most of the day and then brought before a judge and acquitted. The salary he received for the day's work was five dollars.

When he returned to the studio a week or so later, the pepper incident had been forgotten, but a lull seemed to have fallen over employment. A girl extra and Jack Hull kept him in crackers and milk for the duration of this trying period, during which he had to tramp on an empty stomach back and forth to his Main Street hotel. Sometimes a bottle of Coca-Cola was his only nourishment, but just around the corner his main chance was waiting, he was sure.

Mae Marsh in *The Birth of a Nation*. Von Stroheim played several parts in this film as a stunt man and extra

D. W. Griffith directing battle scenes in the California hills for *The Birth of a Nation*. Billy Bitzer's camera in foreground

4

John Emerson and
Douglas Fairbanks

O NE day during the lunch hour, a strange-looking man
passed through the deserted cattle yard. His head was
bowed and he appeared to be lost in deep thought. The most
outstanding thing about him was that he was dressed in evening clothes, apparently for a part he was playing, and a narrow
ribbon was fastened across his stiff-bosomed shirt front.

From a fellow extra, von Stroheim learned that the man was
John Emerson, who for many years had been a stage director
and playwright with the Charles Frohman Company in New
York. He was planning to direct Ibsen's *Ghosts* for D. W.
Griffith and enact the role of Alving himself. Von Stroheim
knew the Ibsen play well and remembered the great Austrian
actor, Josef Kainz, playing Oswald at the Burgtheater in
Vienna. If the film version was not to be a comedy, the

grotesque decoration of Mr. Emerson had to be corrected.

Von Stroheim took a deep breath and stepped up to him. "Pardon me, sir, but I have heard you are to play Alving in *Ghosts*. Is it to be a drama or a comedy?" he inquired.

"It's a drama, of course," mumbled Emerson, a bit irritated and about to move on. Suddenly he turned, with a puzzled look. "Why did you ask me that silly question?"

"Because in that case it is the ribbon rather than my question that is silly."

"Are you Norwegian?" demanded Emerson.

"No, sir, Austrian, but I was an officer and I know about decorations and could supply you with the proper one."

"All right," said Emerson. "Get me the right one, but it must be quick. We start work tomorrow."

Von Stroheim dashed off, borrowing carfare for the ride to downtown Los Angeles, where he also borrowed a small sum of money from his patient landlady, telling her of his luck and begging her to do a bit of sewing for him, once he had purchased the materials for the ribbon at the department store.

In three hours he was back at the studio gate, but the gate-man stood in his way. "Siegman's told me not to let you in any more," he said.

"But this is an important package for Mr. Emerson."

"Emerson ain't here no more and he ain't going to direct. He had a row with Frank Woods (the story-department editor) and left about an hour ago. Henry Walthall is going to play the part instead, and Nichols is slated to direct."

This was bad news, but von Stroheim thought quickly. "Then I must deliver this package to Walthall," he said. "I'll only be a minute, and I'll make sure that Siegman doesn't see me. Where's Walthall?"

"Bungalow number seven," replied the gateman to the young man already hurrying past him.

Von Stroheim knocked on the dressing room and a deep voice called, "Come in!"

The sensitive-featured Walthall stood in his underwear, struggling to get into his dress-suit trousers, a Scotch highball at his side. Then, having pulled on his pants, he sat down and drank. When von Stroheim finished his recital and opened the package to show him the ribbon and decoration, Walthall laconically inquired, "How much does it cost?"

"Nothing—if you put me on the picture at five dollars a day," von Stroheim said. "I could supervise your wardrobe. You will need the uniform of a consul in another scene. They will want someone like me who knows about these things," he added.

Walthall poured out a second glass of whiskey and handed it to his visitor. "Here's how!" he toasted, as von Stroheim took the glass and clicked his heels in tribute.

George Nichols cheerfully agreed to take on von Stroheim —over the expected objections of Siegman—and even proved more generous, making him his new wardrobe assistant and also giving him a bit part, his first non-stunt role, in the film.

Ibsen would certainly have disapproved of the screen adaptation of *Ghosts*. The alterations made in the play afforded von Stroheim his first lesson in American censorship. Though syphilis was prevalent in the United States at the time, any public mention of the malady was taboo. To avoid touching on the forbidden subject, Consul Alving was shown as a dipsomaniac who died of delirium tremens and whose son, Oswald, inherited, not syphilis, but presumably his father's weakness for alcohol. Mary Alden, a noted actress in the theater, starred as Mrs. Alving and the film was received as a superior one— because it at least aspired to present a well-known intellectual drama.

During the editing, Nichols summoned von Stroheim to the

Henry B. Walthall as Alving and Mary Alden as his mother in
Ghosts. John Emerson was replaced as director by George Nichols

projection room and the young man sat amazed as he watched himself for the first time on the screen. What he saw hardly coincided with his own conception of himself, but here was the image that was to make him famous.

"You've got something, boy," said Nichols with glee as he reached for his hip flask. "You've got something that nobody can take away from you—screen presence. When you enter, people look at you—even if they don't want to. I've watched these scenes at least ten times and I'll be damned if I remember what Henry and Mary are doing in them. Each time, I was watching you. Here, let's celebrate!" shouted Nichols, handing his companion his flask.

Despite Nichols's enthusiasm, von Stroheim's screen presence was not in immediate demand. After *Ghosts*, he was demoted once again to the cattle yard. Shortly afterward John Emerson returned to the Reliance-Majestic Studios and, coming through the cattle yard, caught sight of von Stroheim and walked over to him.

"I'm sorry that I disappointed you a few months ago," he apologized. "But I heard you gave Walthall the right decoration and got a part in the picture, so your work wasn't wasted." Then, after a moment's pause, he asked if von Stroheim had ever heard of the play *Old Heidelberg*.

"Why, of course," came the prompt reply. "I saw it three times in Vienna, and I have read it too."

"Have you ever been in Heidelberg?" pressed Emerson.

It would have been very easy for von Stroheim to lie, but he had only been in Germany once, when he traveled from Vienna to Bremen.

"No," he answered. "But I do know the students' customs and costumes, as we have student corps in Austria, too."

"I am going to direct *Old Heidelberg*," declared Emerson. "How would you like to be my assistant?"

Von Stroheim could scarcely believe his ears.

"I can't pay you much—fifteen dollars a week is all I can afford—but it's the chance of a lifetime. Are you willing to accept?"

"Am I willing to accept! Do you know what this means to me after waiting in this yard month after month?"

"Where do you live?"

"Downtown in a hotel on Main Street."

"You had better find yourself a room near the studio," advised Emerson.

"I won't be able to move until I get a few weeks' salary. I owe quite a lot of rent."

"How much?"

"About fifty dollars. I wouldn't have to pay it all at once." Emerson took his wallet from his hip pocket and gave his future aide thirty-five dollars. "That's for the old rent, and ten for moving and the new rent which you'll have to pay in advance. I'll deduct five dollars a week from your salary. Is that all right?"

Needless to say, von Stroheim agreed.

"Now," continued Emerson curtly. "Call for me at the Rex Hotel tonight at eight. We'll have dinner together and we can talk things over." Emerson walked off, and a band of extras crowded about von Stroheim wanting to know about his conference with the director.

That night von Stroheim was Emerson's guest at Levy's Restaurant on Spring Street, where film notables usually gathered. He learned that Wallace Reid was to play Prince Karl-Heinz in *Old Heidelberg* and that Dorothy Gish was to be Kathl, the beer-garden waitress to whom he loses his heart and whom he must abandon when his uncle's death calls him to the throne. Emerson and his new aide discussed the choice of an actor for the part of the prince's tutor, and it was decided

Dorothy Gish and Wallace Reid in *Old Heidelberg*, with von
Stroheim in background. John Emerson directed

that von Stroheim himself would appear as the prince's snobbish valet, Lutz. He was also to be in charge of all other casting, being entrusted with securing the proper student "types" and with supervising their dress.

Two days later von Stroheim commenced his multiple duties. These consisted of casting minor parts and bits, engaging the crowds, providing the players with their costumes—which required his going with them to fittings early in the morning and late at night—seeing that the costumes were promptly delivered, controlling makeup, advising on the ladies' toilettes, ordering transportation, arguing with the chauffeurs who refused to take more than seven persons in one car, supplying the box lunches from a caterer when the company went on location, and arranging for police permits to shoot in parks and in the streets.

Each morning the von Stroheim "student corps"—all of whom had been subjected to a German haircut—would "fall in" in military fashion on an open stage to stand roll call, inspection, and a rehearsal drill. This martial spirit was not appreciated either by the "students" or by such bystanders as Siegman and Sutch, who looked on with ill-concealed sneers. The war was worsening in Europe and anything Teutonic was suspect.

Freed from petty worries, Emerson, however, was delighted, as he was now able to give his full time to the direction of scenes. The animosity of the extras diminished at least outwardly when they realized that von Stroheim was empowered to "hire and fire." They postponed their revenge until after the filming of *Old Heidelberg*, when von Stroheim was again back in the cattle yard. There he was the daily target of their abuse, being jeered at for his past arrogance in commanding them.

His wages from *Old Heidelberg* were soon swallowed up,

and he found himself with only a few dollars left and had to hock his wristwatch at a Main Street pawnshop. The time for radical action had come. He would take his case to D. W. Griffith, who made his permanent residence at the Hotel Alexandria.

Informed by a studio chauffeur at what hour Griffith would pass through the hotel lobby, von Stroheim lay in wait. When Griffith stepped out of the elevator, he found himself confronted by an excited young man whose face he vaguely remembered. Motioning his uninvited caller to a sofa in a corner of the lobby, he gave him audience.

Von Stroheim related his enthusiasm for motion pictures and his suppressed desire to direct them. He had written a scenario —*The Pinnacle*. Would the master give him a chance and let him direct and act in it? He told how he had starved and struggled to get a foothold in the growing medium. Griffith, ever reserved, was struck by the Austrian's sincerity and fire. He promised to confer next day with Frank Woods, chief of the literary department, and he did so. But the studio's decision was that von Stroheim had had too little experience to be entrusted with the making of a film. Instead, he was made a member of the studio's stock company. Though this elevated his status, he found no demand for his services as actor or assistant for many weeks.

One day von Stroheim was in desperation in his rooming house. His rent had gone unpaid for weeks, and any day he expected to be thrown into the street. He was back on his Coca-Cola diet and in a weakened condition physically and morally. But Emerson had not forgotten him. A telephone call came to report to the studio.

He reached Woods's office in a state of perspiring anxiety, and the story editor glared at him ferociously and angrily demanded where he had been and what he had been doing. "Well, get this!" Woods shouted. "Mr. Emerson wants you to go East with him as his assistant on his next picture. The train leaves the Los Angeles depot at noon. Pack and report to Mr. Emerson's hotel. Them's orders!"

Von Stroheim had very little to pack and had no wish to return to his rooming house for a showdown with his landlady. Instead, he asked for an advance on his salary and hurried to a department store to buy shirts, socks, a toothbrush, and a razor. He arrived at Emerson's hotel to find his employer impatiently seated at the wheel of his sports car.

"Come on, come on, Von!" he urged. "We've got twenty-five minutes to make the train." And his assistant, burdened with bundles, slipped into the seat beside him. Emerson was a fast and reckless driver and they sped to the Santa Fe station, more than twenty miles away, with indifference to the whistles of policemen and red traffic lights. Flirting with death, Emerson's car wove in and out between cars, trucks, wagons, motorcycles, and alarmed pedestrians. They arrived after the scheduled departure time, but the station master, a movie fan, had received a message from the studio and had held the train. Panting and perspiring, they scrambled aboard.

In his drawing-room compartment, Emerson, still out of breath, pulled his whiskey flask from his hip pocket and handed it to his companion. Both men relieved their jangled nerves with a quick, bracing drink. Luncheon was then ordered, and as they sat over the meal, Emerson explained why they were in such haste. He had read an excellent original story by Anita Loos, *The Social Secretary*, and it had to be made on location in New York, most of it on the streets.

Miss Loos was already a well-known screenwriter. A wisp of a girl with large, dark, sad eyes, she was the daughter of a San Francisco journalist. In her teens she had written a

Anita Loos, who wrote Douglas Fairbank's early scripts, and her husband, John Emerson, who directed them

scenario and posted it to D. W. Griffith's company. Never suspecting that it was the work of a precocious child, Griffith bought and filmed *The New York Hat*, with Mary Pickford and Lionel Barrymore as its stars. The Loos scripts were so consistently good that the studio deemed it wise to place this unknown under permanent contract. Everyone was amazed when the promising scenarist, invited to visit Griffith in Los Angeles, turned out to be a schoolgirl. She was so piquant and pretty that Griffith offered her a screen test, but her mother vetoed this proposition. Later Miss Loos was to marry Emerson, and write her witty novel, *Gentlemen Prefer Blondes*.

On the long journey across the continent, Emerson talked of his own rise in the theatrical profession. As a young man he had been ordained a Protestant minister, but he had forsaken the cloth to join a touring stock company. His early disappointments were as bitter as those of his Austrian assistant. He, too, had starved and strived to make a place for himself. These experiences had left him with a haunting fear of poverty. After almost a decade of barnstorming, he had at last been engaged as a member of Mrs. Fiske's distinguished company. Afterward he had directed plays on Broadway for the Shuberts and Charles Frohman, leading managers of the era. He had written and acted in a successful play with a Civil War setting, *The Conspiracy*, and had entered moviemaking at the request of Griffith.

The economic insecurity of his trouping days had made him a cautious spender, something of a miser. Von Stroheim was amused by one of his moneysaving devices. Emerson rang for the Pullman porter and drew a ten-dollar bill from his wallet. When the smiling attendant appeared, the ex-minister tore the note in two and handed one half to the porter. If the service was satisfactory, the man would receive the other half of the note at the end of the trip; otherwise, not. Von Stroheim wondered what Emerson could do with the useless half of the bill if he was displeased with the service.

In the restaurant car one evening, the two men dined with Norma Talmadge and her mother. Miss Talmadge, already a well-known screen actress, was to be the star of *The Social Secretary*. A dark beauty, she maintained the pose of a movie empress and grew chilly when Emerson introduced his traveling companion as his assistant. Her estimate of assistants was not high. Her icy attitude thawed as the conversation brightened and she learned that the assistant had had an education, had been an officer, and was well read. Next morning, when the foursome reunited at the table for breakfast, she addressed him familiarly as "Von" and from then on treated him as an equal.

Emerson and his aide worked rigorously on the shooting script, completing it before they reached Chicago, where there was a brief stopover to change trains. This halt allowed von Stroheim an opportunity to buy a suitcase for his cumbersome effects. He wanted to arrive in New York in style, as Emerson had booked him a room in his own hotel, the Algonquin. From Grand Central Station they taxied to West 44th Street. Frank Case, the usually aloof hotel owner, greeted Emerson profusely at the door and an impressive group of stage folk seemed to be waiting for Emerson's arrival, providing a sort of informal reception committee, although they were probably gathered there on other business of their own.

There was bleary-eyed John Drew, the elegant veteran actor; his niece, Ethel Barrymore, and her waggish and handsome brother, John, who began to intone, "To be or not to be in Hollywood—that is the question," as he greeted Emerson. A swarthy, swaggering, youngish man, Douglas Fairbanks, vaulted over an armchair to make his way to the film director. Fairbanks was then appearing in a patriotic melodrama, *Haw-*

thorne of the USA, on Broadway, his last stage role before entering the cinema under Emerson's auspices. Mrs. Fairbanks and their little son, Doug Jr., a plump five-year-old, came up to shake hands.

When Emerson introduced his new assistant, there was an ill-concealed animosity, as the newcomer acknowledged the presentations with a bow and click of the heels. At that time the German and Austrian armies were advancing on all fronts. When his Teutonic name was uttered, the group's displeasure was so visible that von Stroheim politely withdrew to take the lift to his top-floor room.

Emerson, however, did not share the prejudices of his friends. He had an increasing regard for von Stroheim's intelligence and resourcefulness and he enjoyed his company. He had had the good luck to find an invaluable assistant—and at a salary that would not strain his budget. The liking was mutual, but the assistant now saw his employer's faults more clearly: Emerson's films in no way could be compared to those of D. W. Griffith. *Old Heidelberg* happened to be running on Broadway and von Stroheim studied it, sitting through it again and again. His own art work embellished it and lent it the required atmosphere of the dreamy university town. His appearance as the stuffy valet, Lutz, had won him a favorable comment from an important trade journal, though his name was not given in the cast. Wallace Reid as the German prince was acceptable, but Dorothy Gish, a skillful comedienne, was entirely wrong as the wistful daughter of the innkeeper the prince loves but cannot wed. The whole picture, the assistant concluded, lacked heart and soul. Many of the poignant scenes that in the theater had drawn tears from millions of playgoers had been botched on the screen and remained flat and ineffectual.

Emerson, in von Stroheim's opinion, was first and foremost a stage director. He had not mastered the new techniques of the motion pictures. He clung tenaciously to the photographic reproduction of static "stagy" scenes devoid of movement, preferring the old approach—"as seen from the theater audience's angle." Emerson's attitude toward the cinema was one of contempt. He disliked Hollywood and was at home only in familiar surroundings like those of the Algonquin. Here—and in the restaurants, cabarets, and dressing rooms of Broadway —he was looked upon as a celebrity. He was a leading spirit of the Lambs and the Friars, and later on he was to organize Equity, the actor's union. He was proud of his friendship with the Barrymores, the royal family of the American stage. Through him, von Stroheim met most of the Broadway notables of the day, Elsie Furgeson and Emily Stevens; David Belasco, the producer-author, who affected a clerical collar (which caused von Stroheim to address him as "Reverend Father" on being introduced); George M. Cohan; the elderly Charles Frohman, soon to go to a watery grave when a German submarine torpedoed the *Lusitania*, on which he was a last-voyage passenger; and Flo Ziegfeld.

During the filming of *The Social Secretary*, in which von Stroheim had a small, uncredited bit as a snooping yellow journalist, the ambitious assistant sought to enliven Emerson's stodgy direction by adding a few realistic touches to the street scenes. He arranged for fire engines and ambulances to dash by, to suggest the movement of the metropolis. A white-uniformed, white-helmeted street cleaner was seen sweeping up horse dung. Picturesque characters occasionally passed in the background: for example, one caught sight of an Italian organ-grinder with a monkey on his shoulder churning out a hurdy-gurdy tune. These were initial steps in the directorial technique that von Stroheim was now determined to master.

Emerson, who insisted on working in his beloved New York whenever possible, now arranged to make his second film in the streets of Manhattan. The script was written by Anita Loos. This was *His Picture in the Papers*, a jaunty farce that starred Douglas Fairbanks. In one scene, a realistic effect was comically if deceptively achieved. Emerson and his crew set up their cameras before the Vanderbilt mansion on Fifth Avenue, an imposing replica of a French château. The sequence was to picture Fairbanks as a carefree, wealthy man-about-town calling on one of his society friends. As the cameras clicked, Fairbanks with characteristic bounce bounded up the steps of the handsome town house and rang the bell. As expected, a butler appeared and admitted him. Thus the social status of the character had been established on celluloid. Behind the door of the palatial dwelling, Fairbanks explained that he must have mistaken the address. His comrades on the sidewalk, who had the shot in the bag, were jubilant.

Von Stroheim had little leisure during this prolonged stay in New York. He often worked at his desk until after midnight, sketching out the plans for the next day's filming. After hours of shooting and an inspection of the rushes, he interviewed prospective bit players in his cramped hotel room. It was while searching for types that he made the acquaintance of Norman Kaiser, an actor's agent.

Kaiser was a husky, broad-shouldered six-footer. He was what the French call *un bel homme* and looked more like an actor who could set feminine hearts aflutter than most of his clients. When the United States later entered the war, Kaiser, aware of the rising patriotic fervor, changed his surname to Kerry, gave up agenting, and went on the stage. Some years later von Stroheim engaged him to play the Viennese nobleman dandy in *Merry-Go-Round*. This made Norman Kerry a star. He later played the romantic leading roles in such Universal super-productions as *The Hunchback of Notre Dame* and *The Phantom of the Opera*.

60

As his professional position at the time was relatively low, von Stroheim was often ill at ease in the company of Emerson's famous friends, whose condescending attitudes he resented as much as they resented his close-cropped hair and stiff military bearing, so symbolic of the Hun. His shaven head suggested something else to a house detective at the Hotel Astor. Sitting in the Astor lobby one afternoon waiting for an acquaintance, von Stroheim was approached by a detective who had been scrutinizing him. The plain-clothes man flashed his badge and commanded the surprised loiterer to follow him to the manager's office. There von Stroheim was questioned and a telephone call was made to the police. He had been mistaken for an escaped convict from Sing-Sing, where all the felons had their heads shaved. The manager apologized profusely when the detective's error was discovered; a more mercenary-minded man than von Stroheim would have brought a damage suit against the hotel for false arrest and insult.

One rainy evening, coming out of a Broadway theater, von Stroheim collided with a young woman on a street corner. When she raised her umbrella, he was face to face with May Jones, the girlfriend of his first years in New York. He was happy to find her again and invited her to supper. There he recounted his adventures in the West, his collapsed business career, his marriage, and, more proudly, his entrance into moving pictures. She, too, had much to tell. Her dress establishment had prospered and she was designing costumes for the theater.

"Why don't you move back to our apartment for the rest of your stay here?" she suggested. "Mother always asks about you and calls your room 'Erich's room.' It's there waiting for you."

This touching invitation appealed to Erich. It offered him companionship and an escape from Emerson's continual surveillance—and May Jones was very charming. Going back to his top-floor room at the Algonquin, he quickly packed his belongings, while Miss Jones waited in a taxi. The move did not interfere with his working schedule, but it was to lead to a change in his future.

Some months later, Miss Jones was on the station platform to wave a tearful farewell, when the train carrying Emerson and his assistant pulled out of Grand Central.

5

Assistant on *Intolerance* and *Macbeth*

Foreseeing his return to the cattle yard, von Stroheim on the journey West made a desperate plea to Emerson to intercede for him with Griffith. When they reached California, Emerson took the matter directly to Griffith, strongly recommending von Stroheim as an experienced and efficient assistant.

Griffith immediately summoned Siegman, who was still his first assistant. The latter's dislike of von Stroheim showed in his face as soon as Griffith announced his intention to place the Austrian on the payroll.

"What have you against him?" Griffith demanded.

"He's too damned officious and militaristic to suit me," said the burly Bavarian, who boasted that his father had been awarded the Iron Cross in the Franco-Prussian War.

"Maybe a little of that Teutonic efficiency wouldn't do

us any harm," remarked Griffith. "He'll start tomorrow."

"Between you and me and the gateman," Emerson confided to von Stroheim in recounting this interview, "you *could* be less positive in your ways. Forget that soldier stuff. You aren't in the army any more."

"Why should I be less positive?" von Stroheim asked. "You wouldn't want me to say 'maybe' or 'perhaps,' instead of giving a precise answer to a precise question, would you? If I don't know something, I say so frankly. If I do, I am positive about it. People like Siegman are afraid that Griffith will recognize my superior competence and that I'll become a potential danger to them. Militaristic? No. I don't agree about everything the Germans and Austrians are doing, but after all I am an Austrian by birth. It's only natural that I should be proud of my country's achievements in the field."

"I guess it's hopeless to try to make you see things in a different light," said Emerson. "Anyway, you've got the job, and I know you'll make yourself a career. Good luck."

Griffith was about to begin shooting on his colossus of a film, *Intolerance.* Actually, it was to be composed of four separate films inter-edited into an ensemble that would run for over three hours. It was the most extravagant venture that the cinema had yet attempted, either in the United States or in Europe, though the grandeur of its Babylonian scenes owed something to the gigantic Italian spectacles *Quo Vadis?* and *Cabiria,* as well as to Griffith's earlier film, *Judith of Bethulia.*

In making his plea for tolerance, Griffith sought in some degree to atone for his own intolerance toward the Negro in *The Birth of a Nation,* which lauded the birth of the Ku Klux Klan in the post-Civil War South and tacitly supported white Protestant supremacy. It had caused race riots in Chicago, and the liberal press denounced it as a public menace. Griffith's scenario was based on a lurid, inflammatory novel, *The Clans-*

man, the work of a Southern minister, the Reverend Thomas Dixon. Though Griffith had had a little trouble raising money for the production of *The Birth of a Nation*, it was a sweeping box-office hit. It had played a two-performance-a-day run at the Liberty Theater in New York for eleven months. It had raised the motion picture to a level of prestige, and it was hailed as the official coming-of-age of the movies as an art.

It was thought that Griffith's new epic would surpass the earlier film as that had surpassed all the previous films ever made. Bankers were eager to invest and reap the profits. Though a monumental movie, widely seen and admired, *Intolerance* proved a financial failure in its initial engagements. Griffith used a vast canvas to depict the senseless persecutions that have troubled mankind through the ages. The four episodes were linked by the image of a mother eternally rocking the cradle. The first story was of the fall of Babylon; the second pictured the trial and crucifixion of Christ; the third painted a gory vision of the massacre of the Huguenots in Paris on St. Bartholomew's Day, 1572; and the fourth, set in modern America, showed the last-minute reprieve of an innocent workingman about to die on the gallows. Scenes of one episode were contrasted with those of the others in a sort of all-time-is-simultaneous effect. Griffith's technique here, as elsewhere, had tremendous influence on the future of the screen; his juxtaposing of unrelated scenes to achieve dramatic excitement was imitated by the Soviet directors Eisenstein, Pudovkin, and Dovzhenko, who called it *montage*.

For the making of *Intolerance*, Griffith mobilized every resource available to him. The cast included Lillian Gish, Mae Marsh, Robert Harron, Mary Alden, Miriam Cooper, Walter Long, Monte Blue, Bessie Love, Constance and Norma Talmadge, Colleen Moore, Carol Dempster, George Fawcett, Seena Owen, Elmo Lincoln, Josephine Crowell, Alma Rubens,

Carmel Myers, Tully Marshall, Eugene Pallette, Sam de Grasse, Pauline Starke, and George Walsh—all of whom were to play conspicuous parts in American movies. In addition, Sir Herbert Beerbohm Tree, DeWolf Hopper, Owen Moore, Donald Crisp, Tammany Young, Nigel de Brulier, and Douglas Fairbanks made guest appearances in bit roles. The celebrated dancer, Ruth St. Denis, and the Denishawn troupe were engaged to execute their ballet, "Virgins of the Sacred Fires of Life." Billy Bitzer was, of course, first cameraman, with Karl Brown as his aide. Associate directors Tod Browning, Jack Conway, Christy Cabanne, Lloyd Ingram, and George Nichols were assigned to supervise various units of the production. Ingram and Browning also appeared in the film as actors, as did George Siegman, who was to have a long career as a brutal heavy on the screen. Von Stroheim also appeared in the Judean sequence of the film, as the second Pharisee who mocks Christ.

Bowing to the stern command of Griffith, Siegman was now forced to accept von Stroheim as a second assistant. He made a gruff show of goodwill, shook hands with his old enemy, and mumbled something about letting bygones be bygones. Other assistant directors were John Henaberry, who had played Lincoln in *The Birth of a Nation* and who later made two of Rudolph Valentino's films; W. S. Van Dyke, and the inevitable Bert Sutch.

The walled city of Babylon with its temples and floating gardens had risen on an empty lot near the Reliance-Majestic Studios on Sunset Boulevard, a set on a scale of grandeur Hollywood had never seen. The first day of shooting happened to coincide with General Pershing's entry into Mexico on his "punitive expedition." But whereas "Black Jack" Pershing had only an army of fifteen hundred men, D. W. Griffith went into movie battle with two thousand. The assault on the

A scene from the Judean sequence of D. W. Griffith's *Intolerance*—the woman taken in adultery. Von Stroheim is one of the Pharisees. *Photo from the Billy Bitzer Collection, courtesy of Mrs. Bitzer*

towering city of Babylon was costly in casualties. The first hour saw over a hundred wounded extras. Some were splattered by the boiling oil poured from the turrets of the besieged city; others were struck by cardboard rocks hurled from above; an old man, whose helmet had been pierced by a spear, suffered a cracked skull.

The assistant directors were clad in costumes, in case the cameras picked them up as they mingled among the mob, shouting commands and herding the untrained extras into some semblance of military formation. The first assistant received a salary of fifty dollars a week, while second assistants were paid twenty-five dollars for their six days and nights of toil. But to an ambitious young man in Hollywood, more interested in making movies than in making money, the job was a godsend. The economic strain was forgotten in the pride of being able to say that one was "an assistant to D. W. Griffith."

Griffith insisted on absolute accuracy in everything. Even when it seemed impossible to satisfy his desire for authenticity, his disciples made superhuman efforts to try and get what he wanted. The duties of a Griffith assistant, von Stroheim discovered, were manifold. In addition to the fieldwork of commanding extras on the set—and day-shooting was sometimes followed by night-shooting—the assistants had to find extras to make up the necessary crowds, for no central-casting office existed at this time. Von Stroheim went to the Jewish quarter of Los Angeles to enlist—at three dollars a head—old men with patriarchal beards. Other chores of the Griffith staff were the inspection of costumes and makeup—Old Testament whiskers had to be combed and curled—and the rounding up of slackers who hid in the shade behind the sets, playing cards and drinking and appearing only at the day's end to collect their pay. The feeding of the two thousand warriors also had to be supervised, and medical care provided for the wounded.

Griffith, enthroned on a canvas camp chair on an elevated stand on the battlefield sidelines, issued directions through his megaphone. "There is an empty space on the right, about twenty feet from camera Number Five," his deep, velvetlike voice would boom. "Fill it in with the dead." Stock players, who had been appointed as group leaders, would urge and coax their lazy followers to more energetic action whenever the whistle signal for shooting pierced the air. It was often difficult to stop two thousand men from fighting, once they had been whipped into fury. Finally, a bugler was posted to sound Retreat when the order to cease hostilities was given by Griffith. The bugle notes restored peace, and the excited men stopped fighting.

Once Griffith asked von Stroheim to find him a real priest's soutane and biretta and a real blessed pyx, for the actor who was to portray the prison chaplain in the modern sequence of *Intolerance*. The soutane and biretta were easily procured, but the pyx was more difficult to find. Von Stroheim called on at least six priests, but none was willing to lend his viaticum outfit; it was not only consecrated and would have been profaned by such use, but the priest might have real need of it at any moment. Finally a venerable Spanish priest of an old Mexican church on Los Angeles Plaza suggested that the ardent searcher buy a whole kit at the Catholic religious-goods store. He then blessed it for von Stroheim, as he would have blessed a rosary, and the assistant returned with his prize to the master.

There was method in Griffith's thoroughness, and from this von Stroheim learned the technique of making superior motion pictures. There was a Griffith system in movies, as there was a Stanislavski system in the theater. Griffith applied psychology to obtain the best possible performances from his actors. In his early training of actresses like Mary Pickford and Mae Marsh, he employed several young girls to rehearse in turn the scenes that the others would subsequently play; from each he appropriated some effective girlish trick or bit of business that the actual player could improve on when she finally played the scene. Griffith also understood that actors must be correctly attired in new and well-tailored costumes, equipped with all the accessories down to the most insignificant detail. Thus, the actors became on the set what they were not in real life and, being more convinced themselves, could be more convincing to the spectator.

In scenes in which physicians, engineers, artists of any sort were needed, Griffith always engaged a real professional to stand by during the scene to explain and demonstrate the technical procedures of his work. When the director had absorbed the "mechanics," he instructed his actor what to do and what to omit. Griffith knew that total reproduction was not art and was apt to bore an audience. He possessed the gift of separating the necessary and the pictorial from the unessential.

It was also Griffith's habit not to work from a script. He never referred to notes, for he never made any. He never wrote out his scenarios, perhaps originally to protect himself against the piracy that was practiced so ruthlessly in those pioneering years. The complicated, interwoven plot of *Intolerance* existed only in his head, until it was all recorded on celluloid. Yet the filming itself was only the beginning: the unified work of art was forged and perfected in the cutting room. When the rushes were projected, Griffith would explain to Billy Shea, his invaluable wizard of the shears, exactly what he wanted—where precisely to interrupt the action and impose another image, where precisely to resume the earlier action. The cutting room was his cinematic laboratory and he labored there with the tenacity of an alchemist over his potential gold. Here he brewed and distilled ideas that, when projected on the screen, amazed the people who had worked with him on the original elements. In this humble study in a wooden shack the master moviemaker brought to flower notions that would sway the emotions of millions. Von Stroheim saw Griffith as a magician of fabulous powers. Certainly, his disciple believed, what Griffith wrought from his snatches of celluloid was greater than the sum of the parts. His films made those of the less imaginative and less adventuresome directors of the day look like the inferior work that they were. *Intolerance* was the first cinematic attempt to create a fugue, and a close study of its crosscutting even today will show that it has never been surpassed, not even by the Soviet directors who admitted that they were greatly influenced by it.

Griffith's knowledge and memory of classical music and literature was vast. When he recited verse, however, he was inclined to exaggerate as old-fashioned actors did. His sonorous voice would become stagy as he proclaimed a speech from Shakespeare or snatches of Keats or Walt Whitman. When in the studio surrounded by his "stand-by" stars—Lillian and Dorothy Gish, Blanche Sweet, Mae Marsh, and Bobby Harron —he would suddenly start to sing an aria from *La Bohème* or *Madame Butterfly*, which the three-piece orchestra, ever present, would instantly pick up and carry to its conclusion.

To an analytical observer like von Stroheim, Griffith's loudness of dress appeared in sharp contrast to the sensitive man it clothed. He who had given the world its first film poetry had a deplorable penchant for checked shirts and suits, and delighted in overcoats that seemed to belong on a race-track tout.

Yet von Stroheim knew that if Griffith had worn overalls, he would have attracted attention. There was majestic cadence in his walk. He never hurried. Perhaps it was the former actor in him that made him behave as he did, feeling that thousands of eyes were always watching him, thousands of ears listening. The younger directors under his banner—Christy Cabanne, John Henaberry, Jack Conway, and von Stroheim, too—imitated the master's tastes, even adopting his incongruous wearing apparel as the only possible fashion. Those whose circumstances permitted bought a poor-man's imitation of the Griffith panama hat, and their shirts had colored stripes and checks. Cabanne on his set often burst into arias from *La Bohème* and added a bit of *Tosca* for good measure.

Griffith was one of the first to attempt to remedy the shortcomings of the silent film with appropriate music. Musical accompaniment at that period was left to the resources of the movie-house pianists, who might well strike up *Hearts and Flowers* for the scene of the Nazarene's martyrdom or a Sousa march for the bloodbath of St. Bartholomew's Day. Until all hours of the night, Griffith sat in the musty projection room with his musical director, Louis Gottschalk, telling him scene by scene what music he wanted. He sang and hummed the melodies, while Gottschalk at his piano improvised and recorded the score on music sheets.

Whereas practically everyone wore his shirt open at the collar on the set, Griffith always kept his buttoned up and sported a neatly knotted tie. He never wore jewelry of any kind, not even a watch. Time did not exist for him. Sometimes his players were only freed for lunch at four or five in the afternoon. He was so absorbed in his work that he failed to realize how hungry others could become at the regular eating time. He never ate or drank on the set, but now and then he smoked an Egyptian cigarette, holding it in the peculiar fashion of the Chinese and throwing it away after a few puffs.

He was always extremely polite in giving orders, and never indulged in making sarcastic and slurring remarks to his players as, for example, Cecil B. DeMille did. He never, even in nerve-straining moments during battle scenes, raised his voice. He never resorted to vulgar language or profanity.

"No man is ever anything but a swindle," Jean-Paul Sartre has observed. Griffith, as he appeared to those around him in his years of glory, may well have been only the ingenious invention of the man who had failed as an actor and had failed as a dramatist (his only play, A *Fool and a Girl*, had gone on for one week's performance in Washington) and who had, in middle age, at last found success in a new medium after a hard apprenticeship. If so, Griffith remained impressively faithful to his pose. He acted the role of the Olympian artist with consummate skill. Anita Loos, a shrewd observer of men and pretensions, was in such awe of Griffith that she can still remember every word he ever said to her. Lillian Gish, whom he developed into one of the screen's most remarkable actresses and who was his close friend for forty years, still refers to him with great respect as Mr. Griffith.

Sudden wealth and unexpected renown had made his low-born contemporaries in the film industry ridiculous. They wallowed in their newfound luxury and became a laughing-stock; tales of their unbridled vulgarity and ignorance made Hollywood a byword for crass stupidity and illiteracy. Unlike them, Griffith purchased no Beverly Hills mansion (with or without swimming pool). He continued to live simply in his quiet quarters in the Hotel Alexandria and he rode about in an old, rented sedan automobile, a chauffeur at the wheel, for he had never learned to drive. He had so little interest in money that it was discovered years later that he had left some fifty thousand dollars in the vault of his hotel, forgetting that it was there. He did not entertain lavishly, nor did he mingle with his plutocratic colleagues. He kept his social circle small. His only friends were the Gish girls, Blanche Sweet, Mae Marsh, and

Bobby Harron. He had been married but was separated from his wife, who in those years lived in the East. It was said that she would not divorce him.

One thing he loved: dancing. He even frequented the dance palaces where the two-step, the fox-trot, and the Gaby Glide were in vogue and where everyone was trying to tango. He wanted not only to dance but to search for new material, to observe types and characters, and to study the rapidly changing behavior of the nation's youth. The inhibited attitude of the Puritan land toward sex was on the wane and a new freedom was in the air. But despite the new ways, Griffith remained constant to the old standards. His etherealized concept of women, with its mid-Victorian vestiges, is to be found in all his films.

These modest, blushing maidens of Griffith might have stepped from the pages of Charles Dickens. They were lovely, wistful, and charmingly old-fashioned, a souvenir of grand-mother's girlhood by 1916. They might be "betrayed" into a liaison, but it was always unwittingly, and they fought to the end for their "honor." Only "bad" women had any knowledge of sexual matters or welcomed amorous advances, and only cads and bounders would take advantage of a young girl's in-nocence. In Griffith's films cads and bounders were always do-ing so, however, for sex has been the strongest draw of the motion pictures since they were invented. For example, *The Birth of a Nation* contains two attempted rapes.

Griffith had a natural dignity that von Stroheim once com-pared to that of an American Indian chief. His manner simply forbade intimacy. He was never pompous, but no one would have dared to slap him on the back, in the American fashion of the day, and ask him to have a drink. Nor would anyone have ventured to tell him a low barroom joke. He was an individual-ist, by instinct. Most men in professional life band together and join lodges; Griffith did not. His Austrian admirer was to emulate him in this—as he emulated his private comportment in many other matters.

During this apprenticeship under Griffith, von Stroheim regained something of his former self-assurance. His many reverses and calamities had worn off much of his Viennese polish and veneer. Now that he was "an assistant to D.W.G.," some of this style returned. He had befriended two English actors, Courtney Foot and Douglas Gerard, who also had the air of gentlemen. This trio seemed sufficiently well-bred, in the judgment of headwaiters, to warrant a good table at Levy's, where on Saturday nights the cinema elite gathered.

One Saturday evening was particularly fortunate, for they found themselves seated next to John Emerson, who was host to Sir Herbert Beerbohm Tree and his leading lady, Constance Collier, both recently arrived in Hollywood. Emerson, who for some reason was one of the few movie notables not connected with *Intolerance*, invited von Stroheim to join his party.

Sir Herbert Beerbohm Tree was at this time the leading actor-manager of the British theater, a position he had held since the death of Sir Henry Irving. He had built a theater of his own in London, His Majesty's, and there had staged Shakespeare in some memorable productions. Oscar Wilde, Stephen Phillips, and Bernard Shaw had written plays for him. Only a season before, he had created the role of Professor Higgins in Shaw's *Pygmalion*.

It was clear that the spectacle film was now in vogue. The triumph of *The Birth of a Nation* and Griffith's announcement of his plans for *Intolerance* had spurred his competitors to imitation. Cecil B. DeMille, at the Famous Players lot, was in the process of producing a spectacle about Joan of Arc with

On the set of *Macbeth* in 1916. From left to right: John Emerson, the director; Constance Collier as Lady Macbeth; De Wolf Hopper and Dorothy Gish, visitors; Sir Herbert Beerbohm Tree as Macbeth; Douglas Fairbanks.

the opera star, Geraldine Farrar. Thomas Ince was making a spectacle, *Civilization*, which would be advertised as "the picture that will keep America out of the war"—a vain boast. John Emerson had decided it was time for him "to do something big." He told von Stroheim that *Macbeth*, with Beerbohm Tree as the Thane of Cawdor and Constance Collier as Lady Macbeth, would make a marvelous spectacle. Just consider the cinematic possibilities of Birnam Wood—an army of camouflaged soldiers—moving on Dunsinane Castle! Emerson laughed with delight at the idea and Sir Herbert applauded this wonderful vision, while Miss Collier seemed a bit skeptical. When Emerson asked if von Stroheim would volunteer to be art director and assistant, the Austrian promptly accepted.

Sir Herbert said he knew little about the movies, except that on a recent tour of the battlefields he had discovered that Charlie Chaplin was the idol of the Tommies. He was about to do the bit part in *Intolerance* for Griffith. He thought that Emerson's suggestion that he star as Macbeth, a role in which he had shone on both sides of the Atlantic, suited him perfectly.

When von Stroheim asked if he would receive screen credit for *Macbeth*, and decent pay, Emerson agreed heartily to both. The distinguished visitors, finding this newcomer rather fascinating, toasted his decision. When his duties on *Intolerance* were completed, von Stroheim reported to take part in bringing Shakespeare to the screen.

Macbeth, as Emerson had envisioned it, finally emerged as a spectacle—but it was not a successful one. For one thing, Emerson lacked Griffith's epic conception. A mob of extras were treated under his direction as supers are in the theater. He could not dramatize mass movement as Griffith, Ince, or DeMille could. For another, his principal actors found it next to impossible to forget their stage mannerisms in front of the camera. They had played *Macbeth* so often that they insisted at first on mouthing every Shakespearean line, until they were reminded that the words would never be heard.

Sir Herbert's film career was brief. Although his contract called for two films to follow *Macbeth*, the studio was now anxious to be rid of him. He was next assigned to play a New England farmer in *The Old Folks at Home*, with Josephine Crowell, fresh from playing Catherine de Medici in *Intolerance*, as his dowdy wife. Beerbohm Tree was not insensitive to this absurd humiliation, but he was determined to be paid what he had been promised. When he was told he would be cast as a servant in his third film, he could stand no more and refused. His refusal constituted a breach of contract and he returned to the stage, where he had great success as Cardinal Wolsey in *Henry VIII*.

6

"The Man You Love to Hate"

EMERSON sadly and gracefully acknowledged his defeat in the field of screen spectacles. He now proposed that von Stroheim—in the multiple capacity of assistant-director-actor —accompany him to New York again, there to make another film with Douglas Fairbanks.

Having finally been granted screen credit on *Macbeth*, von Stroheim was in a bargaining position. Emerson was not Griffith, but if his salary were raised to fifty dollars a week, and if he could have an assistant, he would go. Emerson agreed and, at his aide's suggestion, engaged Emmet Flynn as second assistant. The cameraman was to be George Hill, an ace film photographer who was later to become a high-ranking Hollywood director in the early talkie days. Emerson, Fairbanks, and the three younger men boarded the New York train a few days later.

Emerson's Pullman compartment was transformed into a conference chamber on the five-day journey across the continent. Fairbanks, breezy as a spring robin, was a natural entertainer and kept his companions rocking with laughter at his anecdotes. He reveled in being the center of attention. His exuberant energy made it impossible for him to sit still for long. Being cooped up in the railroad car oppressed him, and he was always jumping up from his seat to illustrate some point.

The son of a German acrobat, Fairbanks had inherited his father's athletic prowess; breathtaking stunts were to be one of his specialties on the screen. To him, the movies were a new toy. They made him known and loved far and wide and brought him fabulous wealth. No male star, save Chaplin, was ever to surpass him in international popularity. Women swooned over Valentino, but the whole family came out to see a Fairbanks film. To movie goers around the world, he represented the one-hundred-percent American at his best—courageous, democratic, full of fun, and always the protector against evil forces, usually personified by a band of bad men whom he, alone and sometimes with one hand tied, could beat into a humiliating retreat. The United States never had a better goodwill ambassador than this exponent of bravery and wholesomeness. Boys everywhere wanted to be like Douglas Fairbanks.

Fairbanks was bubbling with ideas to be injected into the Emerson film, and von Stroheim had several notions as to how to build up his small part. In one scene Fairbanks was to hit him over the head with a bottle. The alert assistant quickly made a mental note to obtain some bottles made of sugar to avoid head injuries and then suggested that the scene, instead of taking place in a bar, be acted on top of a moving train. To make the villain more sinister, von Stroheim proposed he wear a black patch over one eye and have a paralyzed right arm, the hand of which would be encased in a black glove. Fairbanks greeted all this with a pleased guffaw.

Hill and Flynn bunked with von Stroheim in a stateroom. Neither of these young men liked their fellow traveler. Hill viewed him as a conceited snob, and Flynn, remembering the disastrous incident of the flag-pole ride at Griffith Park, rankled at being under the command of the man whom he had bullied into a dangerous tumble. But on better acquaintance they revised their earlier estimates of the foreign intruder, rating him as a "regular guy."

"But why do you pose, Erich?" inquired Flynn.

"*Pose*? What do you mean? I don't pose," returned von Stroheim indignantly.

"Well, why don't you let your hair grow like the rest of us? And why do you strut around as though you were the Kaiser's bodyguard? You'll get jailed as an agent of the Wilhelmstrasse one of these days."

"If I wore my hair long, I'd be lost in the rush. No one would notice me," explained von Stroheim. "I actually feel physically sick when I miss my weekly visit to the barber. It's more sanitary to be close-cropped and it's a lifelong habit. So is my military bearing."

The train was to pass West Point on the Hudson River, and Hill, who wanted to see the military academy, pulled up the compartment window and stuck his head out in a windstorm, only to receive a cinder in his eye. Combined efforts to remove it failed and an hour later, when they reached Grand Central, his right eye gushed tears and blinked involuntarily. The three cinematic musketeers were determined not to be quartered at the Algonquin under the continual supervision of Emerson. They hurried to find a taxi and Hill leaned forward to instruct the driver.

"Take us to a good hotel," he ordered, his right eye twitching. The cabbie mistook the blink for a suggestive wink and drove them post-haste to a dubious hotel in the West Fifties. This brothel was an ideal choice, the trio agreed, and they made it their residence.

There was much motion-picture activity in and about New York at this time. Once the Fairbanks film was finished, Emerson signed to direct a Mary Pickford feature at Fort Lee and took von Stroheim with him as his assistant. *Less Than the Dust* was the name of this unhappy venture, and in recalling it von Stroheim would sigh, "What an appropriate title!" Miss Pickford mentions in her memoirs that when a gushing fan rushed up to her on Fifth Avenue and exclaimed, "I have just seen you in *Cheaper Than Dirt*," she thought an even more telling description had been found.

In April 1917, the United States declared war on Germany. The nation staggered under this news, for American neutrality had been guaranteed by President Wilson during his reelection campaign. "He kept us out of war" had been the chief slogan, and *I Didn't Raise My Boy to Be a Soldier* had been the nation's theme song. To bring the message of the war home to the American people, George Creel, a reckless rabble-rouser, was appointed propaganda chief. Newspapers and magazines were flooded with war propaganda. German-language courses were suspended at schools and universities. German dishes disappeared from the bills of fare, "Sauerkraut" being renamed "Liberty Cabbage." German operas were removed from repertories; the drive against German music culminated in the arrest of Dr. Karl Muck, the elderly conductor of the Boston Symphony Orchestra, who was accused of being in league with the Hun.

Having received only his first citizenship papers, von Stroheim was still technically an Austrian subject. His position was dangerous and embarrassing, but the temper of the times was to benefit him professionally. Fort Lee was gallantly answering the Creel call for inflammatory propaganda. The War Department had set up a branch there for the manufacture of training and recruiting movies, while the studio's commercial output was devoted almost exclusively to "hate" films. These productions were shot on an accelerated wartime schedule and speedily dispatched across the country to ignite indignation.

Von Stroheim—with his stiff military bearing, his cropped head, his bull neck, his strong face imprinted with dueling scars, his brutal scowl, and his aristocratic sneer—was just the man to personify the loathsome Hun to the American masses. Was there any male of fighting age who did not want to rescue a pretty Red Cross nurse from the lascivious embrace of this repulsive beast, with his sadistic leer and undemocratic monocle? Recruiting posts were set up outside movie theaters so that young men who had just seen these horrors on the screen could instantly respond to their country's call.

Not only did von Stroheim look the part of the ruthless Prussian officer, but there were whispered speculations that he was one. He was quickly and indelibly "typed" and was now much in demand. Sometimes—as in the Norma Talmadge film *Panathea*—he was cast as a Russian, but even as a Russian he was very Prussian. This characteristic had a long life: later when he acted in *Foolish Wives*, his Tsarist officer appeared more Prussian than Slav. In rapid succession he was a Hunnish menace in *Sylvia of the Secret Service*, which George Fitzmaurice directed and in which the dancer, Irene Castle, starred; a Prussian monster in *For France*, which gave von Stroheim both a good role and acting credit; a villainous Hun in *The Unbeliever*; and an evil Junker commander in a propaganda film for which he also acted as military adviser.

Von Stroheim as the Hun in Vitagraph's *For France*, 1917. Edward Earle at left

A naïve public accepted him at his screen value. Often people in the streets would shout insults at him, which roused his defiance and made him cultivate his on-screen mannerisms. When it was noticed that he bore a likeness to the German Crown Prince Wilhelm, von Stroheim made every effort to imitate the royal heir. This was madness at a time when patriotic emotions had reached a feverish pitch. One sunny day, clad in the glittering regalia of a member of the Kaiser's military staff, he hired an open carriage to drive through Central Park to some location site. The spectacle of a German warrior in full-dress uniform, riding haughtily through the park, caused astonishment and mounting displeasure. A crowd formed and began to jog-trot after the vehicle, shouting insults and threats. Von Stroheim, sensing the seriousness of the situation, judiciously ordered the coachman to whip up the horses. As the carriage rolled on at a brisker pace, its occupant produced a monocle from his white tunic and gave his angry pursuers a parting glare.

Shortly after this narrow escape, von Stroheim was once more engaged by Emerson to be the art director of *In Again, Out Again*, another Anita Loos confection for Douglas Fairbanks. The trusty assistant was also to have a part as a Prussian-Russian officer, and supervision of all property matters were to be among his duties. He would now, of course, have full screen credit, but it was deemed best to drop the "von" from his name for the duration of the war. He stubbornly refused to abbreviate his name off-screen, which turned out to be an error in judgment. Explosives were required for a scene in *In Again, Out Again*, and von Stroheim rode to some neighboring town near Fort Lee to order a supply. In his best Crown Prince manner, he told the nervous clerk what was needed and signed the delivery slip with a bold flourish: "Von Stroheim." As soon as he departed, the clerk telephoned the police. A German—

"von something"—had just ordered a supply of high explosives to be delivered to an address in Fort Lee. Secret Servicemen rushed to the Fort Lee studios to investigate, and the clerk's warning of possible sabotage was soon laughingly explained away. But Douglas Fairbanks, despite his quick sense of humor, was not amused. He was fervently pro-Allied, an important figure in the Liberty Bond drives and perhaps a bit uneasy that his own German ancestry might now come embarrassingly to public attention. He demanded that von Stroheim be dismissed, and Emerson was forced to accede to his star's command.

A gloomy future presented itself to von Stroheim. The Fairbanks edict had closed all doors at Fort Lee. Lonely and depressed, he moved into a cheap boarding house on New York's West Side. It was here, oddly enough, that he happened to read Frank Norris's novel, *McTeague*, a former boarder having left a tattered copy behind in the room. Von Stroheim had never heard of Norris and picked up the book, vaguely attracted by its subtitle: "A Story of San Francisco." He loved San Francisco. Soon he was deeply absorbed and devoured the novel in a nonstop reading that terminated at four o'clock the next morning. He knew he had found a story that he could transform into a fascinating motion picture. He read it over and over again, learning it by heart.

One of his few friends in New York at this period was a Dr. Ralk. The discharged film actor was not anxious to go out, as it was midwinter and he had pawned his overcoat. But Dr. Ralk invited him to dine in a little restaurant off Broadway and, hoping to cheer him a bit, informed him that the morning papers had announced the arrival from Europe of D. W. Griffith.

Griffith and his company had been visiting London and the battlefields of France for background shooting of a new film, an epic of the war, the rest of which would be made in California. It had a Wilsonian title, *Hearts of the World,* and it was said to equal *The Birth of a Nation* in scope.

"Now, why don't you go and see Griffith?" queried the helpful physician. "He's hired you before, and he likes you. Maybe he'll have a job for you."

Von Stroheim, thoroughly disheartened, was skeptical. Perhaps Griffith, like Fairbanks, had become a super-patriot and would believe it his civic duty to turn his former assistant over to the police. Then, too, the out-of-work Austrian always seemed to be down on his luck whenever he went to see the master. Besides, he didn't even have an overcoat. But the doctor drew a promise from his low-spirited guest that he would come to his office the next day at two o'clock.

Though von Stroheim had decided firmly not to call on Griffith, he kept his appointment at Dr. Ralk's office. There he was told to roll up his left sleeve and the physician injected a hypodermic needle into his friend's arm. What the injection contained remained a medical secret, but the swift treatment was followed with the blunt advice: "Now go and see Griffith!"

Without delay the patient walked down Broadway with a confident swagger, suddenly relieved of his mental depression and feeling astonishingly fit. For weeks he had avoided his friends, but now he held his head high as he hurried to Griffith's office. In the waiting room, an officious office boy stood in his way and asked him his business. Von Stroheim vaulted over the balustrade and went directly to the door of Griffith's inner sanctum and knocked. A familiar deep voice asked him to enter.

With a click of the heels and a courtly bow, von Stroheim reintroduced himself, and Griffith seemed very glad to see him again. After the preliminaries, the famous director inquired what his protégé's salary was now.

87

"For you, Mr. Griffith, I would work for a ham sandwich a day."

There was a slight pause. Griffith smiled. "You are leaving tonight for Los Angeles, Von. I need you."

The man who on the previous evening had been doubtful that he had a future was "in pictures" again, and at the request of the master.

Back in Hollywood, von Stroheim found himself set for double duty in *Hearts of the World*. He was promoted to be Griffith's personal first assistant, advising on military matters and uniforms, and a part for him was written into the script, the part of yet another merciless officer of the Kaiser's elite. Though this role was now a von Stroheim specialty and his shaven head was so familiar to the moviegoing millions that soldiers went to barbershops demanding a "Von Stroheim haircut," several imitators had sprung up. Wallace Beery scored strongly in a film about the German submarine menace, *Behind That Door*, in which, at the end, he is taken prisoner and as punishment is skinned for his sins. The epidermis of the culprit is vaguely seen dangling behind a door. This grisly melodrama was a great hit at home and in all Allied countries. Bull Montana, a Western bad man, also took to portraying the scoundrel Hun warrior. A cauliflower ear, the souvenir of his youth in the wrestling ring, was a natural asset in his cultivation of a repulsive personality. Yet another rival in Hollywood's growing Prussian army was von Stroheim's old enemy, George Siegman. It was Siegman who took over the role that Griffith had orginally designed for von Stroheim in *Hearts of the World*.

This role—that of an agent of the German autocracy—even bore an abbreviated form of its model's name, von Strohm. On second thought, Griffith felt that it would be wiser to entrust it to the more seasoned Siegman. Griffith, though he liked von Stroheim and admired his pluck, was slow in recognizing his disciple's abilities. He had hesitated over according him the opportunity to direct and had passed the decision on to Woods, who quickly vetoed the offer. Now he had his doubts about von Stroheim's acting talents in an important part. Lillian Gish remembers how bitterly disappointed von Stroheim was when he learned of the change in casting. On the verge of tears, he sat on a bench in the studio yard commiserating with a group of friends.

As compensation, Griffith supplied him with another role, that of a Prussian lieutenant who harassed French peasants in an occupied village. When *Hearts of the World* was released, the superiority and histrionic cunning of von Stroheim's performance outshone the routine work of Siegman. The film was another triumph for Griffith, being acclaimed the outstanding motion picture of the war.

Just as the shooting of *Hearts of the World* was being completed, May Jones, the daughter of von Stroheim's New York landlady, reappeared, arriving on the set one morning in the company of the Gish girls and their mother. Miss Jones's venture into theatrical costuming had led to her designing clothes for motion-picture actresses, and Griffith had engaged her to come to work at his California studios. This unexpected meeting embarrassed the actor at first. She had been away in Canada and he had not written her in many months. But she was forgiving, and soon they were spending their evenings together. When his first wife's divorce decree was granted, he proposed to Miss Jones. Their wedding—a civil ceremony—was quietly celebrated. The second Mrs. von Stroheim bore her husband a son, Erich, Jr., but the marriage was unhappy and short-lived, terminating in divorce in 1919.

After *Hearts of the World*, von Stroheim did one more film at the Griffith studios. This was *The Hun Within*, directed

In Griffith's *Hearts of the World*, 1918. Von Stroheim had become "The Man You Love to Hate"

by Christy Cabanne, with Dorothy Gish, George Fawcett, and Douglas McLean. It had to do with the subversive operations of German espionage agents in the United States and humanely stressed the staunch loyalty of most German-Americans. Von Stroheim, to no one's surprise, was the German German, the horrible Hun attempting to enlist Americans of German origin in his sabotage enterprises, one of which was the blowing up of an army transport ship carrying soldiers to France.

The war in Europe, however, was drawing to a close and the violent propaganda film had about had its day. Nevertheless, a sizable production, *The Heart of Humanity*, which Allen Jolubar optimistically announced as "the picture that will live forever," was in the making at Universal City. Von Stroheim was summoned there to portray another obnoxious German officer. In this final fling at the crumbling Central Powers, his last wartime film, von Stroheim surpassed himself at movie villainy. He received featured billing as "The Man You Love to Hate," and did not disappoint those who came to hiss him. He reveled in a veritable orgy of brutal misconduct; not only did he attempt to violate the leading lady, Dorothy Phillips, but he nonchalantly tossed a baby out of the window.

After the film's première at the Kinema Theater in Los Angeles, he took the stage. His appearance was greeted with hoots and jeers and a man rose in the audience and shouted out that he ought to be shot. Von Stroheim explained that he was only an actor, and an *Austrian*, not a German. "The Austrians like the Germans about as much as the Irish like the English," he hurriedly added, in an effort to quell the anger that his characterization had aroused. The critics, more rational than the fans, praised his performance for its vigorous realism.

Carl Laemmle, the president of Universal, attending the film's opening, was delighted with von Stroheim's suave comportment before the enraged first-nighters. He had just signed an extraordinary contract with von Stroheim and was pleased to witness his new employee's diplomacy in dealing with an embarrassing situation. When von Stroheim came on the stage, the air was electric with hatred. His tactful speech had converted the mob's intense dislike into admiration, and his exit was followed by applause.

PART TWO

7

Laemmle and *Blind Husbands*

C ARL Laemmle was born in Lübeck, Germany, a city that
another native, Thomas Mann, used as the setting for his
novel, *Buddenbrooks*. Laemmle had come to the United States
in 1884 and after several ventures in non-theatrical enterprises
began to rent halls for motion-picture shows at the turn of the
century. By 1908 he controlled a syndicate of nickelodeons and
entered film production in 1910 to supply his theaters with
movies. His original company, I.M.P. (Independent Motion
Pictures), merging with other small movie-production organi-
zations, became Universal in 1912. By 1918 it was a major company owning a vast tract of land in California for exterior
filming, in addition to its studios. Laemmle himself, though as
shrewd a trader as his rivals, was a kindly man whose paternal
image had earned him the affectionate title "Uncle Carl."

Though he lacked formal education, he had an intuitive feeling for drama, backed by cunning in financial dealing, a combination known in the trade as "Laemmle luck." Laemmle spent much time in the East—in New York and Chicago—marketing the Universal products to exhibitors and supervising a weekly advertising column in *The Saturday Evening Post*, which had the largest circulation in the United States at that time. In these outpourings he drew the attention not only of prospective buyers but of millions of fans.

When he visited his studios, he enjoyed mingling with his directors and players, always seeking tidbits to exploit in his column. Whenever he visited *The Heart of Humanity* locations, he invariably found, silently standing by his side, the Austrian actor who played ferocious Prussian officers. As soon as Laemmle stood still, this forbidding character would sidle into his vicinity and take up a silent but resolute position, staring at the president as though to hypnotize him. This unvarying procedure first puzzled and then annoyed Laemmle. What on earth did this man, whose face was so full of iron determination, want? Finally, Laemmle's curiosity brought the matter to a head.

"Do you want to speak to me?" he inquired.

"I do, sir. If you could give me a few moments, it would mean the world to me."

"Now look here," said the businesslike president, "I have just half an hour. We will go to my office and have a chat."

When they were seated, Laemmle asked von Stroheim to state his case.

"I want to make a film for you, one that will cost only five thousand dollars," began von Stroheim.

"Just what sort of film would that be? Even a two-reeler costs more than that."

Seizing this opening, von Stroheim launched into an account

of the scenario he had written, *The Pinnacle*. It had originally taken him four days to write, but for three years he had been trying to find a purchaser for it. He spoke eloquently, relating the incidents in his story with a dramatic vivacity that captured Laemmle's imagination. Sometimes the conversation would slip easily from English into their native German. When von Stroheim finished his recital, Laemmle's eyes were gleaming with pleasure.

"Yes, yes, it's a fine story and I'll buy it," he said.

"No, no, I won't sell it."

"But why not? What is this all about?"

"I cannot let anyone else direct my masterpiece," said von Stroheim. "I must direct it myself."

"But, man alive, you're crazy. You've never directed a picture in your life. You may be insane, but I'm not."

"I may be mad," von Stroheim conceded, "but I know I can make a great film for you."

"For five thousand dollars?"

"No. I only said that to hold your attention. But I could probably make it for ten thousand."

This too was an exaggeration. The film in the end was to cost nearly one hundred thousand, but von Stroheim had won Laemmle's confidence. The promised half-hour session had been extended to several hours. When von Stroheim left the office, he had a contract to direct his scenario and to play its principal role. *The Pinnacle* would be written and directed by, and with, von Stroheim.

In *The Pinnacle*—which was released as *Blind Husbands*— we enter the world of von Stroheim, an intensely personal domain, in which the stamp of its creator is seen in every detail. Unlike Griffith, who never wrote anything down, von Stroheim composed the most thorough screenplays. His scripts are so complete that it would seem a simple matter merely to

follow his written directions—which even include camera angles—and thereby make a von Stroheim film. This is deceptive,
however, for there is an unknown quantity involved. It was
proved some years later when von Stroheim was succeeded on
Merry-Go-Round by another director, Rupert Julian, who
took over his predecessor's scenario and sought to follow its
explicit instructions. Yet critics noted that in the new director's
scenes the master touch was missing.

The Pinnacle was the story of Dr. Armstrong, an American
surgeon, vacationing with his wife in the Tyrolean Alps. A
young lieutenant, von Steuben, who is on furlough, comes to
the same inn. He has an eager eye for feminine charms and on
his arrival is seen studying the comely peasant wenches with a
connoisseur's appreciation through his flashing monocle. He
introduces himself to the Armstrongs, and the wife is amused
and flattered by his polite attention, his hand-kissing, his heel-
clicking, his low bows from the waist. She smiles when she
finds he has placed a sprig of edelweiss on the shoes she has left
before her bedroom door. She senses danger, but her husband's
indifference inflames the lieutenant's courtship. Dr. Armstrong,
enjoying himself in his own way, spends his time reading,
mountain climbing, and renewing his acquaintance with the
Alpine guide, Sepp. Feeling neglected, Mrs. Armstrong is
drawn more deeply into what she considers an innocent flirtation with von Steuben. She makes a vague promise of surrender, but later retracts it in a letter in which she says she loves
her husband and which she slips under the lieutenant's door.
Undaunted by this rebuff, he approaches her room one midnight, but his way is barred by Sepp, whose suspicions have
been aroused and who feels a debt of loyalty to the doctor.

Von Steuben and Dr. Armstrong set out on a perilous mountain expedition next morning and after a rigorous climb reach
the pinnacle. A letter slips from the lieutenant's coat pocket

and the doctor recognizes the handwriting of his wife, but a gust of wind blows the letter away before he can read its contents. His jealousy flames up and he demands an accounting from the officer. The two men are bound together by a rope for their mountain climbing and in the struggle the officer slips to a lower crevice. The doctor threatens to cut the rope if the lieutenant will not tell him the truth, promising not to harm him if he confesses. Terrified, von Steuben lies and replies that he has seduced the doctor's wife. In a rage, Armstrong cuts the rope, leaving the trembling officer to make his descent unaided. Von Steuben tries to climb down the mountain, slips, and is dashed to death. In the valley Armstrong finds his wife's letter and realizes that she is innocent.

Though later presented as a super-special film, on which dizzying fortunes had been spent, *The Pinnacle* was filmed quickly and efficiently on a relatively small budget. Three months saw it through the shooting stage, without delays or mishaps. Its editing—on which the director collaborated with Frank Lawrence, who had prepared the finished version of *The Heart of Humanity*, and with Viola Mailory of the Universal cutting-staff—required a month, and another two weeks were spent in final editing and trimming. Laemmle, having given his approval, did not stint on the necessary production expenses. A little Alpine village, charmingly picturesque as it supposedly nestled in the mountain side, was built on the Universal City acres. For the climactic scene on the edge of a precipice, the director and his staff visited the snow-capped California mountains. The cast contained no full-fledged stars, for von Stroheim in enacting Lieutenant von Steuben was essaying his first leading role. Sam de Grasse, a theater-trained actor, gave a vigorous account of Dr. Armstrong. Francela Billington, a slender beauty, played the wife who unwittingly risks her honor. For the only other important role, that of the rugged mountain guide Sepp, von Stroheim chose a bearded Englishman, Gibson Gowland, whom he had met on the *Hearts of the World* set. (In his mind's eye, he already saw this actor as the burly dentist of Frank Norris's novel, *McTeague*.) The drama concentrated on its four principal figures, but as slight comedy relief there was a pair of young newlyweds on their honeymoon whose endless spooning and kissing was contrasted with the strained state of the Armstrong marriage. A handsome girl of Belgian origin, Valerie Germonprez, was the young bride. Von Stroheim fell in love with her.

On Saturday evenings she and he would be seen at the meeting places where the cinema elite dined and danced. At first she and her family were wary of this man whose Hunnish villains were so convincing, but they relented when they came to know him better. Miss Germonprez became the third Mrs. von Stroheim when *The Pinnacle* was finished. Her brother, Louis, became the director's assistant, working on many of his subsequent productions.

He had first met Miss Germonprez when she had been playing a Red Cross nurse in *Hearts of the World*. One day as she stood in her nurse's uniform beside a glistening white ambulance, von Stroheim had come along in full Prussian regalia, accompanied by a band of prop men. The nurse's blue eyes had caught his attention and he wanted to impress her.

"Now look at this spic-and-span ambulance in the mud of the battlefield," he exclaimed sarcastically. "On the screen it looks as though it had dropped from heaven into the midst of no-man's land. It should be covered with dirt and muck." To illustrate his realistic theories, he bent down and scooped up a ball of mud in his white-gloved hand and threw it at the ambulance. The prop men joined him in flinging mud at the immaculate vehicle, until it resembled a front-line ambulance that had been under fire. Miss Germonprez was both impressed and amused by this, and recalled the incident when the director cast her in his first film.

Von Stroheim chose Ben Reynolds, then little known, as his cameraman. A fruitful association was thus founded, comparable to that of Eisenstein and his Swedish photographer, Edouard Tissé. Reynolds's brilliant photography became a distinguishing hallmark of the von Stroheim productions. It soon placed him in constant demand, and for many years he was the ace director of photography at the M-G-M studios. Greta Garbo insisted that he photograph all the films she made in the United States. He was several times the recipient of an Oscar for his camera work.

Uncle Carl came at last to the projection room to inspect the first film of his protégé. A quintet of Austrian musicians stood by, intending to accompany the film with a concert, but Laemmle waved them away. "Let's see it cold," he ordered.

The beginner director stood at the back of the projection room, trying desperately to control his nerves, chain-smoking and fidgeting. When the screening was over, Laemmle jumped up jubilantly and congratulated the suffering novice. Laemmle's theatrical sense told him that he had a most unusual film and a hit. He said he was delighted and only one small point worried him: the title.

"I don't like 'pinnacle.' People will confuse it with 'pinochle.' We must think of something else." After conferences with his publicity staff, *Blind Husbands* was chosen as the title. Von Stroheim, in his first argument with a producer, disapproved strenuously. Laemmle, never a quarrelsome man, did not insist.

"I'll put the decision up to the exhibitors," he announced, and an avalanche of postcards asking for their opinions was sent forth.

Von Stroheim was furious. Buying a page in the trade journal, *Motion Picture News,* he protested that artistic success should not be sacrificed to commercial success. He declared not only that authors should have more rights than producers, but that "we should assert them more frequently." An ad like this was unprecedented. Laemmle in a reply in the same space the following week hinted that perhaps von Stroheim's public protest was a bit of clever publicity. In answering the charges, he stated that he had fairly left the decision of the title up to the exhibitors. If they chose *The Pinnacle,* he would abide by it.

Meanwhile, with his cunning showmanship, he was seeking to sell *Blind Husbands* to gain the highest possible financial profit. There had been little publicity about it during its shooting, for there was always the possibility that an unknown director might fail. Now that he had an excellent film on his hands, he made it his major release of the year. Critics from the Los Angeles newspapers were invited to see it at private screenings and praised it enthusiastically. There were screenings for exhibitors all over the country and their reports inaugurated a useful whispering campaign. Major Bowes, director of the newly opened Capitol Theater on Broadway, requested a showing. When he booked the film for an engagement at his theater, it was considered a great coup for Universal.

The Universal publicity department started a typical high-pressure campaign and von Stroheim found himself involved in several undignified stunts. He was elected president of a *Blind Husbands* club which held a meeting at the Brown Palace Hotel in Denver. In paid advertisements he held forth on the subject of neglected wives. In "interviews" he gave his opinion on feminine sex psychology.

Blind Husbands—there was no overruling the collective

preference of the exhibitors for the title—had its première at the Capitol Theater on Sunday, December 7, 1919. It had been so extensively publicized that crowds, skipping their Sunday dinner, gathered in long lines waiting to be admitted to its noon opening. Its success went beyond the shrewd Laemmle's most optimistic predictions. Audiences packed the picture houses across the nation.

It was greeted, not as a promising first effort but as a mature accomplishment, by the reviewers, whose reactions were unanimously favorable. The critic of *The New York Times* wrote: "The story is developed to its full power by pictures for which no words are needed—pictures more eloquent than any words ever can be." *Variety* said that it was as superior to the films of its day as a novel by Sudermann or Schnitzler was superior to those of Robert W. Chambers. "Our second thoughts on the first day's showing of *Blind Husbands*," wrote the *Evening Globe* critic, "are more enthusiastic than the first. Bits of direction haunt one. For instance: the Austrian officer is left alone on the knob of the mountain pinnacle. He is dazed at first and does not realize the slow death he is about to face until a shadow floats across the snow— the shadow of a bird. It is too brief to be more than outline, but you suddenly know. And the condemned man knows and the consciousness of his fate creeps into his face as he watches the vulture. This is one of the many things that makes this the surprise film of the year."

In Europe it was thought that the official Puritanism of the producers required von Steuben to pay with his life for having attempted to seduce a married American woman. But this was rather a sardonic von Stroheim plot twist and part of the original script. The film was advertised as a warning to wives inclined to stray, but its creator when questioned about this replied curtly: "I am an artist, not a Presbyterian minister."

He did not go to New York to attend the première of his first film, for he was already deep in the midst of his second. *Blind Husbands* was voted one of the three best films of 1919, sharing honors with D. W. Griffith's *Broken Blossoms*, in which Lillian Gish gave one of her most haunting performances, and James Cruze's *The Miracle Man* with Lon Chaney.

Francela Billington and Sam de Grasse as Dr. and Mrs. Armstrong in *Blind Husbands*. Von Stroheim at right. *Photo courtesy of Herman G. Weinberg*

Lt. von Steuben persists in full view of Dr. Armstrong

A gift of edelweiss

The door is open but the gesture is negative

The concluding mountain scenes of *Blind Husbands*. The guide is played by Gibson Gowland. *Photo courtesy of Herman G. Weinberg*

8

The Devil's Passkey and *Foolish Wives*

THE *Devil's Passkey* was based on a story by Baroness
de Meyer, "Clothes and Treachery." Von Stroheim had
adapted the story under the title, *The Woman in the Plot*.
He made no public objections when his title was discarded,
for in this case he considered the alteration an improvement.
With Paris as its setting, the story developed the theme of
marital infidelity.

A new element was introduced by making the husband an
American playwright, Warren Goodwright. He and his pretty
young wife, Grace, reside in postwar Paris, where she runs
up exorbitant bills at a fashionable dressmaker's, Madame
Malot, who preys on the weaknesses of her clients. When
Grace's debts reach proportions beyond her husband's means,
Mme Malot suggests a handsome American officer, attached

to the embassy, as a solution for her financial embarrassment. This *couturière* maintains a deluxe suite of rooms on the premises, where such difficulties can be adjusted. When left alone with Grace in these suggestive quarters, the officer proves to be a gentleman and does not take advantage of her. However, the incident is reported in the gossip columns, the names being disguised. The dramatist-husband reads the item and welcomes it as the subject for his next play. On opening night, all Paris laughs because the playwright alone is unaware of the real identities. He discovers the truth, but he also learns that his wife is at least technically innocent. Loving and needing the irresponsible creature, he forgives her.

The tone of the film is much lighter than that of *Blind Husbands* with its Gothic premonitions of death and destiny. Midway, *The Devil's Passkey* seems to be heading for tragedy, but it swerves away from catastrophe in its last reel so suddenly that some commentators thought the director had been forced by his employers to compromise. As William Dean Howells once remarked, American audiences like the thrill of tragedy, but demand that tragedies have happy endings. Von Stroheim had produced a second hit which solidly established his directorial reputation. Most critics thought it equaled his first film and some wrote that he had surpassed himself. *The Devil's Passkey* was quite daring and "different" in 1920. The American films that dealt with modern marriage—DeMille's *Don't Change Your Husband* and *Why Change Your Wife?*, for example—were platitudinous, repeating the vulgar clichés with heavy emphasis. D. W. Griffith's version of the ancient homespun melodrama, *Way Down East*, in which a farm girl was turned out in a snowstorm because she had been seduced by a wealthy cad and given birth to an illegitimate child, was also released at this time. Its old-fashioned sentimentality was in vogue, but just barely.

In Germany during the war, Ernst Lubitsch had made a few light sex comedies such as *The Oyster Princess*, but these had not yet been seen in America and von Stroheim's subtle sophisticated approach was an attractive novelty. This innovation was timely; the Puritan standards of the United States had been shaken by the war. The film broke new ground; it made possible a more adult and humorous view of sex, and its influence was seen in many films that followed—in Charlie Chaplin's *A Woman of Paris*, in the work of Lubitsch after he was imported to Hollywood, his *The Marriage Circle*, *Kiss Me Again*, and *So This Is Paris*, and in the films of his American imitator, Mal St. Clair.

Von Stroheim reproduced the French flavor with such skill that many thought the film had been made in the French capital. There was stock footage of the Eiffel Tower, the Arc de Triomphe, the Champs-Elysées, and the Place de la Concorde, but the garden of the Inter-Allié, the stalls of the Comédie-Française, a section of the rue de la Paix (with an alarming inscription on a wall, "DON'T URINATE"), and the haremlike private salon of Mme Malot were constructed at the studio.

The film was starless, and von Stroheim did not appear in it. Sam de Grasse was cast as the American playwright and Una Trevelyan as his incautious wife. For the role of the manly military attaché, von Stroheim engaged Clyde Fillmore, whom he had seen at the Morosco Theater in Los Angeles playing a demobilized lieutenant in Thompson Buchanan's comedy, *Civilian Clothes*. Fillmore was promoted to a captaincy in *The Devil's Passkey* and cut a fine figure as the all-American hero in uniform, too noble to take advantage of the helpless lady in his power. Fillmore had never acted before the camera and his initial experience in the movies made him so nervous and insecure that the dashing soldier would often wilt.

"Remember your rank!" von Stroheim called to him through the megaphone to instill pride in his newly acquired promotion.

"Remember I'm WHAT?" inquired the bewildered actor, a retort that sent the bystanders into howls of laughter.

Maude George, the niece of Grace George, appeared as the insidious dressmaker, who is aided in her questionable trade by her husband Leo White, playing the latter with waxed mustache and much throwing of kisses in the air, a caricature Frenchman. Mae Busch gave an amusing account of the Spanish dancer of the cabarets, La Belle Odera, a piece of acting that was cited as "the high-water mark of the film," a description probably inspired by the scene in which she elaborately prepares to enter a sunken marble bathtub. The director had seen Miss Busch play a coquettish dancer in a musical comedy five years before, *Over the River*.

The four months of shooting on *The Devil's Passkey* ended in January 1920. It was edited down to eight reels by the director and the studio cutting staff, and was ready for release in early spring. But *Blind Husbands* was still running in many cities, and as summertime was then—as it is now—a profitable season for important new motion pictures, its first public showing was postponed. In April it had a press preview in Los Angeles, and the reaction of the critics was so favorable that Laemmle set a nationwide advance advertising campaign in motion. The film's risqué daring was stressed: posters with scarlet demons and dancing devils promised scandalous revelations of "Paris the Wicked, Paris the Wonderful." Stills of the forthcoming film were released to the Sunday newspapers and widely reprinted. Among then-novel scenes in the film were the Longchamps race track

The garden-party scene of *The Devil's Passkey*. Mae Busch, center, plays La Belle Odera. *Photo courtesy of Herman G. Weinberg*

Mrs. Goodwright (Una Trevelyan in white) observing a model being fitted by Monsieur Malot (Leo White). *Photo courtesy of Herman G. Weinberg*

Clyde Fillmore is exposed by Mae Busch, while Una Trevelyan
and Maude George look unhappy, in *The Devil's Passkey*

thronged with fashionable crowds, complete with doubles of such celebrities as King George V, Field Marshal Douglas Haig, Marshal Foch, and General Pershing; the opening of a chic dressmaking establishment, with beautiful mannequins parading the very latest styles; a play at the Comédie-Française; a journey down the Champs-Elysées with its café-lined sidewalks; and an embassy reception at which La Belle Odera appeared almost nude.

The making of *The Devil's Passkey* had gone smoothly and von Stroheim was now a celebrity, a director who was compared by reviewers to his old master, Griffith. Interviewers liked him; he was always good copy. Unlike his fellow moviemakers, he dressed neither like a forest ranger nor like a war correspondent. He was always impeccably and smartly clad, the traditional cap on his head, but wearing well-tailored suits and overcoats, highly polished shoes, and white gloves. Despite his look of the European aristocrat and an imposing manner, reporters found him polite, democratic, and unusually frank. There was no doubt that he had a remarkable career before him.

After the preview in April, he suffered a physical collapse from nervous exhaustion and his doctor ordered him to bed. A six-week vacation was recommended. Von Stroheim, though now a high-salaried director, lived in a small house on a busy street in Hollywood. As he lay sick, Laemmle came almost daily to consult with him. It was Laemmle's suggestion that when he was on his feet again he should combine relaxation with business and attend some trade screenings of his new film in New York. They also discussed projects for the film to follow.

When von Stroheim had found a battered copy of Frank Norris's *McTeague* in his room in a New York boarding-house a few years before, he had written the publisher, Nelson Doubleday, inquiring about film rights. Though he was hardly in a position to make a movie offer, he had hoped to raise sufficient money to option the book. Doubleday, who had employed Frank Norris in his office as a reader in 1900, replied that the novel had already been filmed! It had been retitled *Life's Whirlpool* and Holbrook Blinn, a facile light-comedy actor in the theater, had played McTeague. Fania Marinoff, an actress from the New York Yiddish theater, who later married Carl Van Vechten, had been Trina, the miserly Mrs. McTeague. *Life's Whirlpool*, a four-reeler, had not been a success in 1915. Von Stroheim with his contagious enthusiasm convinced Laemmle that he could make it into such a great film that no one would remember the earlier version. Laemmle wrote Doubleday, to whom the rights had reverted, and obtained an option. But, meanwhile, Laemmle presented another film idea to von Stroheim.

A gambler by nature, Laemmle had recently spent a few days in Reno, Nevada, a wide-open town where gambling, forbidden elsewhere in the United States, was permitted and casinos thrived. Reno was the Las Vegas of its day and it drew visitors from all over the country. It was a sort of mecca for those in search of quick and easy riches. Why not a film about Reno, where divorces were also speedily granted? Certainly a film about money and sex could not fail. Von Stroheim considered the matter and offered a counter-proposition. The basic idea was fetching, but why Reno? Why not the most famous casino in the world—Monte Carlo?

"Genius!" exclaimed the excited Laemmle, shaking the hand of his protégé warmly.

"But we must have a story," von Stroheim pointed out, "and I have an idea for one. I'll start writing the moment I'm allowed to get up."

When he recovered, von Stroheim went for a brief stay in

the mountains. In the sunny garden of an inn near Arrowhead, he mapped out his scenario. The story was fundamentally the same situation as in his first two films, the misadventures of an American couple on the Continent. The social position of the pair, however, was more elevated. The husband was to be the United States ambassador to "Mobaco," and his wife, more cautious than her more lowly sisters, would narrowly escape being seduced by a cynical, European man-of-the-world, a part that von Stroheim himself would play. To suit Laemmle's taste, he would call it *Foolish Wives*. Laemmle read the script and it had his approval at once.

Not only had his faith in his find been reassured by the enormous returns of *Blind Husbands* and *The Devil's Passkey*, but other producers were now trying to lure von Stroheim away from Universal with tempting propositions. The new director had become the movie man of the moment, the most successful Griffith disciple, possessing a fresh viewpoint that matched the postwar attitude. Taking advertising space in the *Motion Picture News*, Laemmle denounced the tactics of his underhanded rivals who were trying to steal his artists. His diatribe was headed "PUBLIC NOTICE TO CROOKED PRODUCERS," and it led off with a threat to mention them by name if they did not desist from urging directors and players under commitment to him to break their contracts:

"When Mr. von Stroheim was unknown and untried as a director, why didn't you gamble on him as Universal did? Failing to do this, why do you hang over him like vultures, seeking to grab him by hook or by crook, with the accent on crook?" He concluded: "Unfortunately for you, von Stroheim comes of good old stock, and your money and your wiles cannot tempt him from the path of honor."

However, to make doubly sure of his prized possession, the

producer offered the director carte blanche to direct and act in *Foolish Wives*.

Von Stroheim went East and in the New York offices of Universal polished the editing of *The Devil's Passkey*, tightening its narrative. Major Bowes booked it to open at his Capitol Theater in August. S. F. "Roxy" Rothafel designed the elaborate prologue for the film's presentation at the Capitol, a version of Felix Foudrain's "Carnival" with its leading vocalist, Bertram Peacock, as Satan leading a masked ball. As Peacock sang the last notes of the concluding number, the stage lights dimmed and the film commenced, a bit of theatricality that was highly praised.

The New York press echoed the advance evaluation of the exhibitors and the Los Angeles reviewers. "Von Stroheim has done another photoplay of exceptional quality," wrote the critic of *The New York Times*. "The scene is Paris and the film was evidently made there," commented the deceived reporter of the *New York Globe*. In the opinion of the *New York American*'s observer, it was "unusual, intelligently handled, sumptuously staged and marks another step forward in cinema performance."

At the year's end, *The Devil's Passkey* was voted one of the best motion pictures of 1920, sharing honors with Griffith's *Way Down East*, Frank Borzage's *Humoresque*, Maurice Tourneur's *Victory* (after the Conrad novel), and *Dr. Jekyll and Mr. Hyde* with John Barrymore.

Laemmle had decided that *Foolish Wives* must be a stupendous production, something that would go beyond anything yet seen on the screen. When von Stroheim returned to his offices at Universal City in late July, Laemmle hurried to see him, proposing a new five-year contract with improved terms and augmented salary. With this contract signed, Laemmle's worries about raiding producers vanished. He went back to his desk to begin signing checks for the construction of enormous sets. The most magnificent of these, covering several acres, reproduced in full scale the central plaza of Monte Carlo with its Casino, the Hôtel de Paris façade, and the huge café. Mistaken information introduced a streetcar line running through the square, but otherwise it was an amazingly accurate replica.

Von Stroheim liked Laemmle and was grateful for the confidence he had shown, but he did feel entitled to some security himself. He was about to engage in a very unusual venture and it was possible that Laemmle and his advisers might balk at his detailed realism. They might well draw back in the midst of production. What then? To avoid such a possibility, he employed the safety measure of making himself the star actor of the film, shooting all his important scenes first. If differences arose, there would be no way out for his backers, for without him they would have to begin all over again at prohibitive expense.

The scenario of *Foolish Wives* has been outlined by its author in the following summary:

"Count" Sergius Karamazin, a Russian émigré adventurer, and his two "cousins," the "Princesses" Olga and Vera Petschnikoff, lease a villa on the sea, near Monte Carlo. When a special American envoy, Andrew J. Hughes, accompanied by his young wife, comes to confer with the Prince of Monaco, the Muscovite impostors are anxious to meet and cultivate them to attain respectable social status.

The Count scrapes up an acquaintance with Mrs. Hughes, who is flattered by the attentions of a polished European. One day while driving in the country the Count and the envoy's wife have to take refuge from a storm in an old hut, where they are forced to spend the night. A witchlike harri-

dan, owner of this hovel, would aid the Count in the seduction of Mrs. Hughes, but the arrival of a monk saves the
honor of the American lady and keeps the impostor from
betraying his true colors. Mrs. Hughes manages to conceal
the escapade and her overnight absence from her husband.

The Count and his cousins escort the Hugheses to the
Casino, where the diplomat's wife wins 100,000 francs. It
is then proposed that the party adjourn to the Count's villa
for a few hours of poker, but Mrs. Hughes excuses herself,
complaining of a headache, and goes to her hotel.

Later in the night the Count sends her a message to come
to his house, as his life and honor are at stake and only she
can save him. He meets her and takes her to the tower of his
villa, where he first wheedles her out of 900,000 francs and
then begins to make love to her. In the meantime, her husband has caught one of the Princesses cheating at poker and
the other operating a crooked roulette wheel and has indignantly departed.

The maid in service at the Karamazin household is also
a victim of the Count's treachery. He has cheated her out
of her life's savings and seduced her, promising marriage.
When she overhears him making love to another woman in
the tower room, she locks the door of the top-floor apartment and sets fire to the house and then throws herself into
the sea.

The Count and Mrs. Hughes are rescued from the tower
by the fire department, which has been summoned to put
out the blaze. The Count reveals his cowardice by jumping
into the net first. Hughes arrives, knocks the Count down,
and orders him and his two female accomplices to leave
Monte Carlo at once.

Infuriated by his folly, which will center suspicion upon
them, the Princesses drive the Count from the villa. He goes
to the home of Ventucci, an old counterfeiter for whom he
has been passing money, to spend the night. The counterfeiter's half-witted daughter is alone in the house and his
bestiality is aroused when he sees her asleep, lightly clad.
He violates her, but she is his last victim, for Ventucci re-

turns, kills him, and deposits his body in a sewer. The corpse is seen floating out to sea with other rubbish as the early morning mist dissolves over the harbor.

The Hugheses are reconciled. The terror of the night has caused the wife to give premature birth to a baby. Her horrendous experiences have taught her that it is best not to flirt with strange men.

On the screen this melodrama came to life with sardonic wit, persuasive atmosphere, and flashes of realism. In its precise detail, down to the buttons of the last lackey at the Casino, it seemed a truthful large slice of decadent high-life on the Continent. Von Stroheim impersonated the rascally Karamazin with undisguised relish, as he strutted the promenade in tight-fitting white uniform and black riding boots of the Russian Imperial Army. His character was revealed by cinematic means. One sees him first breakfasting luxuriously in Russian pajamas in the sunny garden of his villa, while his wolfhounds frisk about. As he partakes of his morning caviar, with oxblood to wash it down, his two mistresses make much of him. His cruelty, as well as his deadly marksmanship, are shown in the scene of the pigeon shoot; his cowardice at the climax, where in panic he leaps before the lady into the rescue net. His insatiable desire for women is a motif throughout. "It is a fine portrayal of the sort of maniac we lock up in America for the protection of our daughters and wives," wrote Quinn Martin in the *New York World*. This is exactly what the von Stroheim characterization intended to show, though some felt he enjoyed himself too much, stressing the male vanity of the part.

In other scenes from which he was absent, the von Stroheim touch was present. The American envoy arrives on a warship, and it is a real U.S. warship with its real captain playing a part. Similarly, the ceremony in which the diplomatic visitor presents his credentials to the Prince was done strictly in accord with protocol. One bit of business often cited had to do with an American marine officer in a cloak. In the hotel elevator he fails to take off his cap when Mrs. Hughes enters, and she gives him a cutting look. Later on the terrace she drops a book while he is nearby and he makes no effort to pick it up. Again she glances with scorn in his direction. On their third encounter, the officer's cloak falls from his shoulders: he is armless. She picks it up, but, before restoring his cloak to his shoulders, kisses the wound strips on his sleeve with a look beseeching pardon.

Few films have ever belonged as completely to one man as this one did, but it was far from a "one-man" show. When it came to casting, von Stroheim wanted no stars. "I believe there is not a man or a woman in the world who could not act in films, given a really suitable role and properly directed," he told an interviewer. He insisted that an unknown girl, a former modiste, who happened to come to the Universal studios on a costuming mission, be given the leading feminine role, that of the foolish wife, Mrs. Hughes. Miss Armstrong had at first balked at even making a screen test, but von Stroheim as usual was a persuasive talker. For publicity purposes she would be the mysterious "Miss Dupont," and in a contest fans would be asked to guess her first name. "Miss Dupont," only twenty-one, contributed a well-modulated performance as the much-harassed Mrs. Hughes.

George Christians, whom von Stroheim had seen on the Vienna stage and at the German-speaking theater that existed in prewar days in Irving Place in New York, was cast as the American envoy. Shortly before the shooting ended, Mr. Christians suffered a heart attack and died. For his remaining scene, Robert Edson, a well-known American actor, was recruited as a substitute. Filmed from behind his back, these sequences were so cleverly faked that the trickery was not detected.

Mae Busch and Maude George, as a reward for their sprightly performances in *The Devil's Passkey*, were asked to play the princesses. Among their many duties was the comic interlude in which they lace their cousin into his corset, a shocking revelation of European military attire to millions of American moviegoers. Dale Fuller was selected as the love-sick chambermaid who sets fire to the villa; her portrayal of the frustrated servant was a histrionic triumph beyond the emotional powers of most of the screen favorites. Cesare Gravina, once a conductor at La Scala in Milan, an expert player of Venetian gentlemen in Goldoni comedies, and the former secretary of the great Caruso (who had returned to Italy to die that year), was engaged to impersonate the avenging counterfeiter. Malvine Polo appeared as his idiot daughter.

As expenses mounted, Laemmle decided to publicize the vast sums that he was spending on his breathtaking venture. The large-scale production was becoming not the exception, but the rule. The public wanted "big" pictures. Over on the Metro lot a young Irish-born director, Rex Ingram, who had been under contract at Universal previously, was making a film version of Blasco-Ibáñez's best-seller of the war years, *The Four Horsemen of the Apocalypse*, with an obscure, young Italian tango dancer, Rudolph Valentino. Metro, in shaky financial shape, was banking its future on this enterprise. Douglas Fairbanks had just started his first elaborate romantic spectacle, *The Mark of Zorro*, and was planning to follow it with *The Three Musketeers*. Mary Pickford was negotiating to import Ernst Lubitsch from Berlin to direct her in a spectacle. William Randolph Hearst announced a historic epic, *When Knighthood Was in Flower*, as Marion Davies's next production.

Shooting on *Foolish Wives*—with Ben Reynolds as chief cameraman and William Daniels as his assistant—covered almost a year, from July 12, 1920, to June 18, 1921, with 32 reels filmed. Much of it was made, of course, on the costly sets at Universal City, but there were location excursions to the Exposition grounds at San Diego, to the cliffs of La Jolla for the mad maid's dive into the sea, and to the lake of a Los Angeles park for the battle-of-flowers carnival-night scenes. At Del Monte, a fashionable seaside resort in northern California, the façades of the buildings along the Riviera promenade were set up along the coast. They were so often clouded in the swift-rising afternoon fog that von Stroheim was sometimes forced to call an early halt to the day's work.

The Del Monte expedition was reported on front pages, because four hundred San Francisco society leaders agreed to appear as extras, their salaries to benefit a charity. They were delighted to be the smart strollers of the Monte Carlo promenade and arrived for a weekend stay in a parade of automobiles. The Burlingame smart set was enchanted to meet the European director and to have a look at moviemaking. They all noted, however, that once he reached for the megaphone he could become extremely rude and blunt.

"You fireman there!" von Stroheim would shout. "Put on those gloves. What do you think you're given them for—to play with?"

Three baby carriages chauffeured by gray-uniformed nursemaids were to pass before the cameras. He spotted a deserted carriage in a secluded corner. "Who's on this baby carriage?" the megaphone would roar. "You are? Well, your job is to wheel that carriage and keep on wheeling it until the baby dies of old age."

When the society visitors, uncertain what to do, huddled together, he shouted: "Move, please move. Show a little life, can't you? Stop looking like a bunch of dead fish. Let's see some spirit and swagger. This is NOT a funeral!"

It finally dawned on Laemmle that he might be in deep waters financially. He was risking the future of his studio with an extravagant gamble. The American tycoon Gates had gained notoriety by his constant repetition of the wager "Bet you a million." Laemmle was betting a million (or so he said) on *Foolish Wives*. So why not advertise it as "the first million-dollar picture"? That would make the public sit up and take notice.

The New York office was alerted to sound the opening drums of the new campaign, months before the film would be ready for release. The East Coast headquarters responded by erecting a commanding electric sign on Broadway. The figures of the forthcoming film's budget blazed out in golden Mazda bulbs. As an additional publicity stunt, the New York fire engines with sirens screaming arrived each Wednesday at noon to change these bulbs to the latest estimate wired from Hollywood. The S in von Stroheim's name appeared on this gaudy billboard as a dollar sign.

Meanwhile, Laemmle held forth in his weekly column on the fascinating subject of how much money he was spending. All this to-do gave a junior Universal executive much to think about. His name was Irving Thalberg, and he was only twenty-five. Dark-haired, of small stature, and very slender, he was a dynamo of nervous energy. His mind was as alert as his body. Thalberg had been spotted by Laemmle when the president visited his New York offices. The young man's drive and "picture sense" had impressed his employer and he invited him to the Hollywood studios.

Thalberg, soon in charge of the Universal studios, was now

contemplating a reform program. As he studied the figures of the rising expenses of *Foolish Wives,* and as he observed von Stroheim's perfectionist technique, with the endless retaking of scenes until the right effect was achieved, he contemplated a plan that would control all directors. Why not appoint a supervisor, acting for the studio, to oversee production matters, casting, expenditures on costumes, settings, footage, location work, salaries? Such a supervisor need not be a dictator, but he would be entrusted to make the final decisions after conferring both with the director and with the studio board. It was from this idea of Thalberg's that the modern producer arose. The producer was soon to overshadow the director in the realization of films—at least in Hollywood.

Although not taking the title of producer officially—either then or later when he was in charge of production at M-G-M—Thalberg inaugurated the practice of his producer theory by entering into long discussion and disputes with von Stroheim concerning the production of *Foolish Wives.* When urgent business called Thalberg to the New York offices of Universal early in May 1921, he appointed Edwin Loeb (one of the two brothers of Universal's law firm, Loeb and Loeb) to act in his stead. Loeb was instructed to keep a watch on von Stroheim and to report to Thalberg if the director failed to obey orders. A violent disagreement soon occurred.

Permission from the municipal authorities had been granted for the night filming of some scenes of the Monte Carlo battle-of-flowers carnival sequences on a lake in a Los Angeles park. This permission extended only until midnight. Von Stroheim objected that this would not allow him sufficient time to take the close-ups. Loeb arranged for the permit to be extended so that shooting might continue all night, but he firmly stipulated that the shooting must be completed by dawn. The next afternoon Loeb received word that von Stroheim and his crew were returning to the park for another all-night session. He had the lighting apparatus removed from the park, but von Stroheim went back and shot in the semi-darkness. The following night, when von Stroheim arrived for still more shooting, the cameras had been confiscated by the studio representatives.

This terminated the filming of *Foolish Wives*. The director had planned to take more close-ups in La Jolla, to match the scenes shot there when the film was in its early stages, but Thalberg, acting through Loeb, refused to consider this.

When the shooting of *Foolish Wives* ended—it had been "on the floor" longer than any film in motion-picture history —von Stroheim retired to the cutting room, where he spent the summer of 1921 clipping the miles of footage into a presentable ensemble.

In its finished form, *Foolish Wives* was in thirty-two reels. The director demanded that it be shown as a full-blown von Stroheim production. "But how?" inquired Laemmle and Thalberg. It would run for six hours. Its creator suggested that it be shown in two parts, released simultaneously in two theaters in each city. Such a plan was insane, argued Thalberg. And the junior executive, having won Laemmle to his side, locked von Stroheim out of the cutting room and gave the editing task to Arthur D. Ripley, who reduced it to ten reels.

Von Stroheim stormed and raged over this adaptation, and a slight concession was made to him. At the New York première a three-hour version would be presented to the press and first-nighters. If they felt it was not overlong, the film would be released in that form. There was gossip now about the behind-the-scenes differences of the Universal president and his star director, and to curb the exaggerated rumors, the president and the director, together with their wives, agreed to attend the world première in New York.

On January 11, 1922, *Foolish Wives* had its gala première at the Central Theater on Broadway. Shown in twenty-four reels, it ran until past midnight. Sigmund Romberg had composed a special score with an ominous hunting-horn effect to herald every entrance of the sinister Karamazin, and with themes for all the other characters.

The first-nighters applauded enthusiastically and the reviews next morning echoed their approval. "I have seen many motion pictures and *Foolish Wives* is the best photoplay I have ever seen without any exceptions whatever," wrote Harriet Underhill in the *New York Tribune*, and the other comments were of a similar tenor, though there were complaints that the film was too long, and some found its scenario "unpleasant" and "in the decadent Continental vein." One editorial writer wanted to know if the censors were on vacation when *Foolish Wives* was granted a license.

Puritanic censorship ruled literature and the theater with a firm hand in the United States in 1922. Such distinguished novels as Dreiser's *The "Genius,"* James Branch Cabell's *Jurgen,* and James Joyce's *Ulysses* were forbidden publication.

The New York State censorship board had made no objections to the twenty-four reel version of *Foolish Wives* and had issued a permit for its public showing. After its première, however, it threatened to revoke the license if cuts were not immediately made. Universal officials were anxious to cut down the running time of *Foolish Wives* in any case. They were able to claim that they were shortening it to make it better entertainment, but in point of fact they complied with all the demands of the censors. The sequence of the premature birth had given offense; some viewers thought it was an illegitimate child by Karamazin. For its road-show engagement, *Foolish Wives* was trimmed to twelve reels; later it became ten reels for general release.

The wartime distrust of von Stroheim had not died and to some people he was still a hated object. He had a particularly unpleasant experience the night after the première, as he and his wife were dining at the L'Aiglon restaurant. A party was ushered in to occupy the table beside him, and on seeing him, one of the women emitted a horrified shriek.

"How dare you place us next to that unspeakable man!" she said in a loud voice, reprimanding the maître d'hôtel. "We'll leave this place at once!"

She and her guests angrily departed, leaving the von Stroheims very embarrassed.

When Miss Underhill of the *Tribune* interviewed the actor-director after the triumphant opening of his new film, she found him in a depressed mood. He regarded her gravely with sad eyes and he seemed to be playing another role, that of a recluse from a harsh and unkind world. She restated her admiration of his film.

"You are too kind," he replied sadly. "Your sympathy is like the handclasp of a friend at the open grave of a loved one."

"What do you mean?" she inquired. "Do you call the Central Theater an open grave? Your 'loved one' is the best picture I ever saw."

"You are too kind," he repeated. "But they are showing only the skeleton of my dead child."

"But you can't run a picture of one hundred reels. People want to go home about midnight."

"I know, I know," he continued, more in sorrow than in anger. "But why not let me do the cutting? I was the proper person to do it, not all these brainless hacks and Puritans. It was *my* brain child."

Miss Underhill tried to cheer him. "There will be more films. I feel that you are going to have a large family."

To Quinn Martin of the *New York World* he outlined his directorial methods. "We can't hope to compete with foreign films until we can conquer two handicaps—the cry from producers, 'Keep down your footage,' and censorship which prevents the delineation of real life, the sort of things expressed in Tolstoy, Turgenev, and Schnitzler," he said. "The spectator's intelligence is often insulted by the screen versions of famous stories, because the director is held down on footage, so he can only show effects without being allowed the space to explain them and approach them properly."

Von Stroheim went on to explain some of his directorial principles: "I believe in the moving background, even during an important dialogue between two principals. Because two characters are conversing in the foreground there is no reason why a streetcar should not be passing in the distance, or a maid should not come out on a balcony and shake out a dustcloth, or people should not be passing near the couple.

"Then there is a great prejudice against allowing actors to wear glasses, because of the halations that take place when the light strikes the edges. As these things take place in real life, why not on the screen? I am very fond of these halations on highly polished surfaces. I insisted on having the windows of the Monte Carlo set made of plate glass instead of the wire screening they wanted me to use.

"The makeup of an actress is another case in point. Why should every little pimple be eradicated? The men in my films, including myself, do not wear makeup at all. I read my scenario to my players as a stage manager does. Then they read their parts separately. We act the scenes out with the people in their proper places, sometimes for two or three days before a single scene is shot."

132

On the whole, this personal appearance in New York was rewarding, and von Stroheim impressed his interviewers as an artist with his own point of view.

The censors, however, continued to strike at *Foolish Wives*. It was banned from showing in any form in the state of Ohio. *Photoplay* magazine damned it as "an insult to every American." The D.A.R. in Texas condemned it and requested that it be withdrawn. A clergyman in San Francisco, the Reverend Walter John Sherman of the Central Methodist Church, called a meeting of the Women's Vigilant Committee and urged it to take action against the film. "The picture," thundered Dr. Sherman, "is the result of a man's idea of sex appeal. It is a disgusting story of lust. Not only is gambling shown, but men and women are seen brazenly smoking cigarettes."

San Francisco is a liberal-minded city and its public was eager to see *Foolish Wives*; yet Puritanic power was such that a police corporal, representing the Vigilant Committee, called on the theater manager and obtained a few cuts in the film's scenes. Laemmle, von Stroheim, and Thalberg, returning from the San Francisco opening, read in their Pullman drawing room the accounts of Methodist meetings at which they had been denounced as "foul" and "filthy" and were accused of trying to corrupt the American people with their Prussian degeneracy. The Puritans had imposed Prohibition on the country, but their proposed legislation for "clean books" and "clean plays" had failed to become law. They were reduced to these unofficial attacks, hoping in vain to gather public support behind them.

The Casino, Hotel and Café de Paris at Monte Carlo reconstructed
in Hollywood under von Stroheim's orders, for *Foolish Wives*

Maude George and Marguerite Armstrong ("Miss Dupont") with von Stroheim in *Foolish Wives*

(OPPOSITE) The bogus "Count" and his friends (Mae Busch at right) live it up

The U. S. Ambassador's wife gets more than she bargained for in
Foolish Wives

9

Merry-Go-Round and Departure from Universal

THALBERG and von Stroheim at this juncture discussed a new film. Circus stories seemed to be popular. In New York they had seen the Andreyev play *He Who Gets Slapped*, about a heartbroken clown, which had already been purchased by Metro. Molnar's *Liliom* also had a sort of a circus background, the Budapest carnival grounds. Thalberg suggested a circus film with a Continental setting. In a sudden flash, the Vienna Prater, the pleasure park with its show booths and cafés, its Ferris wheel and merry-go-round, rose in von Stroheim's mind. Here was the real meeting place where the rich and the poor of the city rubbed elbows democratically on holidays. His eyes lighted with a wave of memories of his birthplace.

"Got an idea?" questioned the alert Thalberg, noticing that his companion was smiling to himself.

"*Half* an idea," answered the cautious director. "Let's wait until we get back to the studio and look over the stories on my desk." It was piled high with manuscripts when he arrived at his office at Universal. A rapid reader, he scanned them with repeated disappointment. After a week of drudgery, he informed his employers that he would take a brief mountain vacation and outline a notion for his new film.

Merry-Go-Round, the fruit of a few weeks at Mount Whitney, was, its author believed, the best story he ever wrote for the screen. It had a background with which he was intimately familiar and, like *Old Heidelberg*, its central plot revolved about the impossibility of marriage between an aristocrat and a girl of the people. This theme is almost as old as drama itself, and was the subject of countless comedies and operettas before Meyer-Förster placed it in the setting of Heidelberg's gleaming spires. It was the Meyer-Förster version, with its wistful melancholy, bittersweet charm, and tale of youth and lost love, that appealed so strongly to von Stroheim. Thomas Mann has written of that play's curious power to draw sentimental tears; the caustic American critic, George Jean Nathan, listed it as one of the ten finest plays of the modern theater.

The germ of the idea, a "circus" film, grew in the writing into an allegory of Vienna before, during, and after the Great War. A young count is commanded by the Emperor to wed a princess of the court. The count has no affection for his fiancée; imperious and spoiled, he leads a dissipated existence. Regretting that his gay bachelor life is soon to end, he goes in mufti with a brother officer to carouse in the Prater. There he encounters a sweet-faced girl who turns the handle of the carousel's organ. He lies to her, telling her that he is a necktie salesman, and later takes her to a *maison de rendezvous*, intending to seduce her. But her purity and innocence awake his tenderness and he restrains himself, realizing that he has at last fallen in love. The girl has a bitter time of it. Her mother dies and her savage employer treads on her foot to make her smile as she cranks the hurdy-gurdy. On several occasions he tries to violate her, but her old father—a circus clown who runs a puppet show—and a pathetic hunchback boy who loves her secretly, intervene to protect her honor. The boss is a repulsive sadist who beats his wife, the cashier of the carousel on the fairgrounds. He also enjoys driving a caged gorilla into fury with his taunts. One night the hunchback leaves the cage door open and the animal climbs out, finds the boss while he is slumbering, and wrings his neck. When the forced marriage to the princess takes place, the girl understands the count's deception. Then World War I breaks out, and the count is sent to front-line duty. Vienna suffers revolution and starvation and the bright lights of the Prater are dimmed. After the war the count, impoverished and humbled, comes back to find the merry-go-round maiden. His wife has died and he proposes at last to his true love. Behind the bushes the hunchback, whom the girl has promised to marry, overhears her confession of love to the count. He creeps away to commit suicide, leaving the lovers to wed.

Von Stroheim's cinematic imagination is shown in the use of a motif—a diabolic giant seen capriciously lifting in his mammoth hands the tiny figures revolving on a merry-go-round. He examines them as they struggle in his grasp, and then sets them back or wantonly tosses them away. He roars with laughter as the carousel that encircles him spins about. This macabre symbol of tragic destiny provides the keynote of the film and is reintroduced at climactic points in the narrative.

A vista of Vienna with its sparkling lights dissolves into a shot in which a suicide leaps from a bridge into the Danube.

The gay masque of the Prater with its pleasure-seeking crowds is followed by a scene showing the bestial Huber dining with his terrified wife. He cuts himself a huge hunk of sausage and throws her a tiny sliver as if she were an animal. Later, when the puppet-show performance draws the spectators away from his carousel concession, Huber pushes a heavy flowerpot off the overhanging balcony onto the puppeteer's head. The old man continues to play his part, his head bleeding, until he is taken away in an ambulance. With such harsh strokes von Stroheim painted the milieu and the people of the Prater, exposing the tragedy and brutality that lay beneath its tinsel surface.

The aristocracy he satirized in a more witty tone. The count is first seen as he is being roused from sleep in a magnificent bed in his palace. The obsequious valet has drawn his bath, into which his Great Dane dog has already ventured. The ceremony with which he dresses, his eye-opener cocktail —all help to create the pampered, self-indulgent dandy. The psychology of the bride chosen for the count arouses one's curiosity at once. In the stable she seizes her groom and passionately kisses him, and then strikes him with her riding crop when he tremblingly reciprocates. The pair, embracing, sink down on the straw of a stall as a horse turns its head to look on. She is next seen in her boudoir, where she throws herself on a divan and lights a long black cigar. When her maid attempts to pull off her riding boots, she kicks her over.

The script is crowded with the unusual and bizarre, and cynical humor is alternated with tragedy. Luxurious high life, photographed with dazzling sheen, is contrasted with the grim sub-world of misery and brutality. Fellow officers celebrate the forthcoming marriage of the count with an orgy at which a naked girl steps from an enormous covered champagne-filled bowl in the middle of the table.

The striking emotional conflicts of *Merry-Go-Round* marked an advance in von Stroheim's style both as a writer and as a director. As he recited his "circus" story to Thalberg, the young executive listened intently, whirling his watch chain and nodding approval.

"It's sold!" cried Thalberg, jumping up from his desk when the author had described the final scene. "Congratulations, Von! It's great!"

He had, nevertheless, a few reservations. The count in returning from the war must not be maimed. In the first draft, the count was to be minus an arm and so reduced in fortune that he was driven to shining the shoes of war-profiteers in an arcade booth. The author conceded this point, but when he was told that the part he had written for himself—the count—must be played by another, he flew into a temper and used strong language. Laemmle sided with Thalberg on the casting decision. Von Stroheim would direct, but he would not play the leading role or any other role.

Norman Kerry, whom the director had met in New York as an agent some years before, was now under contract to Universal. A fine figure of a man, though a bit stiff in his acting, he was selected to be the playboy count. For the brutal Huber, von Stroheim insisted on Wallace Beery, who had just played Richard the Lion-Hearted in Douglas Fairbanks's *Robin Hood* and whose reputation as a character actor would soon make him a star. George Hackathorn, another contract player, was cast as the hunchback. Sidney Bracey, who became a standard fixture of von Stroheim productions, was cast as the count's valet, and Captain Albert Conti was engaged to be the count's confidant. He cut a convincing military figure and, like von Stroheim, had served in the Austrian Army.

There were other von Stroheim favorites—Maude George as the madam, Cesare Gravina as the old clown, and Dale

Fuller as Frau Huber. After quite a delay (she was making a film at another studio), Dorothy Wallace came to enact the perverse princess-bride. Anton Wawerka, another Austrian Army veteran of Czech birth, was recruited to impersonate his former commander-in-chief, Emperor Franz-Josef.

Construction work on the series of elaborate sets—including a complete reproduction of a section of the Prater—began at once. Elmer Sheeley and Richard Day were art directors of the unit, with Archie Hall as technical director. Edward Sowders, von Stroheim's first assistant, and Louis Germonprez, his personal adjutant, interviewed a large number of applicants, eliminating all but those reviewed by the director for parts as soldiers or hired hands in the Prater.

Uniforms, medals, swords, and other relics of Austria's glory under the Habsburgs were imported from Vienna, including the late Emperor's golden coach. When the news-wire services carried a report that the ex-Emperor Karl and his wife, the ex-Empress Zita, were destitute in their exile at Funchal, Madeira Islands, Laemmle cabled them offering them a quarter of a million dollars if they would come to California and appear in a motion picture being directed by their former subject. They never replied.

Von Stroheim had had a certain player in mind as he wrote the script. Two years before, he had been delegated by the studio to serve as judge at a beauty contest in Chicago, the winner to receive a film contract at Universal. A nineteen-year-old Chicago girl, fresh from high school, had been in his opinion the prettiest of the Midwest beauty contestants. Her name was Mary Philbin. No one seemed to have much faith in her; she was just another pretty face on the lot and, though she had appeared in several pictures, professionally she was nowhere. Von Stroheim had thought of her as he created the character of Mitzi, and now he wanted her to play the role.

The production was an expensive one and Laemmle and Thalberg were skeptical about Miss Philbin's talents, but as the players under von Stroheim's direction seemed always to display hitherto hidden abilities, they reluctantly agreed.

On August 22, 1922, von Stroheim with Ben Reynolds and William Daniels as his cameramen, began shooting on *Merry-Go-Round.* Laemmle was on hand at the zero hour as the director bawled out through his megaphone the initial "cammmmerra." Laemmle shook his hand, wished him luck, and then departed for a vacation in Europe, leaving Thalberg in full charge of the studio.

Merry-Go-Round, though it was a special Universal production, was not announced as the "second million-dollar picture." Thalberg believed such boasting might encourage the director to surpass his reputation for wasteful spending; he intended to keep a close watch on expenditures. No sooner had the battery of cameras begun to grind than Hollywood was flooded with the most extraordinary rumors. Now that Laemmle was absent, it was said, von Stroheim and Thalberg were heading for a terrific clash. Silly stories about the director's autocratic behavior and incredible extravagance were widely spread and believed. In the scene in which the count steps from his bed, he is seen in a monogrammed nightgown. This fact was soon distorted by gossips who said that all the soldiers in the film wore monogrammed underwear, stamped with the Imperial coat-of-arms. Hours were being wasted while the director drilled troops in the goose-step. If an orderly failed to give the absolutely correct salute, the whole production was held up until he did. Every shot was being taken fifteen times or more. There was no way to prevent such talk, and the studio was not particularly concerned about curbing it. All such chitchat about the film simply gave it additional importance. Several papers had predicted that *Foolish Wives* would be von Stroheim's swan-song, yet it was playing to packed houses everywhere. Obviously Laemmle had given his blessing to the new project, though the rumor persisted that Universal was anxious to sever its contract with the director.

The film, contrary to the usual procedure, was being shot more or less in sequence, as von Stroheim wanted his players to grow into their parts as the drama progressed. Mary Philbin was responding wonderfully to his direction.

After five weeks of filming, the principals and a crowd of extras gathered on the huge outdoor Prater set for night shooting. All evening von Stroheim had been rehearsing Mary Philbin and Wallace Beery in an important scene, while Thalberg stood watching on the sidelines. It was past midnight and Thalberg had gone back to his office, when von Stroheim climbed the high stand where the cameras stood to register a commanding view of the pleasure park. There was a chill in the early-morning air, and the director reached for his hip flask to take a warming swallow of whiskey. No sooner had he done so than an attendant tapped him on the arm and handed him a message: report at once to Thalberg's office.

Pale and taut, a challenge in his dark eyes, Thalberg faced von Stroheim in the dimly lighted executive suite. Fearing perhaps even a physical attack, he trembled as he spoke.

"Von, you're off the picture!" he announced.

Von Stroheim glared at him and then, turning on his heel, walked out. He went directly to his own office. The news reached the set in a matter of minutes, causing panic and bewilderment. Everyone there had been personally selected by the dismissed director. Would they all now be out of work?

Mary Philbin burst into tears. "I can't act without Mr. Von," she said pathetically.

Wallace Beery proclaimed in a loud voice: "If Von is off, so am I," and stalked from the Prater. But though loyalty for the director was high, the others dared not follow. In the late-night cafés of Hollywood the word was being spread: "Von Stroheim's through at Universal." The long-circulated rumor was now a fact.

William Wyler, then a young assistant, heard the news as he sat with some friends in a restaurant. An employee at Universal and a distant relative of Laemmle, he telephoned the studio for confirmation. Yes, it was true. And he knew what it signified. The power of a great director in the American cinema had been broken by a producer. The era of the director was over. Henceforth, the movies would be under the rule of the producers.

Von Stroheim's complete and docile surrender to Thalberg surprised Hollywood observers and the general public. A more sensational showdown, with at least a fistfight and perhaps even a gunfight, had been expected. It was disappointing that the ex-soldier had not battled for his rights. It was probably the last opportunity for a strong director to take a public stand against the money-men who were profiting so handsomely from his work.

When, after Laemmle's departure for Europe, the ambitious Thalberg had begun to badger von Stroheim, the latter had meditated secretly on a fantastic plan. He thought of organizing his followers on the lot—and they numbered several hundreds—into an underground group. On a given night they would seize the Universal City post office, wire Laemmle that his studio had been occupied by the director's troops, and keep Thalberg from entering its gates. This would have been, indeed, a magnificent gesture and a publicity stunt to surpass even those of Laemmle. But its execution was vetoed by Mrs. von Stroheim, whom the director always consulted. One does not do such things in America, she informed him. His attorney not only agreed but warned him that such a move might put him in prison. Thus, most unfortunately in his own view, he restrained himself from realizing one of his most amusing notions.

He was also advised by his attorney to make no statement to the press until Universal released the news of his dismissal officially. He was told it would be unwise to bring suit against the studio, as his contract would be settled as a matter of course, whereas a suit might take months and prevent him from accepting other offers.

His scenario of *Merry-Go-Round,* having been purchased by Universal, was the property of the studio and Laemmle and Thalberg could do what they wished with it—which they proceeded to do. Rupert Julian, best known for his wartime *Beast of Berlin* film, was appointed director of the film. With one exception, the original company was retained, as all its members had already been registered in the film. Wallace Beery, who refused to return, was replaced ironically by von Stroheim's old enemy, George Siegman. The original scenario was revised and shortened, and some early scenes made by von Stroheim were included in the released version. It finally appeared and proved a great success in the summer of 1923. Only Rupert Julian received screen credit.

Von Stroheim now found—as Laemmle had long suspected—that he was in great demand. The American movies were changing and his sophisticated treatment of sex, despite the censors, was in vogue. D. W. Griffith's *Orphans of the Storm,* a version of an old melodrama of the French Revolution, had opened the same week as *Foolish Wives* in New York. *Orphans of the Storm* was to be the old master's last

great popular success and the last film in which Lillian Gish
was to appear under his direction. Acclaimed as the screen's
outstanding tragic actress, Miss Gish formed her own company, Inspirational Pictures, in 1922. Engaging Henry King
as her director (he, too, had come to the fore this year with
'Tol'able David'), she went off to Italy to make *The White
Sister.*

One reason why von Stroheim had few regrets in leaving
Universal was that he had been forced to work under supervision. He demanded complete independence, and it was generally agreed, in the offers that now flooded his desk, that he
should have it. Inviting proposals arrived from Vienna, Berlin, and Rome; W. R. Hearst sought to woo him for his new
company, Cosmopolitan Pictures.

It was the Goldwyn Company he decided to join. At Goldwyn, which was being reorganized with Metro, June Mathis
had been engaged to take an important post as chief of the
scenario division. It was Miss Mathis who had chosen Rex
Ingram to direct *The Four Horsemen of the Apocalypse* and
Rudolph Valentino to play its leading role. This film had
saved Marcus Loew's Metro Corporation from threatening
bankruptcy. Miss Mathis's word was law at the new Goldwyn studios, and when she suggested that it would be a
tremendous coup to sign von Stroheim, an irresistible offer
was made to him.

He was to have carte blanche and to direct the major
Goldwyn pictures. Their most valuable property was *Ben
Hur,* planned on a stupendous scale. Though Griffith had
been considered as its director, it now seemed that von Stroheim was the man of the moment. When early in December
1922 the refugee from Universal signed his attractive contract
with the new company, the occasion was celebrated with a
dinner party at the Hotel Ambassador, and there was specu-

lation in the trade papers that *Ben Hur* would be his first film. The trusted Miss Mathis was at work on the adaptation. She too thought that von Stroheim would be the ideal director to undertake it, but the script and casting and organization of the production would require time.

Meanwhile, he was asked if he had another film he wanted to do. Now was the moment to propose his favorite project, a film of Frank Norris's *McTeague*. The company acquired the novel's screen rights, and before Christmas von Stroheim was in San Francisco searching for locations.

When the critics voted on the ten best films of 1922, *Foolish Wives* was given a high place, together with *Orphans of the Storm*; Harold Lloyd's *Grandma's Boy*; *Blood and Sand*, with Rudolph Valentino; Robert Flaherty's *Nanook of the North*; Rex Ingram's *The Prisoner of Zenda*, another boost to the fortunes of Metro; *When Knighthood Was in Flower*, with Marion Davies; Douglas Fairbanks's *Robin Hood*; *Oliver Twist*, with Jackie Coogan as Oliver and Lon Chaney as Fagin; *Smilin' Through* with Norma Talmadge; and *Tol'able David*. *Merry-Go-Round* did not make the list.

One of the opening scenes of *Merry-Go-Round*: the tradesmen's entrance at the palace. *Photo courtesy of Herman G. Weinberg*

The Prince (Norman Kerry) and his valet. *Photo courtesy of Herman G. Weinberg*

The cigar-smoking Countess (Dorothy Wallace) in her boudoir.
Photo courtesy of Herman G. Weinberg

Dale Fuller sells carousel tickets to Norman Kerry and his festive
friends at the Prater. *Photo courtesy of Herman C. Weinberg*

Mary Philbin as Mitzi, Cesare Gravina as her father, and George Siegman as the brutal carousel owner. *Photo courtesy of Herman G. Weinberg*

A censored scene cut from von Stroheim's part of *Merry-Go-Round*:
the Countess's affair with her groom (Sidney Bracey) amuses her more
than him. *Photo courtesy of Herman G. Weinberg*

Emperor Franz-Josef (Anton Wawerka) at the wedding. *Photo courtesy of Herman G. Weinberg*

10

Greed

F<small>RANK</small> Norris's *McTeague* was published in 1899. Written in imitation of Zola, it was the first naturalistic American novel and exercised a profound influence on Theodore Dreiser and other native realists. Norris, a young Californian of distinguished family, had been educated at Harvard and had studied art in Paris, where he fell under the spell of Flaubert and Zola. He planned and wrote two volumes (*The Octopus* and *The Pit*) of a trilogy of novels that was to form "an epic of wheat," before his early death at thirty-two in 1902. In addition to writing fiction, he worked as a journalist in San Francisco. Newspaper accounts of the murder of a charwoman caught his attention and he investigated the case himself. In doing so, he found such color and drama in the city's lower-middle-class life that he decided to use it in the writing of a milieu novel, with the murder case as its climax.

He gave *McTeague* the subtitle that captured von Stroheim's eye, "A Story of San Francisco." He drew on his own knowledge of the city, arranging the details of petty-bourgeois conduct and standards as he, a wealthy young man slumming in the poorer quarters, had observed them. He added vivid descriptions of the bay and of the Mojave Desert. Von Stroheim has summarized the story as follows:

McTeague, a car-boy in the Big Dipper gold mine of the California mountains, is the son of a miner who dies of delirium tremens. His mother is a worn-out drudge who slaves in the camp's kitchen. McTeague is "a human beast" —after the Zola model—a giant of abnormal strength and slow wits. He is a victim of circumstances and environment, unable to guide the destiny that is beyond his stupid comprehension. He can battle men, but not inexorable fate. On the surface he is placid and gentle, good-natured and well-meaning. But within him a savage brute lies dormant.

A traveling dentist visits the mining camp and, noting McTeague's powerful hands ("already like mallets"), employs him as a tooth-extractor. When the dentist leaves, McTeague goes with him to learn his trade. Having mastered the rudiments of dentistry, McTeague some years later opens a dental "parlor" in Polk Street, San Francisco. Small shopkeepers and laborers of the quarter are his patients; his practice thrives. He has made a fast friend in Marcus Schouler, an arrogant, vulgar blow-hard who is employed as an attendant in a neighboring dog hospital.

Marcus introduces McTeague to Trina Sieppe, his cousin and fiancée. Trina, the daughter of Swiss-German immigrant parents, is a shy and frightened maiden of the late Victorian era. Her relatives, always anxious to demonstrate a hundred percent Americanism, carry the Stars-and-Stripes when they go on picnics. On one of these excursions, Trina falls from a swing and breaks a tooth. She makes an appointment for treatment with "Doctor" McTeague.

He administers a gas anesthetic to spare her the pain of extraction. As she lies unconscious in the dental chair, a sudden passion for her is aroused in McTeague. He struggles to conquer his desire to take her there and then. After her visits end, he pines secretly for her, and finally confesses to Marcus that he has fallen in love. Marcus, with a false show of magnanimity, sacrifices his sweetheart to his friend.

There follows a formal and grotesque courtship; in a few months Trina and McTeague marry, the event being celebrated with a wedding breakfast at which friends and relatives gorge themselves disgustingly. On the eve of the wedding Trina, who has bought a lottery ticket for a dollar, is informed that she has won five thousand dollars in the drawing. This unexpected turn of good fortune for the McTeagues infuriates Marcus, who would have profited financially had he not generously given away his fiancée.

Marcus broods and snarls and one night, in a seizure of envy and frustration, throws a knife at McTeague as the dentist sits tranquilly smoking his pipe and drinking beer in a saloon. Then the former friend plots a terrible revenge. He informs the state medical authorities that McTeague is practicing dentistry without a license, and McTeague receives an official notice that he must discontinue his practice at once.

Trina, haunted by fear of starvation, has turned into a miser and will not spend a penny of her lottery winnings. The McTeague belongings—including the huge gilded tooth that hangs outside the dental parlor's window—must be auctioned. The ex-dentist and his wife sink slowly into poverty, McTeague taking to drink and Trina accepting work as a charwoman. McTeague seeks unsuccessfully to wring money from Trina by tormenting her; he bites her fingers. Finally he abandons her. Her sole comfort now is the five thousand dollars, of which she will not spend one cent. She draws it from her bank in the form of gold coins and keeps it in her shabby back room in a schoolhouse where she works as a washerwoman and concierge. At night she spreads the coins on her mattress and lies on them. Finally McTeague, hungry and intoxicated, breaks into her quarters and demands money. She refuses him again and, losing his temper, he murders her and flees with her gold.

He leaves San Francisco, returns to his mountain birthplace, and from there sets off across the desert, hoping to escape justice. Trina's murder is discovered and a high reward is put on the capture of McTeague. Marcus joins in the pursuit, but the police posse balks at following the refugee into the heart of the Mojave Desert: Death Valley. Marcus takes on the mission alone.

Spurred on by his greed for the reward and the stolen fortune, Marcus hunts down McTeague in the sun-scorched salt-flats of the wastelands. When in this inferno he at last overtakes the murderer, they are a hundred miles from the nearest desert post. The temperature is 130 degrees. Only one mule has survived and, as it starts to wander away with the water supply on its back, Marcus fires a shot at it. The mule falls in its tracks, but the bullet has pierced the canteen and the water trickles out before they can stop it.

The two men fight in the clouds of powdered dust of the cracked salt-flats. McTeague deals Marcus a fatal blow in the head but, in a last spurt of energy, Marcus locks a handcuff on his wrist. McTeague, manacled to the corpse, must die in the desert with the gold beside him.

There are two sub-plots in the Norris novel. The first concerns Maria Macapa, a half-crazy Mexican chambermaid in the boarding house where the McTeagues and Marcus lodge. Maria continually repeats a meaningless phrase: "Had a flying squirrel and let him go." She often speaks of her family's former wealth in Mexico and of the dazzling orange-gold table service that was to be her inheritance. Zerkow, an old Polish junkman, who lives in an alley behind the rooming house, is intrigued by her fables. He, too, is a victim of greed and the gold fever and dreams of one day recovering the lost treasure. He marries Maria in this hope. In a lucid moment, wearying of her mania and despondent over the death of their deformed child, Maria confesses to him that the gold service never existed. Zerkow falls on her with a wild fury at this awful disillusionment and cuts her throat. Then, clasping some old pots and pans, which in his madness he mistakes for the gold service, throws himself into San Francisco Bay. This secondary plot serves to counterpoint the main story of the downfall of Trina and McTeague. The other sub-plot, a frail ray of sunshine in an otherwise somber narrative, has to do with Old Grannis, an elderly Englishman who owns the dog hospital where Marcus works. He is also a tenant in the rooming house and is secretly in love with another boarder, Miss Baker, a spinster of his own age. He is too timid to declare himself and the ridiculous flirtation of this old couple makes a gentle passage in the total symphony of greed. Yet even the quaint romance of this pair expresses the idea of dissolution and decay.

Von Stroheim, who for *Foolish Wives* had built some of the most lavish sets Hollywood had ever seen, had very different notions for the production of *McTeague*. It would not be a studio film at all. He planned to shoot it in its entirety against the natural surroundings of San Francisco and the Mojave Desert, even penetrating into Death Valley, though the last seemed an impossibility when first suggested. On his preliminary tour of inspection he took with him his trusted art director, Captain Richard Day, a British Army veteran who had served in the Prince of Wales Regiment in the First World War. Captain Day, who had previously conjured up replicas of the Austrian Tyrol, Paris in the spring, Monte Carlo at Mardi Gras time, and Vienna in its imperial glory for von Stroheim, now began to reproduce the low life of San Francisco on the screen. The director and his scenic designer

162

were hampered in their realistic research by several problems. The city that Frank Norris wrote of in *McTeague* had been largely destroyed by the earthquake and fire of 1906. Polk Street, the meanness of which Norris had minutely reported, was now a prosperous and respectable avenue. The houses of the ladderlike streets of Telegraph Hill had been rebuilt. But the teeming waterfront and the harbor where river boats and schooners for Australia and Asia lay at anchor had not changed. Oakland, where the Sieppes of the Norris novel had a house and where von Stroheim had been married, and Shell Mount Park, the picnic grounds, were exactly as they had been in the nineties. A tenement section of the 1900 era was a necessity for the treatment that the director had in mind; weeks were devoted to its discovery. It was finally found at the corner of Hayes and Laguna Streets.

"What a find!" von Stroheim exclaimed as he showed his friend Idwal Jones, the Welsh-born writer and drama critic of the San Francisco *News*, through a rambling old structure on which the Goldwyn Company took a year's lease. "Right here in the bay window will be McTeague's dental chair. Just around the corner will be the car conductor's coffee joint, where the dentist used to gobble up suet pudding and hot meat on a cold plate. Just across the street is the saloon where he listened to Marcus Schouler's socialistic talk. And in the back there is an alley where you can almost smell murder. That's where Zerkow's junk shop will be."

Then he dragged Jones to the top of the building. Lying flat on the roof, he pointed with his leather cane into the alley below, reciting the Norris description almost word by word from memory. The tour of the old house continued.

"And this is Maria Macapa's room," he said, pointing to a cavelike chamber. "And the bathroom. Isn't it remarkable for its deep, tin tub encased in wood, and its high washbasin? Here's how my film will begin. Marcus Schouler, McTeague's pal, will be reading the *Police Gazette* in this tub while all his neighbors—McTeague and Grannis, Maria —are impatient to get in themselves."

As Idwal Jones later reported to his readers, "Von Stroheim can quote you *McTeague* from beginning to end, like a sailor boxing a compass. For two months he has burrowed into the newspaper files, rounded up old-timers, tramped the city over, all to get the atmosphere."

Von Stroheim also visited Charles Norris, Frank's brother and a celebrated novelist himself, the author of *Salt*, *Bread*, and *Brass*, at his Palo Alto home. Charles's wife, Kathleen, one of the country's most popular writers at that time, had some graphic recollections of her brother-in-law. Both the Norrises were deeply impressed by this foreign artist who knew *McTeague* by heart and had such detailed knowledge of San Francisco.

In Oakland, Captain Day found the house where the Sieppes, McTeague's in-laws, lived. It was a little box at the foot of 34th Street. Though it seemed unfit for use, it was occupied. "Five people lived in that house—gloomy, filthy, musty. They could not understand why I came to offer them money for the use of their home. They stared vacantly and were relieved when I left," Captain Day reported.

Von Stroheim felt more at home in the Pacific port than he did in Hollywood. When a banquet was given him at the St. Francis Hotel by the city's social leaders, and he stated that censorship was keeping the cinema in its infancy, he was cheered. Mayor Rolph received him at the City Hall and presented him with a wooden Indian. This relic was placed before a cigar store in the street scenes to aid in re-creating the old days before the fire. The police chief issued orders that the streets were to be cleared on notice for von Stroheim's day and night shooting. The director returned this favor by engaging the chief's son, a Marine veteran and boxing champion who wanted to enter the movies as an actor. His name was George O'Brien. Before *Greed* was released, he had become a star in other films.

Von Stroheim returned to Culver City to write the scenario, with June Mathis collaborating on its continuity. He felt that a change of title was required. Norris had at first wanted to call his novel *The Golden Tooth*, the treasure on which McTeague's heart was set, his ambition being to have projected from his window a huge golden molar with enormous prongs. It was the only ambition he achieved and he was deprived of it. *The Golden Tooth* was not right for the film either. In the end, *Greed* seemed the ideal title for a film of the scope von Stroheim intended to give it.

For the role of the boorish dentist, he had in mind Gibson Gowland, who had played the lumbering Tyrolean mountain guide in *Blind Husbands*. He always saw the giant figure of Gowland as he read the book. Gowland, despite critical acclaim for his performance in *Blind Husbands*, had received no advancement in his film career and had gone back to his native England. Von Stroheim cabled him to return.

June Mathis suggested either Claire Windsor, an actress under Goldwyn contract, or Colleen Moore for the role of Trina, but von Stroheim was intrigued by ZaSu Pitts. She was a frail, wistful girl from Kansas, who had had minor success in whimsical comedy parts. After he tested her, the announcement was made that she would have the prize dramatic role of the year.

It should be noted that the majority of the players in *Greed* were recruited from the comedy lots of Hollywood. This was not a coincidence. Von Stroheim believed that comedy roles made greater demands in characterization and comedians were therefore better trained. ZaSu Pitts was known only for her comedy performances. So too was Dale Fuller, who was to play the mad Mexican maid. Chester Conklin, the former Keystone Cop, was to contribute a juicy slice of caricature as the officious German paterfamilias, Papa Sieppe. So were the obese Hughie Mack, cast as the harness-maker, Heise; Tiny Jones, the midget who played his wife; and Frank Hayes, who was to be Old Grannis.

The Danish-born actor, Jean Hersholt, having scored as the villain of Mary Pickford's *Tess of the Storm Country*, was elated when he heard that the role of Marcus Schouler was open. He had read the novel and knew that the part offered him a wonderful opportunity. He at once went to the Goldwyn Company, but at their first meeting, a chance one by the Culver City gates, von Stroheim was obviously disappointed.

"You're not Marcus Schouler at all!" he remarked, as he took a long cigarette-holder from his lips. "Your eyes are too kind." Hersholt insisted that he could make his eyes as evil as he wished and reminded von Stroheim that he, too, had kind eyes, though he had played villains with success.

"But Schouler is a helper in a dog hospital," von Stroheim pursued. "A greasy, smart-aleck type in a loud suit and derby hat, a cigar always between his lips. Your haircut is wrong; his hair was smeared down. I'm sorry, but I don't think you'll do!"

Hersholt, desperate, rushed to Zan's, the makeup parlor in Los Angeles, and had a long session there. One of the finest makeup artists worked over him. He had his mustache shaved away and was given a Bowery haircut. Then he dressed himself in a loud checked suit, purchased a supply of cheap cigars, and hurried back to the studio office. When he faced von Stroheim again, the director clicked his heels and bowed.

"I apologize, Mr. Hersholt," he said. "You are Marcus Schouler. I am glad—and sorry I didn't recognize you at first sight."

The Goldwyn Company announced through its vice president, Abraham Lehr, that it was opposed to the factory system of filmmaking. Its directors were to be invested with complete authority over their productions and were not to suffer interference while they worked. It was this policy that allowed von Stroheim to experiment with ample backing, to select his players not from among the contract performers on the company's list but as he saw fit, and to work outside the studio without the encumbering aid of a producer.

Eleanore Ross, in an essay entitled "Tea with McTeague," summed up the reactions of a San Franciscan and recorded an eyewitness account of the making of *Greed*. A film friend had invited her to come have a look. "We got off the Hayes street car at Laguna, and made our way through the crowd that had gathered near the doorway of an alley, at the end of which a dog fight was evidently in progress, judging from the yelps and growls that were issuing. A good-natured officer of the law greeted us: 'Nothin' going on just now, but the fight,' he informed us, so my friend took me to the junk house a block or so away, adjoining a stable, with its old metal, tin cans, bottles, old stoves, rags and what not, piled up in a filthy yard, the patched-up shack with broken windows, standing starkly at the rear, a melancholy eucalyptus tree sweeping the roof with its branches. 'When they first rented these quarters and put up that sign JUNK FOR SALE, men from all over the city came here to buy,' my friend laughed. 'Just as people used to come and sit around in McTeague's dental parlors waiting for the dentist.' So von Stroheim, always realistic, shot them with the rest of the scene.

"We walked back again to the corner building, whose

whole upper floor had been leased for the film. I looked up at the signs painted on the windows: DR. MCTEAGUE'S DENTAL PARLORS, GAS ADMINISTRATED, PROF. HASSAN, PALMIST AND PHRENOLOGIST, KNOW THY FUTURE, OTTO PLATZMEISTER, PHOTOGRAPHER, BEAUTIFUL LIGHTING AND POSING. The saloon beneath boldly announced (this was during Prohibition): WINES AND LAGER BEER.

"We went up the stairs into the narrow upper hall and immediately we were in Bedlam. Wild yelps came from the dogs in the dirty alley, men stumbled over each other in the passage way, some sort of machine with piercing light was being manoeuvred from a window in the light well to shoot the dog fight. A tall, hook-nosed man in a cutaway with long tails came out of one of the rooms. His make-up included a crop of disgusting boils, which at first I thought were genuine. We picked our way into Miss Baker's rooms, glad to get away from the racket. A little black kitten ran to meet us and then flew under his mistress's skirts, Fannie Midgley, who was busily re-making up for her part. 'I have just heard that we are at last going to shoot the scene,' she said. 'After being ready since eleven o'clock this morning!'

"I glanced around the dirty room. From where on earth had they resurrected such awful mid-Victorian furnishings? Beaded portières, crotcheted table covers, antimacassars, wax flowers in glass cases and soiled lace curtains, plush rockers, a carpet covered with large flowers of unknown species, a small gas plate. 'I always make tea when I am agitated,' went on little Miss Midgley (her name should have been Miss Midget, so small and frail and old-maidish was she, with her bobbing corkscrew curls). 'Won't you have some now?'

"Tea in that room! We murmured something about a late lunch and Miss Midget rambled on: 'We fix up a little when they begin to shoot, but the boys camp here, and it is generally in an awful upset. But then, you know, the untidiness is all part of the set.'

"A cry of *Forwoertz*! came from the hall and at the same time a huge creature pranced into the room. I don't know what Gibson Gowland looked like before he bleached his hair and eyebrows, but at present he is the most extraordinary-looking man. And there is so much of him. 'Come on out,' said he. 'They're shooting the lottery man.' 'Most lottery men ought to be shot,' said Miss Midget, curling up on her sofa for another wait.

"The confusion in the hall had straightened out a bit, the scene centering around the lottery man, who, with an umbrella as long and gaunt as himself, was rapping on a certain door. 'He brings the five thousand dollars to Trina,' said a man near me, 'and not one cent of it does she give McTeague.'

"It was odd how these people spoke of all the characters in *McTeague* as if they really lived and breathed. In fact, owing perhaps to von Stroheim's realism, they do live and breathe. 'Knock again,' someone was shouting. 'Again! Again!' The door opens; Marcus appears; they talk for a while; the door closes. Yet it must be shot again. 'Von Stroheim shot a scene twenty-six times once,' I was informed, 'because it didn't suit him.' We watched the whole proceeding take place again and then again. It was growing monotonous. 'Let's go and have tea,' said McTeague at last.

"We followed him along the dirty, narrow, noisy hall, past Prof. Hassan's suite No. 7, past the dental parlors, in the room back of which McTeague and Trina had set up housekeeping, down the bleak back stairs. 'My part doesn't come until the last rays of the sun just touch that church spire,' confided Gowland-McTeague. 'It's a wonder von Stroheim isn't out here now, yelling that he gave orders for the sun to set hours ago.'

"We passed the curious crowd that gathered on the corner across the street, where heads appeared in various windows —for McTeague was a well-known but always interesting sight in that forlorn neighborhood—and entered the car conductor's coffee joint for tea.

"*Greed* was well named. Sordid, stifling, warping and killing the soul; and ending in the murder of the body!" wrote Miss Ross. "A masterpiece in its way."

After a glimpse of its creation, she added that she felt the urge to go up to the hills for some fresh air, but she would always remember her tea with McTeague and the uncanny re-creation of San Francisco before the fire. It also brought back to her a rush of memories of the Frank Norris she had once known, "the handsome, elegant young writer, a romantic at heart, whose strong jaw-line would harden as he talked with unexpected intensity about *real* life!"

The aura of reality that surrounded the production extended to many who did not actually take part in it. In June a mammoth Easter parade was staged in the streets of the Hayes-Laguna neighborhood. The mayor granted permission for a temporary changing of street signs and even the advertisement of alcoholic beverages despite Prohibition. Some two thousand San Franciscans marched in the biggest mass scene ever seen in the city. Representing "The Polk Street Improvement Club," Jean Hersholt rode at the head of a detachment on a white horse. To older people who watched, the San Francisco of the good old days seemed suddenly and miraculously resurrected.

Another incident of the production's overflowing realism occurred when Trina rushes from Zerkow's junk-house, having discovered the murdered body of Maria Macapa. She dashes into the street talking incoherently. To give it an authentic touch, she stopped passers-by who were unaware of the cameras and hysterically related that she had just found a woman with her throat cut. Alarmed strangers hurried off to telephone the police, and ambulances, receiving emergency alarms, began speedily arriving. One overzealous journalist ran to a telephone and reported to his editor the murder of a woman in the district.

Von Stroheim had drummed the reality of the story into the members of his company so deeply that they "became their parts." He was at once a feared tyrant and a sympathetic friend. He applied a changing psychological approach to obtain the very utmost from them when they were before the cameras. His methods of doing so differed widely. When Frank Hayes as Old Grannis proved shaky in his first scenes, the director did not reprimand him but understandingly and without comment shot the scenes over and over again. Hayes' self-confidence rallied and he began to suggest the grotesque pathos of the kindly elder who had fallen in love.

Cesare Gravina, who had been off on a South American tour with his opera-singer wife, had been summoned back to California to play the old junkman, Zerkow. He had let his thin hair grow long for the part and his eyes glittered madly when the cameras started turning on him. Gentle and soft-spoken in real life, he was transformed into a mad, shrieking fury once he entered into his role. During the filming of a sequence where the crazy Zerkow broods in his hovel over the lost gold service, von Stroheim, dissatisfied, halted the shooting. Then he acted out the part himself. In a flash von Stroheim became the insane miser, glancing over his shoulder with maniacal suspicion. The by-standers applauded and Gravina rushed up gratefully. After that, one take was enough.

For the suicide scene, the old Italian was frightened at having to jump into the bay night after night. The director would taunt him during the day about the forthcoming "dunking," and Gravina, would be in a state of trembling anxiety by the time the zero hour arrived, just the state that von Stroheim desired. He also had to remain floating in the water as the water police dragged his supposed corpse from the bay. Long hooks, though padded, were employed for this operation, and Gravina floated in a semi-paralyzed condition, not daring to move for fear of accident. His nightly diving and floating resulted in his coming down with pneumonia and spending two weeks in a hospital. But even this did not make him resentful. He was an artist, and he also knew von Stroheim was an artist who would literally give his life for his art if he had to.

Gowland was less dedicated. He balked at risking his life or being disfigured. In the saloon scene in which Marcus hurls a knife at him, a professional knife-thrower was engaged to fling the deadly weapon, but Gowland refused to be his target. To reassure him, von Stroheim, the script girl, and others stood against the saloon wall to allow the knife-thrower to demonstrate his skill. But Gowland continued to refuse.

"How can you do this to me?" demanded von Stroheim. "All must be real, real, real! I've brought you all the way from England for this part! Are you yellow?" But neither pleading nor insults would sway Gowland. To the director's almost tearful regret, the knife-throwing had to be faked. A knife with a string attached was implanted in the saloon paneling above Gowland's head, and then pulled away. Shown in a quick reverse process, this gave the illusion that the knife was flying in the other direction, slightly grazing Gowland's right ear. Before the scene in which McTeague and Marcus wrestle at the picnic ground, with their playful grappling turning into a serious struggle, von Stroheim whispered instructions to Jean Hersholt to reach up and bite Gowland's ear when the latter held him on the ground. Hersholt did so and his bite brought blood. Gowland rose, roaring in pain and anger, while the director shouted to keep the cameras turning. A terrible argument ensued with Gowland, as his ear was being nursed. He threatened to bring the matter to court.

"But that's in the book!" insisted von Stroheim. "You should have known what was going to happen!"

In silent films, music was an extremely important element. Films were made to music and shown to music and von Stroheim had musicians on hand for all scenes. There was an orchestral *Greed* motif which violin, organ and cornet, brass and drums played incessantly. Derived from a theme of Leoncavallo's, this somber motif dominated the score. Then there was the melancholy whining of McTeague's concertina—"Nearer My God to Thee" and "Hearts and Flowers" being his favorite renditions; ragtime for picnic outings and the Orpheum vaudeville show. The wedding ceremony—with a funeral passing by in the street—called for mixed musical accompaniment. "O Promise Me!," the most hackneyed of marriage melodies in America, sounded as Trina sees the assembly through her tears; and the sentimental "Call Me Thine Own" broke forth when Old Grannis, nervously fingering his white cotton gloves, looks across the circle at the wedding breakfast to steal a glance at timid Miss Baker, so well-bred and dainty amid the vulgar, sweating guests gorging like hogs.

Edwin Schallert, of the Los Angeles *Times*, came to inspect the production, the most-discussed movie then being made in the United States. He arrived to see the scene in which the disintegration of the McTeague marriage has set in. Through a tangle of electric wires and glaring lights, he came on an alcove room where the action was taking place. A thick, heavy-set, lumpish figure of a man, grotesquely haloed by a mass of peroxided yellow hair, towered over a bed on which there was a quilt of rags. Cringing beside him was a woman whose face was worn and whose eyelids were bloated from weeping. Her heavy black hair was bound in huge coils about her head and she wore a faded gray bathrobe stained with cooking and with tears

"They were Trina and McTeague," he wrote. "There was no mistaking them—to anyone who had read Norris' novel. Light shows down on the faces of the players in this box-like room. The sweating atmosphere literally stifled them as they fought through rehearsal after rehearsal, scene after scene. And the rehearsals were many and the scenes few, for they were driven as few players have ever been driven by the unflagging zeal of the director's will."

"It has always been my determination to produce this story exactly as it was written," von Stroheim informed Schallert in his quarters at the Hotel Fairmont. "They said I was crazy to do an American story. Of course, it is foolish to say that *McTeague* is American any more than *Nana* is French. They are international. You can, in fact, trace the inspiration of Norris to Zola's *L'Assommoir*, and the novel appealed to me more than any other story by an American because it is so universal and because, perhaps, basically in viewpoint and style it shows European influence. In Europe, the audiences laughed at *Blind Husbands* because as its villain I am obliged to expiate for my human longings—my ardor for a woman of charm and beauty. This, of course, was to satisfy the American public that insists on the villain paying for his crimes by the fifth reel. What I don't like is the persistent

174

denial by blubbering sentimentalists of man's basic nature. Away with those who would sterilize life, or, as they call it, 'spiritualize' life. And then this talk about logic! But life, monstrous, unfathomable, beautiful, ominous, is illogical. You can't tie it up with pink paper and baby ribbons. Plot is a pattern, the mechanism by which infantile minds are intrigued. It is a riddle, a puzzle, or the skeleton on which melodrama, comedies, detective stories are hung. But life, raw, immense, swirling, has no plot. Its riddle can never be solved. Our McTeague struggles futilely against the hard swipes of destiny and goes down to death beneath the beating sun out there in the vast lonely desert."

In these remarks von Stroheim summed up his attitude about filmmaking in general. He was not interested in cleverly reproducing neatly contrived plays and novels on the screen. He believed that the motion pictures might make a philosophical comment on life itself, to depict with shattering but compassionate power the tragic plight of human existence.

Abraham Lehr, the Goldwyn vice president, came to San Francisco to study the progress of the film. He was impressed with what was shown him and delighted at the nationwide publicity the production was receiving. But he and his confreres in Hollywood were uneasy about the von Stroheim plans to go into Death Valley for the making of the final scenes. It was one thing to work away from the studio, and another to risk the health and lives of personnel in the desert. The life-insurance company—von Stroheim had already been insured for one million dollars when he joined the Goldwyn ranks—listed the hazards involved. Here are a few of them:

Temperature from 120 to 150 degrees, and not a tree in the valley

Water holes poisoned with arsenic; one drink brings
instant death
    Air pockets of death-dealing gas and poison fumes
    Poisonous reptiles and insects
    Treacherous quicksands
    Long marches in the blinding light, breathing alkali dust
that brings on nausea
    Trackless wastes in which hundreds of parties have been
lost.

Who could resist such blandishments? Certainly not a
movie director fired with putting the torments of humanity
into motion pictures with fearless realism. "Do you think
that I can drag some sand to the studio, put my actors before
the cameras, and tell them to register agony because they are
dying of thirst and tarantulas are crawling over them?" the
determined disciple of Zola inquired, as Lehr listened, won-
dering vaguely if this conference were taking place only in a
nightmare.

For the last time, the Goldwyn executives bowed to the
demands of realism and allowed the director and his unit to
go into the desert. They had hoped he would compromise
by filming the Death Valley climax at a location ranch near
Los Angeles, where most of the Westerns were shot. On his
expedition into the wastelands, von Stroheim took Gowland
and Hersholt; his three first cinematographers—Ben Reynolds, William Daniels, and Ernest Schoedsack (who the following year was to collaborate with Merian Cooper on that
astonishing documentary, Grass); forty-two technicians; his
press representative, Fritz Tidden; and a hardy script girl, the
only woman of the crew.

Seven army trucks were loaded with camera and camping
equipment, and an old Indian guide advised on the rough
trek through the roadless sands. Death Valley is a slit in the

earth in Southern California, several hundred feet below sea level. It is the lowest spot on the globe not covered by water. After three days of round-about trailing, the company entered Death Valley over the Emigrant Trail, so called because hundreds of emigrants have perished of thirst along it.

During the filming the party crossed Death Valley eleven times, the thermometer registering from 125 to 135 degrees. Two trucks were used to go back and forth to Baker, the nearest railroad point from the location, carrying men suffering from sunstroke or heat exhaustion, and bringing back food and water supplies. Tempers were short under this ordeal, and there was such deep resentment of the director that he kept a pistol at hand day and night.

Gowland and Hersholt had to crawl across miles of sun-baked salt-flats, impersonating the murderer and the pursuer. There was murder in their hearts as they dragged themselves along, gasping in the infernal heat, bare to their waists, unshaven, blackened by the sun, blistered, bleeding. When the day of the death fight arrived, they were groggy with misery. As they battled in the caked dirt, the director egged them on by shouting to them: "Fight! Fight! Try to hate each other as you hate me!" As Hersholt lay unconscious, his wrist handcuffed to Gowland's, the latter lets his canary, symbol of his gentle nature, out of its cage in the still air of the desert. When the cameras stopped clicking, *Greed* was at last completed. Hersholt was immediately transported to a hospital, where he spent several weeks recuperating from the ordeal.

Greed had been shot in less than ten months at a cost of $750,000. In Hollywood, von Stroheim began editing it late in August 1923. Had he been able to assemble it rapidly, even in lengthy form, it is possible that the Goldwyn Company might have released it, as he wished, to be shown on two consecutive evenings or as an all-day, all-night movie.

But he worked slowly and exactingly and it was only in January 1924 that he showed his producers and a group of friends (see page 339) his film in forty-two reels.

As his contract called only for his directorial services, he labored without salary for these months. When further cuts were demanded, he went back to his editing and devised a twenty-four reel version. Meanwhile, since he was occupied with his editing, the prize Goldwyn property, *Ben Hur*, was assigned to another director, Charles Brabin, and plans to film it in Rome under June Mathis's supervision went forward.

Unfortunately for von Stroheim, the Goldwyn Company merged with Metro during the spring of 1924. Louis B. Mayer was placed in charge of production in the new organization, and his name was added to its banner. Like a nemesis, he brought with him from Universal, as his new producer-manager, Irving Thalberg. Mayer's ambition was to make the new Metro-Goldwyn-Mayer firm a film factory. He intended to exercise a strong hand on production, and believed firmly in the star system and "box-office" values.

Mayer had inherited *Greed* in the merger, and he foresaw only a disastrous flop. It showed life as movie patrons did not want to see it. It had no glamour, no stars, no soothing optimistic message for the multitudes. It ran counter to Mayer's own personal philosophy of patriotism, sentimentality, and momism. He was a crude, illiterate, self-made man. A financial genius of sorts, he had the contempt of the uneducated for art and the artist. Those who could afford to, like Charles Chaplin, shunned his company. Chaplin in his memoirs describes his reaction when Mayer visited his home on an invitation from Mildred Harris, then Mrs. Chaplin. The comedian hid in the garden hothouse to avoid Mayer, an incident he later immortalized in his film *Monsieur Verdoux*.

In a later public encounter, Mayer punched Chaplin and knocked him down.

Von Stroheim's suggestion that *Greed* be shown in two parts seemed ridiculous to Mayer. Thalberg, of course, agreed. The director had wept as he had cut a scene here, a scene there, to reduce the film to twenty-four reels. Any further shortening would weaken the whole exposition; the result, he thought, would be like a novel with hundreds of pages torn out.

The Dublin-born director Rex Ingram was one of von Stroheim's closest and most devoted friends. In addition to the success of his film, *The Four Horsemen of the Apocalypse*, he had increased Metro's fortunes with his *Prisoner of Zenda* and *Scaramouche*. Marcus Loew, the president of Metro and the Loew's theater chain (with which the new M-G-M was associated), held Ingram in the highest estimation. Ingram had written von Stroheim to beware of Mayer, whom he distrusted. Secretly, von Stroheim sent the twenty-four-reel copy of *Greed* to Ingram in New York. Could he cut it further without damaging it fatally? Ingram cut it down to eighteen reels and sent his friend a telegram: "If you cut one more inch, I'll never speak to you again."

With this message, von Stroheim went to Mayer. The Hollywood "rajah," as Bosley Crowther aptly characterized Mayer in his revealing biography, angrily replied that he cared nothing for the opinion of Ingram or anyone else. *Greed* must be slashed to ten reels. If its director refused to undertake the job, it would be given to someone else. For some reason, the conversation trailed off to a discussion of actresses and women in general.

"They're all whores!" von Stroheim remarked injudiciously, forgetting momentarily that Mayer suffered from a maudlin mother-complex. The producer leaped up from his desk in a wild fury.

"Not *mothers!*" he cried out. "Not *your* mother! Not *mine!*"

Von Stroheim rose, picked up his white gloves from the desk, and took up his cane to depart.

"I suppose you consider me rabble," sobbed Mayer, now weeping copiously.

Von Stroheim made the most insulting reply he could think of. "Not even that," he said.

As von Stroheim crossed the office, Mayer rushed after him and struck him such a forcible and unexpected blow in the neck that von Stroheim fell, gloves and cane in hand, over the threshold of the open door. Mayer's secretary rose in alarm from her desk in the outer office.

"You see, my hands were occupied," von Stroheim said to her, as he got up and dusted his trousers. Mayer, standing behind, collapsed on the floor and sat there in a seizure of moaning hysterics.

Fearing a lawsuit, Mayer was profuse in apologies next day. He was so profuse that von Stroheim half hoped this would lead him to change his verdict on the future of *Greed*. But it was not to be.

Greed was left to the mercies of a hack cutter, who was ordered to slash it to ten reels. The rest of the negative was destroyed to squeeze from it the small amount of silver it contained.

Laemmle, with his gambler's instinct, might have risked releasing the twenty-four-reel or eighteen-reel version. But the film offended Mayer; he thought it opposed all he believed in.

Von Stroheim, who had mortgaged his house, his car, and his life insurance to devote his time to editing his film without salary, was in a state of black despair. Ten months of the most intense creative work had been wasted. He refused even to look at the truncated film that they prepared for public showing. He believed then, and for the rest of his life, that had *Greed* been released in more complete form, it would have enjoyed the greatest success.

W. R. Hearst, whose Cosmopolitan motion-picture unit was now under the M-G-M banner, was a native of San Francisco. Frank Norris had been a foreign correspondent for his newspapers during the South African and Spanish-American wars. Hearst was enormously impressed by a preview of *Greed*, but not sufficiently to demand the reconstruction of the entire film. Hearst announced that it was the greatest motion picture he had ever beheld. Naturally his opinion was echoed in his chain of journals and magazines. Moreover, he wished to honor it by giving it its world première at his New York theater, the Cosmopolitan.

Following its brilliant opening, *Greed* in its general release played prearranged runs in hundreds of Loew's theaters across the country and again on Broadway at the Capitol. Figures on its earnings are not available, but it certainly earned the $750,000 it had cost. There were not, of course, any visible profits for its director to share, as his contract provided. Having disowned the released version, von Stroheim was not surprised at its apparent failure. In Hollywood, the director commiserated in his mortgaged house with friends who had been invited to see *Greed* in its full forty-two-reel glory. They alone could understand his suffering.

A panoramic view of the San Francisco of *Greed*

McTeague (Gibson Gowland) is thrilled to have a golden symbol of his profession

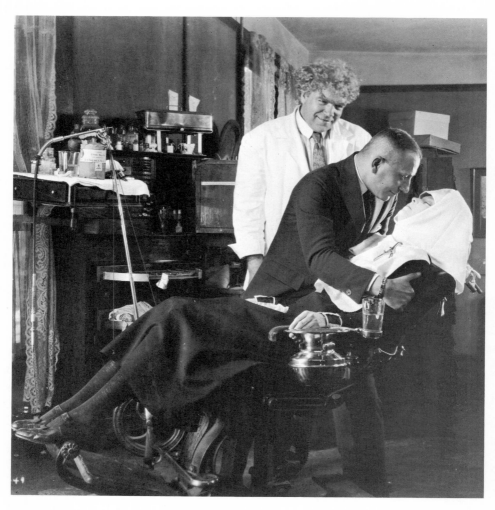

Von Stroheim demonstrates how he wants McTeague to embrace
Trina (ZaSu Pitts) under anesthesia

McTeague and Trina

(OPPOSITE) Von Stroheim in a bit part as a balloon seller at the amusement park

From the left: Jean Hersholt, Oscar and Otto Gottel, Sylvia Ashton, Joan Standing, Frank Hayes, Gibson Gowland, Hughie Mack, ZaSu Pitts, Fanny Midgley, Chester Conklin, Max Tyron, Austen Jewel, Dale Fuller, Tiny Jones

(OPPOSITE) The bridal couple

Wedding night

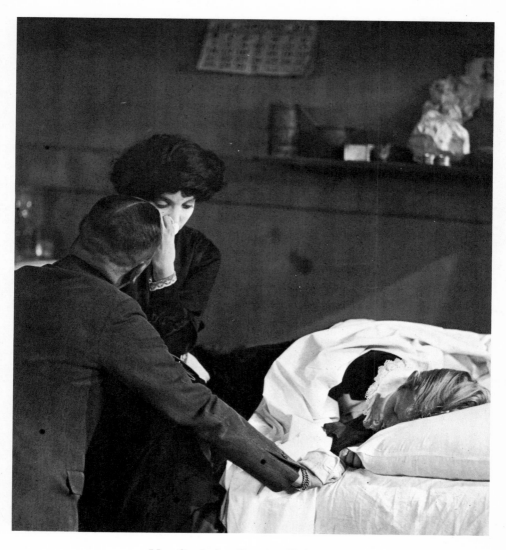

Von Stroheim directing ZaSu Pitts

(OPPOSITE) Sunday picnic in the park

ZaSu Pitts as Trina

(OPPOSITE) Street scene: the crowd reacts to Zerkow's murder of
Maria Macapa

McTeague tortures Trina to get money from her

Trina withdraws her lottery money from the bank

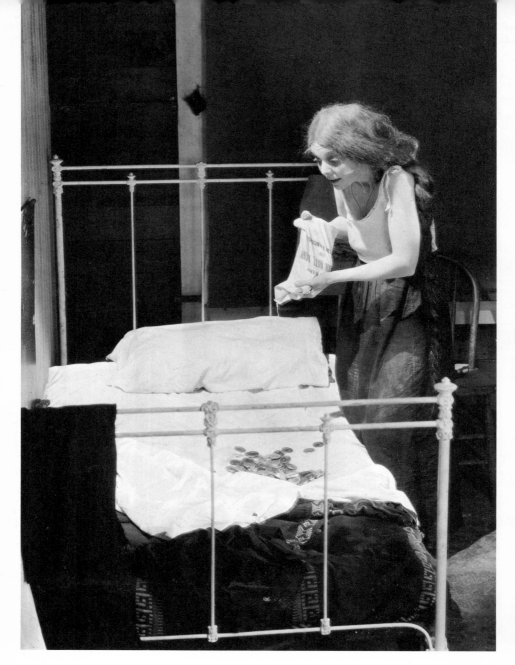

Trina spreads the gold coins on her bed

Von Stroheim's comment on this photo: "*Supprimé*"—suppressed

The final encounter of McTeague and Marcus (Jean Hersholt) in Death Valley

McTeague is handcuffed to Marcus—one of the final shots of *Greed*

11

Mae Murray and
The Merry Widow

I N private life, as in the studio, von Stroheim maintained a "closed set." He did not mingle with producers at poker parties, and he did not relish attending the receptions and dinners given by movie "aristocracy." No doubt this hurt him professionally, but he was not a mixer. Among actors— aside from those who had worked with him—only Rudolph Valentino (with whom he had hoped to make *Ben Hur*) and Adolphe Menjou (whom he had considered for the count in *Merry-Go-Round*) were his intimates. Other companions were Harry Carr, the feature writer and author, who was later to collaborate with him on *The Wedding March*; the novelist, Jim Tully, who wrote about him in *Vanity Fair* and with whom he had sought work at the Reliance-Majestic Studios when they had both been down-and-out years before; Albert

Lewin, a former university professor, who was Thalberg's aide and brain trust; Idwal Jones, the San Francisco friend, who wrote an indignant series of syndicated articles on the cannibalism the studio had performed on *Greed*; the directors Clarence Brown, Victor Seastrom, King Vidor, John Ford; the author John Weaver, and his actress wife Peggy Wood.

Despite his reputation for the diabolic, von Stroheim was a regular churchgoer. "He wouldn't miss Mass on Sunday if President Coolidge asked him to breakfast," Tully, the ex-Catholic, wrote ironically at that time.

The talented Rex Ingram, who had been in Tunis making his film *The Arab*, paid a fleeting visit to the Coast and renewed his warning to von Stroheim about the new management of the M-G-M studio. In his opinion, neither Mayer nor Thalberg was to be trusted and he was convinced (correctly) that both were actively seeking complete control over all directors. When he signed a new contract in New York with the M-G-M president, Nicholas Schenck, Ingram again expressed these views and insisted upon a special clause that he was to be in no way dependent on the new West Coast executives. He thought he would solve the problem by making all his films abroad, at the Vittorine Studio in Nice, which he had purchased as his headquarters. There he would have no interference or snooping to put up with from supervisors. Marcus Loew, who rightly regarded Ingram as his financial savior, promised him full protection. Rex Ingram had his own way for three years, making three excellent films— *Mare Nostrum*, *The Magician*, and *The Garden of Allah*— independently abroad. When Marcus Loew died suddenly in 1927, Mayer and Thalberg—as Ingram had predicted—ordered him to return to Culver City. His box-office success was less important to them than breaking his independence.

Rather than give this up, he severed his connection with M-G-M. Von Stroheim rejoiced in Ingram's temporary good fortune, but he felt he could not very well break his present contract. His salary-less months had sunk him in debt; his wife, on whom he relied for guidance in his business affairs, urged him to stay.

Once *Greed* had been taken from him, Thalberg, who said he admired his talents and his box-office potential, proposed to him that he adapt and direct *The Merry Widow*. It could be as free an adaptation as he saw fit, but it must include two scenes: the one in which the widow and the prince waltz at the Paris embassy, and the one at Maxim's, since they would both be expected by the public that cherished the Franz Lehar operetta. Thalberg added, "A film is as strong as its villain," and said it would be a good idea to have a conscienceless rake to contrast with the playboy hero of noble heart. He also presented the director with a collaborator, to assist in composing the scenario.

This collaborator was Benjamin Glazer, a jolly Hungarian who had translated the plays of his countrymen, Molnár and Vadja, for Broadway production. It was a happy choice, for the two men found they had many interests in common. "The secret of every collaboration is that one collaborator does all the work," Glazer later wrote. "If von Stroheim received any inspiration from me, it must have been from my indolence." Their adaptation of the Victor Leon-Leo Stein libretto was so free that only the basic situation of the operetta even vaguely resembled that of the film. This situation—that of a prince who must court the rich widow of his wealthiest subject to keep her money in the kingdom—had been taken by Leon and Stein for the operetta from a Meilhac and Halévy comedy, *The Attaché*, and is said to have been suggested by an actual incident.

Von Stroheim proceeded to revise the old comic opera's "book." In the screen adaptation, Sally O'Hara, a dancer touring the Balkans with the Manhattan Follies, arrives in a border town of Monteblanco. The local inn is overcrowded, as the royal troops, led by the crown prince, Mirko, and his cousin, Prince Danilo, are returning from summer maneuvers in the mountains. The prince and Danilo are both smitten with the Irish-American performer. Danilo wins her gratitude by ordering the officers to double up so that the itinerant theatrical company can be accommodated. Sally believes that both men are merely army officers, and the three dine together democratically. When the Follies open in the capital a few days later, Danilo comes backstage and asks Sally to supper, his success infuriating his cousin. In a *chambre séparée* at a cabaret he seeks to seduce her, spilling soup on her so that she must change her dress. Their tête-à-tête is interrupted by the crown prince, who is giving a wild party in a neighboring room. He mocks the girl's situation and Danilo defends her by announcing that he intends to marry her.

The crown prince hurries to inform his parents of Danilo's threat to marry a commoner, and Danilo is summoned before the king and queen. The queen persuasively tells him that royalty cannot love where it will and that she, too, in youth loved and lost a man. He writes Sally a note that the queen throws into the fire as Sally, clad in her wedding gown, waits in vain for her royal bridegroom. The crown prince comes to tell her of the broken engagement. Sally finds she has another suitor, the crippled Baron Sadoja, the richest man in Monteblanco. The baron, a decadent old roué, promises her that as his wife she will be the real ruler of the kingdom. Sally accepts his proposal and they are married, but on the wedding night the baron at her bedside suffers a paralytic stroke and dies. Sally is now the richest woman in the land. She takes off for Paris to lead such a gay life that she becomes known as "the merry widow."

The royal family is now alarmed that the kingdom's greatest financial asset will be lost if Sally remarries a foreigner. The crown prince is dispatched to Paris to woo her for his bride, and Danilo, pining for her, follows. Resentful of Danilo, Sally taunts him by pretending a passion for Mirko. Her behavior provokes a duel between the two men. Danilo fires his revolver in the air, but Mirko shoots him down. Sally nurses Danilo back to health and becomes his bride.

As the king of Monteblanco has died suddenly, Mirko returns to succeed to the throne, but is assassinated by an old beggar he maltreated in one of his drunken fits. Danilo inherits the throne and the wedding coronation is celebrated at the cathedral.

The von Stroheim-Glazer script pleased Thalberg and Mayer. It offered opportunities for production display and had a strong dramatic story. Who would play Sally and Danilo? Mae Murray, a top Metro actress whom the new company had inherited in the merger, was suggested, and von Stroheim, who had seen her in the Ziegfeld Follies and admired her beauty and dancing but had reservations about her acting, agreed. He suggested Norman Kerry for Danilo, but Thalberg thought it high time that a young contract actor, John Gilbert, who was showing great promise and increasing popularity, be given the role. He had scored in *The Wife of the Centaur*, and most recently in *The Big Parade*, which was awaiting release. King Vidor had directed these films and in confidence told von Stroheim to take care lest Gilbert (who had also been a director), end by directing in his stead. Gilbert had advantages: he wore uniforms with natural ease; he was a sound actor; he had irresistible charm for women; and he could dance. Despite these attributes, von Stroheim preferred Kerry, with whom he had worked harmoniously. Gilbert somehow reminded him of a ladies' hairdresser.

Von Stroheim had written the role of Crown Prince Mirko for himself, but Thalberg vetoed this proposition. He remembered the impasse over *Foolish Wives*, when the director could not be dismissed because he was also the principal actor. He would not be outwitted again. He simply told von Stroheim to hunt for another player.

Von Stroheim and his wife happened to see *The Clinging Vine*, a musical comedy in which their friend Peggy Wood was appearing at a Los Angeles theater. One of the actors was a foppish schemer whose affected comportment caught their attention.

"Whom does he remind you of?" whispered von Stroheim to his wife.

"He's Mirko to the life," was her reply.

The actor was Roy d'Arcy and he was invited to test for the role at Culver City. He had studied in Germany and had observed the prewar German officers strutting in the streets. In uniform and a monocle, he resembled not so much von Stroheim himself as the effeminate Prussian commander of Maupassant's "Mademoiselle Fifi." This gave an interesting edge to the character, accentuating the spoilt-dandy quality of the cruel aristocrat.

The director again summoned what had virtually become his stock company: Albert Conti as Danilo's adjutant, Sidney Bracey as his footman, Hughie Mack as a fat innkeeper, Dale Fuller as the sinister housekeeper of Baron Sadoja's mansion, and Lon Poff, the lottery man in *Greed*, as a lackey of Sadoja. George Fawcett, an acquaintance from Reliance-

Majestic days, was selected to be the froggish king, and Josephine Crowell, another Griffith veteran, to be the strong-charactered queen. Tully Marshall, who had just played a degenerate millionaire in Victor Seastrom's *He Who Gets Slapped*, was a perfect Baron Sadoja. A newspaper friend of the director, Don Ryan, a war veteran who wrote an outspoken column in a Los Angeles daily, was engaged as Mirko's adjutant. "The part calls for a mean, sadistic underling, as callous and heartless as his superior," von Stroheim said to Ryan. "Just act natural. Be yourself!" Ryan, half flattered and half suspicious, turned movie actor and became the film's historian by writing a novel, *Angel's Flight*, that recounts the filming of *The Merry Widow*.

The Merry Widow started shooting at Culver City in November 1924. All of it—save for some introductory glimpses of the misty mountains of Monteblanco, filmed in the Sierras by the cameraman Oliver Marsh, and the duel, which was staged in the early-morning light in Griffith Park—was photographed on studio sets designed by Captain Richard Day and Cedric Gibbons, chief art director of M-G-M.

The picturesque inn in the mountains; the theater of the capital with signs in Slavonic on dressing-room doors; the Frenchified supper club with its luxurious private dining rooms, suggesting the Hotel Sacher in Vienna; the royal palace; the quaint streets of the Balkan town; the macabre residence of the Baron Sadoja; the Paris embassy; Maxim's, an enlarged version of the original; the cathedral wedding-coronation, all filmed in Technicolor, at least gave the romance pictorial reality.

Mae Murray, visiting New York before the start of the film, had unwisely given some interviews, which came to the attention of her new director. Mae Murray's previous films at Metro had been directed by her husband, Robert Z.

Leonard. Miss Murray, the original model for Howard Christy, had entered motion pictures in 1915. Though forty-ish in 1925, her popularity with the movie public had grown with her series of jazzy comedies in the early twenties— *Peacock Alley, Broadway Rose,* and *Jazzmania.* These films called for little acting on her part and much dancing. In New York, Miss Murray, when questioned as to how her effervescent style would fare under the direction of the realist von Stroheim, replied that such a change would make little difference; she always directed herself, anyway. This was not a statement calculated to please von Stroheim.

Initial trouble flared up when John Gilbert, stung by von Stroheim's comments about his clumsy comportment in an early scene, turned on his heel and without a word walked to his car in the studio yard. Miss Murray was in her dressing room when the news reached her and she rushed out in scant attire to Gilbert's car. Gilbert had started the car's engine and was about to speed away, but at the tearful beseeching of his co-star he relented and promised to return if von Stroheim would come to him and apologize. Miss Murray begged the director to save the situation. When he arrived at Gilbert's cabin, the actor, an incipient alcoholic, had already opened a bottle of Scotch and was drinking deeply. The director told Gilbert of Mayer's order to come to him if there was any misbehavior on the set and explained he disliked Mayer so much (as did Gilbert) that he hesitated to do so. He suggested they keep the matter between themselves and try to work harmoniously together. Gilbert responded and they had a friendly toast to their continued collaboration. Thereafter, all was amicable between them.

Von Stroheim had already voiced his misgivings about the allegedly temperamental Miss Murray to Louis B. Mayer, and Mayer had assured him that he would have absolute command over his new production. The first meeting of Miss Murray and her new director was cordial but chilly. The early phases of filming went smoothly, the star being delighted with her part and at the ingenious photographic treatment she received. Veiled cameras were used for the close-ups, and these soft visions gave her a melting beauty. Von Stroheim tactfully tore away the artificiality of her screen pose and found that she could act, especially in comic and wistful scenes.

But Miss Murray feared her new director's dictatorial attitude. Was it to be her picture or his? She suspected that he wanted to eliminate the famous waltz that would be her big scene, permitting her to display her well-known ballroom technique. Actually, since the waltz takes place at the Paris embassy, he wanted rather to blend it into the reception ceremony and not make it a musical-comedy production number, as she desired. She consulted Thalberg, to whom she related her shock at the way von Stroheim was showing the sordid side of royal private lives. In the apartments of the king and the queen, champerpots were allowed to be visible; the queen's false teeth were kept in a drinking glass on the royal night table!

This news had an unexpected effect on Thalberg. "He's giving the characters depth," he said, greatly pleased.

She then sought an ally in Mayer, demanding audience with him to state her complaints. To her surprise, he proved even more unsympathetic.

"Von Stroheim is boss," he told her. "He's the best director in the business. If he wants you to waltz his way, waltz his way."

Probably as a peacemaking compromise, von Stroheim yielded to Miss Murray on several small points. Thalberg got little sleep, as both star and director would interrupt his slumbers with telephone calls in the early-morning hours.

"I won't be dictated to by von Stroheim," Miss Murray would weep over Thalberg's private wire after midnight, having brooded on her mistreatment all evening.

"I've had enough back talk from that Murray girl," von Stroheim would growl on the phone. "Don't expect me back in the morning."

Thalberg, an expert diplomat, would reason with his highstrung artists and then try to catch some sleep before going to the studio to prevent a blow-up before shooting time.

Miss Murray had brought an extravagant wardrobe for her role, without consulting the director. She had selected a long ball gown with a high fur-collar coat for the scene in Maxim's. Von Stroheim thought the dress exaggerated even for a movie of 1925, but passed it with an ironic remark or two. In the end he also decided to clear the floor for her waltz scene and let her exhibit her fancy steps, clad in a tight black dress, feathered headdress, and diamond necklace. He considered her ensemble more suitable for a Follies finale than for the visit of a wealthy widow to an embassy reception, but he tried to hold his tongue.

There was tension on the set as the great waltz was danced before the cameras. This scene was shot in its entirety without the usual breaks for different set-ups, a battery of cameras recording the dance from different angles. It was repeated and repeated, while three hundred extras, standing in the background, attempted to register delighted astonishment as Miss Murray danced over and over again. At last von Stroheim, irritated by the unreality of the scene, which he had agreed to against his better judgment, could not resist an acid crack.

"If the dance is rotten," he called out to Miss Murray, as

he ordered the cameras to stop, "it won't be my fault. You had the whole floor to yourself." He then stalked off.

"You Hun!" screamed Miss Murray. "You *dirty* Hun!"

The director was already out of earshot. She threw her peacock-feathered fan on the floor, stamped her foot, and repeated her charge with fury. She expected the extras to rally to her defense; she was defying a Prussian who wanted to be the dictator of Hollywood. But her insult was met by a very different reaction. The extras responded by hissing her. Many of them were members of what was known as "von Stroheim's army," a contingent of ex-servicemen, German, Austrian, Russian, British, American, and whatnot, whose soldierly bearing had brought them parts in all his films. The director's staff was not long in reporting that Miss Murray had publicly insulted him. This time he rejected peace talks and hurried to Mayer's office.

Mayer was closeted with visiting exhibitors when he learned by telephone that von Stroheim was on the way to see him. "Gentlemen," he announced to his guests. "You are about to witness an historic occasion. I am going to fire von Stroheim here and now."

Von Stroheim walked into the room fully composed, but before he had uttered a word the emotional Mayer, who always rose to dramatic occasions, jumped up from his desk. "Mr. von Stroheim, you are *through*," he declared. The director stood still and then, in his best military style, executed an about-face and departed.

Next morning Monta Bell, a director under M-G-M contract, arrived on the ballroom set to take over. His appearance was met with a loud roar. At first, he thought he was being cheered for his daring, but then it became clear that the extras were demanding the return of von Stroheim, bravely risking their salaries by their protest.

"We want von Stroheim! We want von Stroheim!" was the battle cry.

Mayer, accompanied by Eddie Mannix, one of his numerous stooges, hurried to the set. He found it in a state of anarchy, with tempers running so high that open mutiny seemed likely. As he crossed the ballroom floor, a musician of the orchestra made as if to strike at him, but the musician was quickly knocked down by the agile Mannix, a former pugilist. Obviously, work could not continue under these conditions. The extras were already registered on camera in the waltz scene. To discharge three hundred of them would lead to union trouble, perhaps a strike. Even if this could be avoided, the scene was too expensive to be remade. Mayer bowed to the inevitable, but it did not increase his affection for the director. He must reengage von Stroheim. To the press he announced—though several exhibitors knew better —that he had not dismissed the director. It was the director who had walked out, thus breaking his contract.

The M-G-M president emerged in the newspapers as the trucemaker. Star and director were called to his office to meet the journalists. A show of friendship by all parties was photographed and reported, just like a movie scene: Von Stroheim kissed Miss Murray's hand and remarked that moviemaking was often a nerve-racking business, Mayer and von Stroheim embraced and walked to the set, arm-in-arm. The clash of temperaments and its aftermath appeared in the newspapers across the country, lending the film unexpected publicity. In Los Angeles it was the most important news of the day, overshadowing world events. "MAE–VON SIGN PEACE" was the banner headline of the Los Angeles *Record*.

With everyone holding his temper, *The Merry Widow* was completed, having taken only twelve weeks to film, a record for a project of such size. Again, its editing was a problem, and von Stroheim, brooding over his wrongs at the hands of Mayer and Thalberg, took such a dislike to them that further collaboration with them was impossible.

Los Angeles Record

LATEST
EVENING
EDITION

Twenty-ninth Year   Two Cents   Entered at Los Angeles postoffice as second-class mail, under act March 3, 1879   THURSDAY, JANUARY 29, 1925   Published Daily Except Sunday at Record Building, 417 Wall Street   Number 9350

MAE---VON SIGN PEACE

PRINCIPALS IN STUDIO ROW

STROHEIM WINS IN SETTLEMENT

CULVER CITY, Cal., Jan. 29.—This city is quiet today after a wild night of fear and rumor.

Peace was signed by Erich von Stroheim and Mae Murray at midnight in the office of Louis B. Mayer, head of the Metro-Goldwyn-Mayer studios.

The terms of the treaty have been withheld, but it is learned that Von Stroheim won his demand for absolute authority in the direction of "The Merry Widow."

Demobilize Veterans

The treaty also provides, it is understood, that Von Stroheim's armed forces, led by officers who served in the world war, will be demobilized. They will retain their uniforms and side-arms supplied for the picture.

Leaders of the warring forces, at first obdurate, according to report, soon drooped to a compromise mood by Mayer's dovecey plea for cessation of hostilities before the league of nations intervened.

Von Stroheim walked onto the Merry Widow set this morning with Peace Commissioner Mayer assigned and putting him on the job.

Here is Mae Murray, screen star, whose shout to Eric von Stroheim, during the filming of a scene of "The Merry Widow," precipitated one of the most heated and bitter clashes in moving picture history. Mae simply called Eric a "dirty Hun," after which Stroheim resigned.

Crown Prince Mirko (Roy d'Arcy), Sally O'Hara (Mae Murray), and Prince Danilo (John Gilbert)

Baron Sadoja (Tully Marshall) dies on the night of his marriage
to Sally O'Hara

(OPPOSITE) The musical sextet at Mirko's orgy

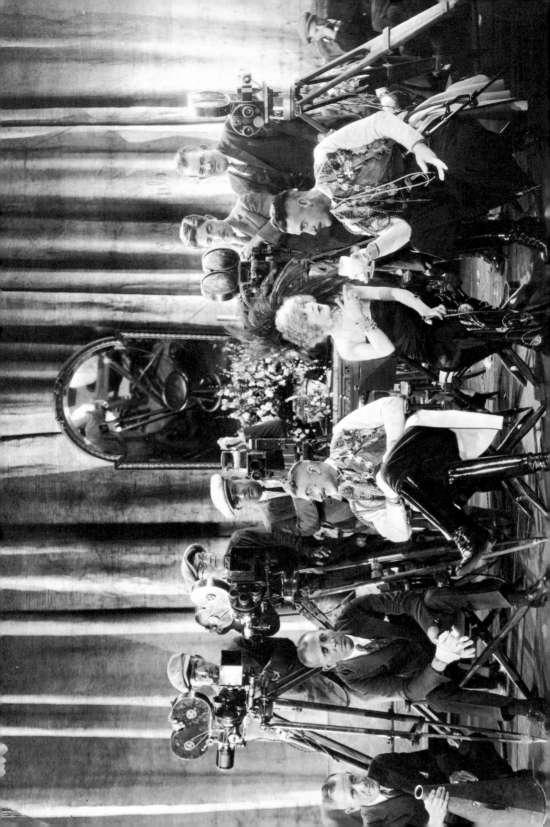

Von Stroheim regards Mae Murray quizzically, as John Gilbert grins

(OPPOSITE) The camera crew and stars of *The Merry Widow*: photographers William Daniels and Oliver Marsh, top right; Eddy Sowders, assistant director, with megaphone, at left

12

The Wedding March
at Paramount

Von Stroheim owed M-G-M at least one more film under his old Goldwyn contract, and Thalberg, who had bought the screen rights to *The Student Prince*, the Sigmund Romberg operetta, thought it ideally suited for von Stroheim's direction. Von Stroheim, however, had another story in mind, *Nine to Nine* by the Viennese author Leo Perutz, a tale of a poor student who is killed trying to escape the police. It had been brought to the director's attention by his friend and agent, Paul Kohner. Universal had acquired it for him and M-G-M had now bought it from Laemmle.

Despite these inviting prospects, von Stroheim had reached the point where he could scarcely stand looking at Mayer and Thalberg daily. Their very faces reminded him of the great defeat of his life, the slaughter of *Greed*. One day, in a rage, he told them that he could no longer tolerate them. His relations with M-G-M were finally severed.

This meant that he would have no hand in the editing of *The Merry Widow*, but it was not a film in which he took great pride. In any case, he felt that if he could not have independence, he might as well retire from directing. In mid-April 1925, when his departure from M-G-M was announced, other studios at once sought his services. Fairbanks, Mary Pickford, and Chaplin wanted him to join them at United Artists. Oliver Morosco, the theatrical producer and husband of the screen star Corinne Griffith, volunteered to finance his productions for U.A. release. He finally accepted a proposal from Joseph Schenck, president of First National and husband of Norma Talmadge, to adapt *East of the Rising Sun*, a novel set in the Balkans, by George Barr McCutcheon. The adaptation was to be a starring vehicle for Constance Talmadge, Schenck's sister-in-law.

In June a preview of *The Merry Widow* took place in Pasadena, the tranquil, highly respectable suburb of Los Angeles. Thalberg and Mayer—but not the director—attended and, in the middle of an audacious love scene between Mae Murray and John Gilbert, the house lights were turned on. The film stopped and the movie executives were invited to meet the Pasadena police chief in the manager's office.

"I can jail you both for showing an obscene film," he said to the frightened producers. Mayer, a quick and able talker, presented a convincing defense.

"We knew you had the strictest censorship in this community and that is why we chose Pasadena for this preview," Mayer explained. "This fellow von Stroheim is a genius, but he often goes too far. We wanted your opinion on how far he is to go. Thank you for your action. I will come back to this town after the film is released, and we will see it together and you will agree with me about its high artistic quality."

The police official, flabbergasted by this novel explanation, allowed the showing to continue. Afterwards the bolder aspects of the seduction scenes were eliminated in the cutting room.

The Merry Widow had its world première on Broadway late in August. The critics raved over it and von Stroheim received some of the best reviews of his whole career. James Quirk, the chauvinistic editor of *Photoplay*, who had denounced *Foolish Wives* as "an insult to every American" and found *Greed* incomprehensible, considered *The Merry Widow* the best film by its director. A poll of national critics voted von Stroheim the best director and *The Merry Widow* the best film of 1925. Since it was the year that also saw the appearance of Chaplin's *The Gold Rush* and Vidor's *The Big Parade*, von Stroheim's sense of irony deepened.

The Merry Widow was a smashing commercial triumph, one of the great drawing cards in film history. It is officially recorded to have made five million dollars—in an era when the dollar's value was much greater than it is today. But its creator did not share in its profits. Technically, the studio lawyers said, he had broken his contract by walking off the set to go to Mayer's office, which was not true because the waltz scene had been finished. Mayer also argued that the contractually promised percentage on any profit had been "lost" on *Greed*. Since von Stroheim was more interested in movies than in money, he did not pursue the matter legally, as he might justifiably have done.

The appeal of *The Merry Widow* was unusually wide, even attracting the intelligentsia. They appreciated the satiric twist with which the popular formula scenario was narrated, its sly comic digs, the sharp irony beneath its "romance," its literary flavor nearer in style to the European cinema than to Hollywood. Baron Sadoja, for example, was a case out of Krafft-Ebing, but the medical ignorance of the censors had not touched his scenes. To the censors he was just a sick old man, not a pathological specimen representing the diseased power of money. Even the intelligent Thalberg had not understood what was wrong with this character. He was puzzled when he saw the rushes of Tully Marshall kneeling to rummage in a cabinet filled with women's shoes. The frenzied fashion in which Tully always gazed at Sally's feet also caught his attention.

"What's all this about?" he asked von Stroheim.

"He has a foot fetish," replied the director.

"Mmm. Well, you have a footage fetish," remarked Thalberg.

But the baron was obviously also a syphilitic, though von Stroheim neglected to mention this—save pictorially in showing his *locomotor ataxia*. He had borrowed this character from French literature, the original being the country gentleman in Octave Mirbeau's *Diary of a Chambermaid*, a novel the director hoped one day to film.

With the release of *The Merry Widow*, von Stroheim reached the zenith of public prestige in his career. "He is, in my opinion, the most important figure in motion pictures, not excepting Chaplin and Jannings," wrote the influential Richard Watts, Jr., in the New York *Herald Tribune*.

Though *The Merry Widow* was a tremendous box-office success all over the United States and abroad, it met opposition in one country, Germany, at the hands of the growing Nazi Party. German nationalists had already placed von Stroheim on their black list. When *Greed* was shown in Berlin, late in 1925, Nazi rowdies booed it from the screen. *The Merry Widow* was accorded a similar reception, and certain critics protested that the Austrian intriguer had destroyed Hitler's favorite musical comedy. This sentiment was echoed in Vienna, but not by the operetta's composer, Franz Lehar, who wrote an open letter stating his admiration for the film and its direction. He added that if he had not already written the score, the motion picture would have inspired him to do so.

For reasons of his own, Schenck at this point postponed the pending production of *East of the Rising Sun*, the projected Constance Talmadge vehicle, and von Stroheim was free again to accept other offers. P. A. Powers, an independent producer, approached him to write and direct a film for Peggy Hopkins Joyce, another famous Ziegfeld Follies beauty, whom Powers was anxious to launch as a picture star. Powers, a genial and canny Irish-American, had begun life as a policeman in Boston and, accumulating a fortune in banking, he invested in motion pictures, having had holdings at one time in Universal.

When von Stroheim lunched with him and Miss Joyce at the Hotel Ambassador, Powers recalled that in 1921, as a Universal backer, he had visited the set of *Foolish Wives* and heard von Stroheim announcing that he would suspend shooting "because relatives are approaching." The incident had amused and appealed to Powers's own sense of Irish independence and truculency. He was certain that the great director could make an actress out of Peggy Hopkins Joyce, of whom he was enamoured.

Von Stroheim, still smarting from his experience with Mae Murray, had no wish to start Miss Joyce on her screen career, and Marshal Neilan unsuccessfully undertook this experiment. But he did have an idea for a film, and Powers was soon hypnotized by his counter-proposal. He outlined the story he had in mind, to which he had already given a title, *The Wedding March.*

Prince Nicki is the son of impoverished parents who are seeking to keep up appearances in the Vienna of 1914. His mother and father are anxious that he marry a rich heiress and save the family. He is willing, but by chance he falls in love with a poor girl whom he meets when his horse shies and injures her, as he is on parade during the Corpus Christi ceremonies. Nicki visits Mitzi as she is recovering, and he later frequents the wine-garden run by her mother, where she plays the harp in the orchestra. Her mother wants to discourage this love affair, but the prince returns one night while her parents are asleep, and the modest maiden gives herself to him.

Nicki's father has finally found a bride for him, the daughter of a wealthy corn-plaster manufacturer eager for his child to marry into the aristocracy. The marriage contract is signed when both fathers are in a state of intoxication in a brothel. The manufacturer's daughter, a lonely, unhappy girl, has one defect: she limps. The wedding is arranged when Prince Nicki, at first repelled, is finally convinced by his mother's pleading. Meanwhile, Mitzi's local suitor, the butcher, learns that she has been betrayed by the prince; he threatens to kill the culprit when he comes out of the cathedral after the wedding ceremony. He is dissuaded from doing so only when Mitzi promises to marry him if he will spare her unfaithful lover.

The second part of the scenario concerns the honeymoon of Nicki and his crippled bride in their Tyrolean castle. The wretched butcher, even at his wedding to Mitzi, sees that she is still pining for the man who abandoned her. In fury, he comes to the castle and fires through a window at the prince, but the bullet strikes the bride and kills her. The butcher dies escaping down the rocky mountain. Nicki is now free to wed Mitzi, only to learn that she has taken holy vows and entered a convent. The prince rides off with his regiment as the world war breaks out, and the old era begins to crumble.

Pat Powers, known to his business associates for the cool poker-faced fashion with which he conducted million-dollar negotiations, was enraptured by this story. He thought it might be even more popular than *The Merry Widow*. Powers also felt he would have two films for the price of one, because the second half, the drama of the honeymoon, could be released as a sequel, an entire film by itself. The usually laconic Powers could not contain his enthusiasm.

Jesse Lasky was so impressed with Powers's unconcealed jubilation, when he related his coup in signing up von Stroheim, that Lasky himself welcomed the venture wholeheartedly. He at once took a share in the project, arranging for the film's release through Paramount, and later bought the controlling rights from Powers. Paramount at this time was preparing a program of spectacular productions: *Beau Geste*; D. W. Griffith's *Sorrows of Satan*; *Old Ironsides*, to be directed by James Cruze, who had made *The Covered Wagon*; and a heroic spectacle about the Air Force in World War I, *Wings*. *The Wedding March* would now join this parade of large-scale films at Paramount.

Of course, it was well known that von Stroheim was difficult to handle, Lasky warned. He advised extreme caution with von Stroheim. He would have a free hand and probably produce a great movie, but it would be a sound idea to appoint a collaborator. Powers also thought this a wise move. Harry Carr, a level-headed newspaperman and a friend of the director, would approve or disapprove the finished scenario and work with von Stroheim on its construction.

The two men rented a villa in La Jolla, then an unspoiled

town on the Pacific seacoast below San Diego. Carr was amazed at his collaborator's zeal and thoroughness. His ability to stay at his desk while the bright sunshine shone, and with the inviting beach only a few minutes away, was impressive. When he found that his charge preferred working at night, they hit on a compromise, spending the afternoons on the beach and beginning work at sundown, continuing until three or four o'clock the next morning and occasionally until dawn. Von Stroheim, always superstitious, was convinced that the villa was haunted. Some evenings he would leave the work table to search for the ghosts that he was certain were conducting "haunting parties" in the darkened bedrooms upstairs, while the lights burned in the library. After setting many futile traps to surprise the spirits, he decided to keep all the lights in the house on all night. This evidently drove the phantoms away: there were no more creakings and scurries in the distant bedrooms or the staircase.

Carr discovered that von Stroheim, in drawing characters, would sketch out their family trees. When he came to describe the corn-plaster magnate's lame daughter, Cecilia (a part he was preparing for ZaSu Pitts), the director began to talk about her dead mother.

"But the mother won't appear in the film," objected Carr.

"No, but how do you know the real truth about any girl unless you know something about her mother?" von Stroheim asked.

He then explained to Carr the Zola system of character analysis, everyone, in his opinion, being the product of both his heredity and his environment, with the inherited qualities dominating. "His films were better than anyone else's because more went into them," Carr later wrote. "He had to be convinced that his characters had a real existence, and

225

were living human beings, before he could set them in dramatic motion."

In March 1926 they returned to Hollywood with the completed script. Carr gave it to Powers and Lasky with his enthusiastic approval.

It had been agreed from the outset that von Stroheim would star as Nicki, a more sympathetic character than he had ever played but a far cry from the Hollywood hero. This screen lover wore no halo. Away from Mitzi and the wine-garden bower, he sought other female company in a brothel frequented by his cynical old father.

Von Stroheim had several players in mind as he wrote the characters of *The Wedding March*. The prince's father was visualized in the screenplay as George Fawcett. "He gives one of Fawcett's quizzical looks" is a stage direction in the script. The unhappy bride had been conceived as a part for ZaSu Pitts, for von Stroheim believed her to be the greatest tragedienne of the screen, on the basis of her performance in *Greed*. He described her rare qualities in an interview he gave at the time: "It is difficult to explain why I consider ZaSu Pitts a great emotional actress. There is an elusive something that is the secret of her personality, and therein lies her greatness. Mystery—she breathes it. A woman of sweet, gentle moods, capable of tenderness. A woman of fire, capable of conflicting emotions smouldering within her. One looks at ZaSu Pitts and sees pathos, even tragedy, and a wistfulness that craves for something she has never had or hopes to have. Yet she is one of the happiest and most contented women I have ever known."

The director-author had thought of Wallace Beery for the part of Schani, the butcher, a crude lover but a determined one—the archetype of lumpenproletariat. But Beery was now a star occupied with other commitments: he was actually at

226

work in Cruze's *Old Ironsides.* So Matthew Betz took the part, establishing himself by doing so as a formidable screen heavy. He was subsequently seen in many gangster melodramas, such as the early talkie *Tenderloin.*

The loyal von Stroheim army, which had tended him a banquet and presented him with a gold cigarette case embossed with his family crest and a bar from a Lehar waltz, as a token of their esteem when *The Merry Widow* was finished, was again recalled to active duty. Cesare Gravina was assigned to play Mitzi's gentle musician father; Dale Fuller found herself his shrewish and determined wife; big Hughie Mack was Schani's father; George Nichols was Fortunnat Schweisser, who arranges the marriage of his crippled daughter to the prince; Maude George was Nicki's mother, a Viennese lady who smoked cigars and took seltzer water with her wine in the masculine manner.

The Wedding March was designed as a lavish studio film, and it was probably the most extravagant of all the von Stroheim productions, surpassing even *Foolish Wives* in opulence. Several thousand extras took part in the Corpus Christi procession, on which weeks of shooting were spent during the summer of 1926. There were thirty-six separate sets, constructed by Captain Day. A group of specialists advised on the details of reconstructing sections of Vienna as it was in 1914, and their work was so successful that when the Archduke Leopold, great-nephew of Franz-Josef, visited the Graben Cathedral set, he stood before it in amazement.

Franz-Josef's golden carriage, brought to the United States for *Merry-Go-Round,* added to the pomp, glittering in the Corpus Christi procession photographed in Technicolor.

Its occupant was again Anton Wawerka, who had portrayed the Emperor in *Merry-Go-Round.* To inspire him with confidence, von Stroheim ruled that the Austrian national anthem by Haydn be played whenever he appeared. This practice was repeated whenever Wawerka visited a café in Hollywood, and its thrilling notes always caused him to adopt the Imperial stride. After the film was finished and his empire gone, he was greatly depressed over the fact that the anthem no longer greeted his arrival. He fell into deep melancholia and suffered a nervous breakdown, another victim of von Stroheim "realism."

One matter held up the production: Von Stroheim had no leading lady. After his nerve-wracking experience with Mae Murray, he was determined not to engage a well-known star. A search was instigated; he reviewed all the young actresses under Paramount contract; and he thought of borrowing Mary Philbin from Universal. Then one day a talent scout, Mrs. Schley, brought a nineteen-year-old Canadian-born girl to his office. Her name was Fay Wray, and after graduating from Hollywood High School a year earlier, she had appeared in some minor Westerns and comedies, creating no great impression. Miss Wray recalls the interview that brought her a long career on the screen:

> The office was rather dark. Von Stroheim sat behind his desk and in a corner sat his secretary. He didn't talk to me at all, but I knew he was watching me as he chatted with Mrs. Schley. Presently he said, looking at me at last:
> "Are you sure you can do the part?"
> "I know I can," I replied, but I was all atremble.
> Then he swung about in his swivel chair.
> "Whom does she look like to you, Mrs. Westland?" he asked.
> "Mitzi," answered his secretary. Not a word more. That was all. Then von Stroheim rose and approached me. He put his hand over mine: "Goodbye, Mitzi."
> I broke into tears. I couldn't help it. That part was right

for me. I knew I would get it when I read it. But when von Stroheim said, "Goodbye, Mitzi," it was just too much.

Mrs. Schley cried, and Mrs. Westland cried, and there were tears in von Stroheim's eyes. They left me there, and I sat weeping in the dark.

Von Stroheim explained the interview as follows: "As soon as I had seen Fay Wray and spoken with her for a few minutes, I knew I had found the right girl. I didn't even take a test of her. Why? Because I select my players from a feeling that comes to me when I am with them, a certain sympathy you might call it, or a vibration that exists between us that convinces me they are right. I could not work with a girl who did not have a spiritual quality. Lillian Gish is to me the supreme artist, having that quality to the nth degree. I chose Mary Philbin because she had something of Lillian Gish. And ZaSu Pitts for the same reason. Fay has spirituality, too, but she also has that very real sex appeal that takes hold of the hearts of men."

The Wedding March was richer in drama and conflict than *The Merry Widow*. It was a more mature and serious work, rooted in reality, with the specter of tragedy in the background. As a symbol of the characters and their world, von Stroheim used the statue of the medieval knight atop Vienna's town hall, which was said to come to life in times of crisis to stalk ominously among the citizenry. To see him meant unhappiness and death. This Iron Man, like Holbein's symbol of death, invaded the love scenes in the blossoming apple orchard and he was present at the fatal wedding march, roaring with laughter over the doom of the participants.

"I am through with black cats and sewers," the director told Louella Parsons when she visited his set in a blooming garden littered with the petals of apple blossoms. It was four o'clock in the morning and he had been shooting all night.

His company was exhausted, but it must work on until dawn. "I am going to throw perfumed apple blossoms at the public until it chokes on them. If people won't look upon life as it is, we must give them a gilded version." There are echoes of *Greed* in the pigsty that borders the romantic garden, and in the attempted rape of Mitzi by Schani in the slaughter house.

Shooting on *The Wedding March* began early in June 1926, and the final scenes were ready to be taken in February 1927. It had been hoped to have the film available for release during the 1926–27 season, and Paramount had announced it as an important feature of its winter program. However, von Stroheim's double assignment as actor and director made it impossible for him to work more rapidly than he did, and actually in the short space of eight months he had made two films, shooting over a hundred reels.

Since one sequence took place in a brothel, rumors had spread that he was shooting scenes that would have to be cut by the censors—in other words, he was wasting time and celluloid. His striving for perfection was caricatured in countless malicious anecdotes, some of which still survive in published estimates of his work. It was said that he had held up production for three days waiting for a toy poodle to sneeze; that he refused to photograph a town because one chimney was not smoking, that he had supplied his army with silk underwear with the Imperial monogram—a repetition of the silly *Merry-Go-Round* rumor.

Eugene Brewster, the magazine publisher, having heard all these wild tales, found a very different state of affairs when he came to view the cathedral wedding scene: "In front of us von Stroheim was being married to ZaSu Pitts. There was music, but far from using a cathedral pipe-organ, a little studio orchestra played 'Here Comes the Bride' in jazz tempo.

The costumes were brilliant and the scene was dazzlingly beautiful and impressive. After Erich had been duly married, he ran to his dressing room and in a few minutes returned dressed in boots, trousers and sleeveless undershirt, and began directing another scene. Then he came over to us. He clicked his heels. The long deep scar across his forehead had been accentuated and he looked the strong, fascinating personality he is. He stands about five feet seven and is powerfully built. His eyes are large, brown, deep-set and brilliant. His nose is large and straight and he carries himself as if born to command. And he does command, but not like a commander— his large flock of associates and helpers follow and obey like idolaters. 'It is no joke running a royal wedding and a cathedral and two thousand extras,' he said, but seemed to succeed admirably, while Pat Powers walked about approvingly."

The military efficiency with which von Stroheim ran his productions struck many visitors who saw him work. Lasky and Zukor now asked him to direct Pola Negri in *Hotel Imperial*, an interesting story about a town on the Polish-Austrian front that was retaken fifteen times during the world war. It had been written by the Hungarian playwright, Lajas Biró, and von Stroheim was attracted by its cinematic possibilities. But when he learned that Erich Pommer, the German producer, was coming from the Berlin U.F.A. studios to supervise its making, he declined the offer. In a formal statement, he announced that he would never again direct under anyone's supervision, though he admired many Pommer productions, especially *Metropolis*.

Maurice Stiller, the Swedish director who had been brought to Hollywood by Louis B. Mayer, inherited *Hotel Imperial*. Stiller, who brought with him his discovery, Greta Garbo, had disappointed Mayer and Thalberg with his direction of Garbo's second American film, *The Temptress.* They had dismissed him and Paramount had taken him on. There had been a general clearing of the lot at M-G-M after von Stroheim's departure. Even Mae Murray had to go. The list of M-G-M refugees included such talented directors as Frank Borzage, Josef von Sternberg, Maurice Tourneur, Rupert Hughes, and Rex Ingram, all of whom complained about the frustrations of working under the Mayer-Thalberg factory system.

Paramount executives next approached von Stroheim about two other projects. Lasky and Zukor had been in league with the Broadway revue producer Florenz Ziegfeld. They had bought and filmed two of his shows, *Kid Boots* and *Louie the Fourteenth,* and were ready to participate in a screen spectacle to be called *Glorifying the American Girl,* the subtitle of all the Ziegfeld Follies. Ziegfeld had suggested von Stroheim as director, feeling certain that he would lend the film the necessary glamour and style. Von Stroheim declined.

Another proposition came from a very different source, the great American writer, Theodore Dreiser. Paramount had acquired the screen rights to the new Dreiser novel, *An American Tragedy.* Dreiser, who considered *Greed* "a great work of art," had asked that von Stroheim direct the film version, and the director was eager to do so. Unfortunately, Will Hays intervened, forbidding any film based on *An American Tragedy* because the book had been banned in Boston. Paramount was forced to obey the Hays edict and the novel was withheld from the screen for several years.

Von Stroheim's intention to film Herbert Ashbury's short story, "Hatrack," was also frustrated by Will Hays when Boston censors banned the *American Mercury* for carrying it. "Hatrack" told of a pathetic prostitute who plied her trade in a small town, transacting her business in the local cemetery. The price of her love was so low that when a traveling salesman gives her a dollar in payment she turns on him in fury to declare: "You know goddamned well I ain't got no change!" Von Stroheim saw "Hatrack" as a perfect vehicle for ZaSu Pitts.

By February 1927 Pat Powers discovered that the production costs of *The Wedding March* had reached $1,125,000. At once he issued an order for von Stroheim to stop filming. There remained only a short passage to be shot, and this could be bridged by editing. Sections of the film had been shown to the press, and the gorgeous pictorial quality of the Corpus Christi procession had received the most favorable comment, though it was impossible as yet to pass fair judgment on dramatic values.

Powers, nervous over his investment, demanded that von Stroheim at once edit the film. Though he received no salary for his editorial services, the director retired to the cutting room with the uncut reels. They were to be divided into two complete and independent films. He was proceeding as rapidly as possible with this work during the summer of 1927, and announced that both films would be completed for showing by October 15, 1927.

Powers had sold a share of his interest in *The Wedding March* to Paramount at the zenith of Lasky's enthusiasm for the project. Lasky and Powers were both eager to place the film on the market as quickly as possible. As a result, on October 8, B. P. Schulberg, chief of Paramount production, informed von Stroheim that he was "off the picture" and that von Sternberg would finish its cutting in his stead, taking only a week or two.

Von Sternberg spent several weeks over the task and his

version proved unsatisfactory to the Paramount officials. The editing was then turned over to Julian Johnston. A bungled version was previewed early in 1928, and met a disappointing response.

Von Stroheim attended the preview and found that his two films had been clumsily chopped. All his scenes of dissipation having been eliminated, Nicki was shown as a typical Hollywood hero. The result was a sentimental and ineffectual *Old Heidelberg*. Sequences from *The Honeymoon* had been tacked onto the first half so awkwardly that the drama seemed confused. Everyone agreed that this would never do, and the film went back to be reconstructed.

Both von Stroheim and von Sternberg were again consulted, and a final version was approved. Of this, von Stroheim had edited only a single scene—that of the first meeting of Mitzi and the prince when he is on parade as a horseguard in the Corpus Christi procession. This final version comprised roughly the first film and concluded with the wedding in St. Stefan's cathedral.

The film was then rushed to the Paramount musical department and J. C. Zamecnik arranged a symphonic score to accompany it and composed a theme song, "Paradise." In March 1928, Paramount announced that it would soon open on Broadway for a special engagement with two showings daily at advanced prices. But this plan fell through when the studio decided to high-pressure the release of *Abie's Irish Rose*, a movie based on the famous comedy about a Jewish youth who falls in love with an Irish girl and their triumph over their families' religious prejudices. The play had run for over five years on the New York stage, but the film version proved a flop. Paramount decided to hold the release of *The Wedding March* until the following autumn and then send it out for general engagements across the country, hoping to recuperate its cost quickly.

The fate of the second part, *The Honeymoon*, remained undecided. Invoking the stipulations of his contract, von Stroheim forbade Powers to release it in the United States in its mutilated state. He could not, however, prevent its being shown abroad, and it was released in Europe in 1931 after *The Wedding March* had completed its first engagements on the Continent.

Powers and von Stroheim had begun to be at odds during the final stages of shooting on the double film. Powers now claimed that the director owed him a second film. Von Stroheim was willing to make another, although he held that *The Honeymoon* constituted the second film, but his employer and he were unable to agree on a subject.

These circumstances were irksome for von Stroheim. He had several other offers but could not accept them, as he was bound to Powers, who kept him inactive. Joseph Schenck, now in charge at United Artists, proposed that the director join the studio to supervise two units there and to direct one major production a year. But Powers stubbornly blocked von Stroheim's acceptance, insisting that the director could work only for him, though he had nothing for him to do.

Being technically idle, von Stroheim received no salary and secretly accepted another Schenck offer. Schenck wanted a scenario for a film starring John Barrymore. With the famous actor in mind, von Stroheim wrote a highly colored script about a Tsarist officer who, having been disgraced, becomes a revolutionary and emerges as a commissar during the 1917 political upheaval. It was entitled *Tempest* and its authorship on the screen was tactfully billed as "From the Austrian," to avoid any objection from Powers. With Barrymore as its dashing hero and with the German beauty

Camilla Horn as the Russian princess he rescues from the firing squad, it became one of the successful films of 1928, and one of the few that Barrymore found worthy of his mettle.

Fay Wray as Mitzi; von Stroheim as Prince Nicki in *The Wedding March*

Officers of von Stroheim's "army" on dress parade for *The Wedding March*

The madam and her staff watch the "Cornplaster Magnate" (George Nichols) applying his product to the corns of Prince Ottokar (George Fawcett) in the wee hours

The bride is ZaSu Pitts and the groom von Stroheim in *The Wedding March*

Prince Nicki bids farewell to Mitzi

13

Gloria Swanson
and *Queen Kelly*

Aᴛ this point, another Irish-American banker from Boston appeared on the Hollywood scene. He was Joseph Kennedy, father of the future martyred President, who at this time was a schoolboy. Kennedy *père* was an able businessman, politician, and diplomat; he was to be Ambassador to the Court of St. James's during the Franklin Roosevelt administration. He was acquainted with his fellow townsman, Powers, and it was due to his urging that the deadlock between Powers and von Stroheim was broken. There was method to Kennedy's intervention. He wanted von Stroheim to write and direct a film for him. Kennedy had come to California to take over the Film Booking Officers of America, an organization that produced B-pictures and was in financial straits. During his stay, he successfully rebuilt it, incorporating it with a new firm, RKO, which was allied with the Keith-Albee vaudeville theater chain. But this was not his only business on the West Coast. He was eager to finance a film to be written and directed by von Stroheim for his friend and favorite actress, Gloria Swanson.

Miss Swanson had been the highest-paid movie star at Paramount. When her commitment at that studio expired in 1926, Zukor and Lasky had tried to persuade her to sign a new five-year contract, augmenting her fabulous salary of $10,000 a week. But Miss Swanson had decided to become her own producer and reap the full benefits of her international popularity. Her first independent film, *Loves of Sonya*, had opened the new Roxy Theater in New York, an ornate temple that held 6,500 spectators. *Loves of Sonya* drew the multitudes and was retained at the enormous cinema palace for several weeks.

Her second independent venture was a film version of W. Somerset Maugham's story "Rain." The play version, with Jeanne Eagels as its heroine, had been an outstanding theatrical success. Will Hays, censor-in-chief, was opposed to the portrayal of a lecherous pastor on the screen, and the Reverend Davidson was defrocked for the picture adaptation, while the title was changed to *Sadie Thompson*.

Miss Swanson was an admirer of von Stroheim's work, especially of his extraordinary feat of transforming Mae Murray from a vapid, twirling flapper into an actress of unsuspected depths. Fresh from her film triumph as Sadie Thompson, she was determined to do something startling. Though she had revealed her uncommon ability as a comedienne in *Zaza* and *Madame Sans-Gêne*, she felt limited by the long string of program-picture roles that she had been forced to play under her Paramount contract. She consulted with Kennedy, a novice in motion pictures, who agreed that the public was weary of the timid products being churned out by the studio bosses. Nor was he deterred by the freely offered advice of these bosses, who warned him that von Stroheim was a madman who would bring him financial ruin.

The director was invited to come and spend a Sunday on Catalina Island with Miss Swanson and Kennedy. Everything conspired to make this a fruitful meeting. The bright sunshine, tempered with the sea breeze, and luncheon on the beach after an invigorating dip in the water, set all three at ease. This preliminary discussion found them "yes-ing" each other to such an extent that Kennedy remarked it sounded like a studio conference.

Miss Swanson wanted von Stroheim to write and direct a film for her which Kennedy would finance. What ideas had he on the matter? As usual, von Stroheim had a story up his sleeve. This one was called *The Swamp*. It was a fantastic tale offering an actress an opportunity to portray both youthful innocence and more mature scenes of dramatic conflict. He told it so well that, by the time the trio boarded the sunset boat back to the mainland, an agreement to film it had been reached.

It recounted the adventures of an Irish orphan, Kitty Kelly, the daughter of a wandering painter who had died while traveling with his child in Germany. Left destitute, she is educated by the nuns in a charity convent school in Koenigberg, supposedly a small German state. The neurotic queen who rules this land is about to be married to Prince Wolfram, whose love affairs drive his jealous fiancée into insane tantrums. One day Prince Wolfram, riding at the head of his regiment on a country road, comes on a procession of convent girls out for a stroll with the sisters. Pretty Kitty Kelly catches his attention and, as the girls are being herded to the side of the road, her panties slip down around her feet.

244

The prince is mightily amused at her embarrassment, and his teasing comments to his adjutant rouse her Irish temper. In fury, she throws her fallen drawers into his face, but to her astonishment he seems to regard this as a compliment, kisses the garment, and puts it in his tunic.

That night—after attending the betrothal banquet given by the queen—the prince and his aide set out to abduct the girl. Scaling the nunnery wall, they start a fire in order to sound the fire alarm. In the resulting confusion the nuns and their charges run about, and Kitty, who swoons in the excitement, is carried to a waiting carriage and driven to the prince's private quarters in the castle. There he declares his love and, as they sit over supper, the queen surprises their tête-à-tête. In a paroxysm of insane jealousy, she whips the girl down the palace staircases and out into the night. Not daring to return to the convent, Kitty attempts suicide by jumping from a bridge. She is rescued and taken to the convent hospital. When she recovers, she is told that her aunt, who owns property in a German colony in East Africa, has sent for her and paid her passage thither.

In Africa the aunt is the proprietress of a dubious hotel which planters and sailors frequent. Kitty becomes a barmaid and her high-toned manners win her the name of "Queen Kelly." Her aunt persuades her to marry a rich planter, who conveniently is stricken soon after and dies, leaving her his heiress. As for Prince Wolfram, who meanwhile had married the queen, he finds that the world war has abolished monarchy in Germany and death has taken the queen. Wolfram comes to East Africa, a humbled man, and he and his convent-girl sweetheart are happily reunited.

It was decided that *The Swamp*, a reference to the jungle territory that surrounds the African colonial outpost, was too somber a title, and the film was renamed *Queen Kelly*. Robert Sherwood, the noted playwright and film critic, on reading the script pronounced it the best screenplay he had ever read. It contained the ingredients of commercial success, in addition to opportunities for the director and actress to exercise their special abilities.

Kennedy, whose associates demanded a tight curb on the director's extravagant ways, appointed William LeBaron as an executive producer. Will Hays approved the script in general but made some cuts that turned the African jungle hostel from a semi-brothel into a semi-respectable hotel.

On a visit to New York in May 1928, in search of an actor to play Prince Wolfram, von Stroheim told journalists he planned to introduce extraordinary realism into the scenes set in the jungle swamp. "It will be a typical von Stroheim film," he announced. "But the shooting schedule is so concise that probably fifteen weeks will see it through."

As a parody of Hollywood "style," when he returned to California with the completed and revised script he engaged two Negroes, clad as Nubian slaves in lion skins, to carry it to Kennedy's office on a silver platter.

At this time, though movie producers were only partially aware of it, motion pictures were undergoing a revolution. The talking film had made its debut in August 1926, when Warner Brothers first publicly demonstrated the new invention, called Vitaphone. Al Jolson's *The Jazz Singer*, the first feature film with a talking sequence, had arrived in October 1927. It was a hit, but it was not as outstanding a hit as *Wings, Seventh Heaven, The Big Parade, Underworld, The Way of All Flesh,* and Charlie Chaplin's *The Circus*, all silent and all strong moneymakers. Neither Miss Swanson nor Kennedy—or von Stroheim—believed at this time that the talking film would eventually replace the silent film. *Queen*

Kelly would be made as a silent and would probably be released with a synchronized musical score.

Though it would employ countless extras, its chief feature would be Miss Swanson's interpretation of her juicy role. A young English actor, Walter Byron, was tested as Wolfram, and Miss Swanson and Kennedy decided he was a perfect choice. Seena Owen, a capable actress who, like her director, had begun her career under D. W. Griffith, was to play the jealousy-crazed queen. Sylvia Ashton was selected as the matchmaking aunt, and Tully Marshall as the loathsome old planter. William von Brincken was the prince's adjutant, and Sidney Bracey was the inevitable valet.

The filming of *Queen Kelly* was underway by the time *The Wedding March* had its world première at the Rivoli Theater on Broadway on October 12, 1928. Paramount had been heralding its release and the studio's publicity agents had been describing its wonders since 1926. It opened at last —with the claim of having cost two million dollars and of having required two full years to make (both these boasts were exaggerated). Public curiosity about it had been thoroughly aroused and in New York it drew capacity houses. Critical estimates varied. The *Daily News* awarded the film four stars, their highest possible tribute. There were qualified endorsements from *The New York Times*, the *Herald Tribune*, and the *Sun*. All the reviewers cited various fine passages, but the majority found the film uneven and its cutting choppy. Several believed that its second part would be the more interesting. It was felt that another von Stroheim film had suffered in the cutting room, but the unified excellence of its acting and the stunning photography (and it was mentioned that though there had been improvement in camera technique since 1926, the film surpassed in pictorial beauty anything seen in 1928) made it a fascinating endeavor. "Von

247

Stroheim certainly knows how to direct women. He has done for the tepid and negative Fay Wray what he did for Mae Murray in *The Merry Widow*. She acts. If she never acts again, she'll have the delightful Mitzi to her everlasting distinction," wrote Bland Johaneson in the *Mirror*.

"He would be the Zola of the screen," wrote the *Times* critic. "His strange characters hold one's attention—if not one's sympathy."

The soft-focused sequence, the admirably cut scene of the meeting and flirtation of Prince Nicki and Mitzi, was pure von Stroheim artistry, as, in an ironic vein, was the scene in which the drunken old prince, Nicki's father, and the socially ambitious corn-plaster king, sprawling on the floor of a gaudy brothel, sign the pact for their children's marriage. The loveless wedding march, with which the film concludes, was acknowledged as a compelling climax. ZaSu Pitts, as the limping rich girl (though after the editing she had but a few scenes), was singled out by the critics as a talented screen tragedienne. Audiences were also delighted to see again "the man you love to hate," though he had mellowed in this new film, his first screen appearance since *Foolish Wives*, seven years earlier. *The Wedding March* was so long in reaching the public that two of its principal actors—George Nichols, who played the corn-plaster magnate, and Hughie Mack, who played Schani's 325-pound father—had died by the time it was seen.

While *The Wedding March* was being reviewed and discussed, *Queen Kelly* was moving on to completion. The making of its European sequences had proceeded rapidly and efficiently, two-thirds of the film being shot within twelve weeks. Gloria Swanson explained to an interviewer how relieved she was to be under the direction of a man in whom she had the greatest trust.

248

"For the first time since my days with Mr. DeMille, I feel that I can relax and at the same time be confident that a seasoned pilot is at the helm. I know pictures, and when one's money and reputation are at stake, one may be excused for taking intense interest in details. But at last I have found a director in whom I have such complete confidence that I feel I can shift all responsibility onto his shoulders. Von Stroheim has the same grasp of fundamentals that makes Eugene O'Neill the greatest playwright of today."

Leaning back among the rose-colored cushions of her studio dressing room, Miss Swanson quoted an old Arab proverb: "He who knows not, and knows that he knows not, is ignorant—teach him. He who knows not, and knows not that he knows not, is a fool—shun him. He who knows, and knows that he knows, is wise—follow him." She added: "I have found the man who knows, and who knows that he knows—and I am eager and willing to follow him."

She followed him now into the African sequences, but as these were being shot, her faith began to wane. First she noticed that all the scenes that had been deleted from the script to meet the demands of Will Hays were reappearing, though they were not restored to the rewritten scenario. The hotel run by Kitty Kelly's aunt was not shown as an open brothel, but girls were seen going upstairs with customers from the bar.

In the original screenplay, a black priest administered the last rites to the dying aunt. Hays had thought this interracial relationship, though logical enough in Africa, might offend Catholics and would certainly draw the wrath of the Ku Klux Klan. But the black priest duly reported for work and the scene was made. Then, too, Miss Swanson felt that far too much footage was being devoted to the squalor of Africa, with filthy jungle-town riffraff comporting themselves disgustingly to overstress the sordid surrounding. She consulted over the long-distance telephone with Kennedy, who was vacationing in Florida.

Kennedy had withstood the Hollywood producers who warned him against associating himself with von Stroheim. He was by nature a courageously independent man, but rumors now reached him that he, an eminent Catholic layman, was financing a film about a runaway nun! Will Hays's spies reported to their master that a very different script than the one he had approved was being filmed, and he complained to Kennedy. While Miss Swanson and Kennedy, both of whom had only contempt for gossipmongers, might have risen above the lies that were spread, another problem now arose.

By mid-winter of 1928 the talking film had definitely established itself. At first, Miss Swanson thought of injecting some talking sequences into *Queen Kelly*—and even of reshooting it as an all-talking film. The expense of this would be prohibitive, she learned. As it would be released with a synchronized musical score, she toyed with the idea of at least singing a song in it, for she had a pretty voice. But Kennedy, informed of the sensational success that the Jolson film was enjoying, abruptly told her that the wisest possible business decision would be to terminate shooting on *Queen Kelly* at once.

She had gone directly from the set to her dressing room to take this fatal telephone call from Kennedy. After speaking with him, she ordered her automobile and went home. Later in the day von Stroheim, who had gone to another set to do some shooting on a scene while he awaited her return, was handed a message that he was "off" the film.

His sudden dismissal stunned the director. Everything had progressed on schedule and to everyone's seeming satisfaction. Many people had expected temperamental fireworks on the set, but the star and the director had disappointed these ill-wishers. A blunt announcement was now issued that, in the light of the success of talking films, the producer and star of *Queen Kelly* had agreed that a silent film was unmarketable.

Miss Swanson, eager to join the talkie rush, quickly prepared *The Trespasser* with Edmund Goulding, a British author-director. It was ready for release at the end of the summer of 1929 and proved one of the star's most popular vehicles. The song Miss Swanson sang in it, "Love, Your Magic Spell Is Everywhere," became a hit too.

Though Miss Swanson shelved *Queen Kelly*, she hoped to be able to doctor it for release one day. Later she shot a tragic ending to the scenario's first part, the abused convent girl succeeding in her suicide attempt, with the prince swearing eternal love at her bier. This banal finish was made under the auspices of Irving Thalberg, one of his few directorial chores. Though *Queen Kelly* could not be released in this abortive version in the United States without von Stroheim's permission—and, of course, he refused to give it—it was shown in the early thirties on the Continent and in South America.

The unexpected cancellation of *Queen Kelly* was a terrible blow to von Stroheim. His Hollywood enemies, pleased over the disaster that had overtaken him, said: "Well, we've always told you so."

In the palace corridor

(OPPOSITE) Kitty Kelly (Gloria Swanson) and the Queen (Seena Owen) on the palace stairway in *Queen Kelly*

Prince Wolfram (Walter Byron) tries to protect Kitty from the Queen's riding crop

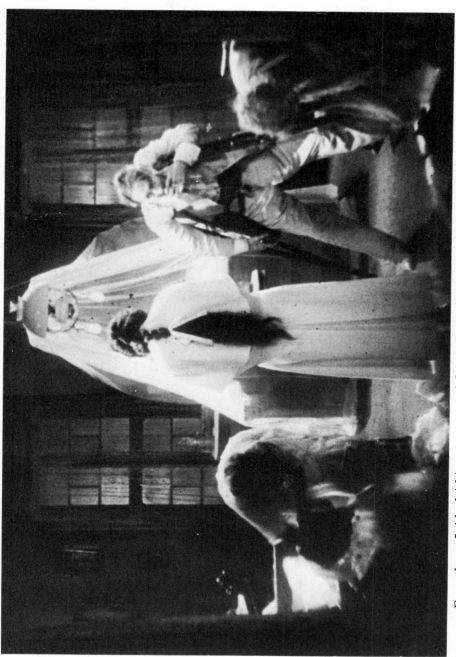

From the unfinished African sequence of *Queen Kelly*: Tully Marshall as the old planter greets his bride-to-be, Gloria Swanson, in her aunt's brothel. *Photo courtesy of Cinémathèque Française*

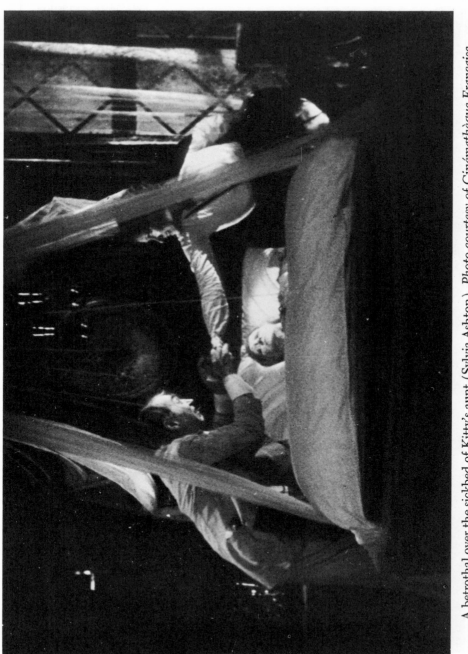

A betrothal over the sickbed of Kitty's aunt (Sylvia Ashton). *Photo courtesy of Cinémathèque Française*

The wedding ceremony. *Photo courtesy of Cinémathèque Française*

The aunt receives the eucharist. *Photo courtesy of Cinémathèque Française*

The bridal couple. *Photo courtesy of Cinémathèque Française*

PART THREE

14

The Comeback

Von Stroheim had a friend and admirer in another director, James Cruze. Cruze, greatly impressed with von Stroheim's successful return to acting in *The Wedding March*, offered him the starring role in his new film, *The Great Gabbo*. This was a Ben Hecht story about a self-destructive megalomaniac, a vaudeville ventriloquist, whose egoism drives him to ruin and madness. Though somewhat perturbed at temporarily losing his directorial status, von Stroheim—hoping to return and complete *Queen Kelly* when Miss Swanson finished *The Trespasser*—accepted the role.

In this, his first appearance in talking films, he achieved a personal triumph. *The Great Gabbo*, an early "all-talking, all-singing, all-dancing" spectacle, was interlarded with revue numbers in blatant color. It was not one of Cruze's most dis-

Von Stroheim in the title role of James Cruze's *The Great Gabbo*, 1929

tinguished accomplishments as a director, but the sequences in which its star appeared—with Cruze's wife, Betty Compson, as leading lady—raised it intermittently to real drama. This gave an uneven quality to the film but, it emerged as both a critical and a financial success. Von Stroheim's acting in the film was compared favorably to that of Emil Jannings.

Von Stroheim as actor seemed an ideal solution to the Hollywood producers' dilemma. He was unquestionably a drawing card, but they would never now entrust him with dictatorial powers over a production. After his hit in *The Great Gabbo,* Warner Brothers approached him, offering him a starring role opposite Constance Bennett in a remake of the World War I espionage melodrama, *Three Faces East.* He was to be a German agent, disguised as a butler in an aristocratic English mansion. Miss Bennett was to pretend to fall in love with him and trick him into revealing his secret.

Both Miss Bennett and the director, Roy del Ruth, resented the arrival of von Stroheim, Miss Bennett because she feared he would steal the film from her and del Ruth because he envied his rival's exalted reputation as director. After a scene in which the unwelcome actor was called upon to kiss her, Miss Bennett shouted to her maid to bring her mouthwash at once. Not to be outdone, von Stroheim, after the next kissing scene with Miss Bennett, ordered his dresser to rush up to him with a bottle of Listerine. Del Ruth's dislike of his leading man increased when von Stroheim, seeking to improve his role, wrote a few lines and took them to the producer, Darryl F. Zanuck, for prior approval. Zanuck, a shrewd moviemaker, was aware that von Stroheim was a better author than the scriptwriter and gave him a free hand to add as many lines as he wished. He also urged Jack Warner to offer von Stroheim a contract with the studio as author-actor-director. When del Ruth learned that von Stroheim had been granted powers to revise his role, he was furious and took what petty revenge he could. Miss Bennett added to this ugly situation by demanding that scenes be reshot because von Stroheim spoke a line too slowly, or too fast, or made a gesture that drew attention from her.

Receiving a call to report for night shooting on the seacoast, von Stroheim decided to fortify himself against the chill by taking with him a thermos bottle filled with hot coffee. As the early morning wind began to whip about the improvised set, he took a swig of coffee. As he swallowed the gulp, he found his mouth full of glass. The interior of the thermos bottle had cracked and he was alarmed that he might have swallowed the glass particles with the coffee. When he told del Ruth, the director replied, "Well, we'll shoot your stuff first in case you die later."

Another example of del Ruth's determination to humiliate him was related comically by von Stroheim to Wilson Mizner, the writer, who was also a Warner employee at the time:

> When I first reported for the picture, I rode out in my car with ten uniforms. All the way out I kept saying to myself, "Erich, don't lose your temper, whatever you do. Erich, keep your mouth shut." I went to the hotel, where del Ruth had a whole floor, and I asked him most politely where I should dress. He said to me, "Dress in your car, where else?" So I went to my car. I tell you that very few men, women, and children in Beverly Hills missed seeing me in B.V.D.'s that day, climbing in and out of uniforms, putting my body in and my head out of that damned car. I swore continually, I ripped my trousers, I bumped my head.
>
> I said to myself: "You are getting paid and it's money you're in great need of. Don't let me hear another word out of you." So, despite these embarrassments, I went through

with the picture. That is called a comeback. To me it is a go-back, a fall-back, and a back-flip. I tell you my luck has been just too damned bad.

Though von Stroheim joked about the absurd indignities he had suffered, he was privately worried about his future. *Three Faces East* was a letdown for him, he felt. Here he was, after a titanic struggle to become one of the greatest film directors, acting in unworthy roles. At the same time, *The Wedding March* was enriching his fame in Europe. During the winter of 1929–30 this film was an enormous hit abroad, breaking records at the recently opened Paramount Theater in Paris and at the Plaza in London. Even in Berlin, where the national prejudice against its director ran high, it received gratifying praise. The Nazi-minded critics still carped a bit— but less than they had over his other films. A Bavarian weekly, strongly pro-Nazi, published a selection of "stills" to illustrate the magnificence of this screen re-creation of Imperial Vienna. Though acknowledging the quality of the film, the accompanying article cast slurs on its creator's origins and motives. He had not been a Schnitzler-like lieutenant at all, it said; he was really the son of a Viennese laundress. Not being able to gain rapid promotion in the Imperial Army, so ran this fable, he had resigned from the service and gone to America. Now in Hollywood, he was taking his belated revenge by maliciously mocking the society that had scorned him. Jewish bankers were eagerly financing him for their own reasons. The malicious tone of this article evoked an ironic guffaw from its subject. In Vienna *The Wedding March* was a sensation, but its première found its audience at political odds. The Socialist element booed the sight of Franz-Josef; the monarchists cheered. When the aristocracy was seen in a drunken orgy in Madame Rosa's luxurious brothel, the Socialists cheered and the monarchists hissed.

In Hollywood *The Wedding March* and its European reception seemed far away to von Stroheim. It began to seem that his directorial status had been completely forgotten. He wondered if he had taken the wrong turn in appearing under someone else's direction in *The Great Gabbo*. At least it had harvested him praise as a superb actor. But, with *Three Faces East*, he feared he was back at one of the starting points of his career—that of the wicked Hun. A best-seller that year was *All Quiet on the Western Front*, Erich Maria Remarque's fine novel, which von Stroheim greatly admired. It was a new era of pacifism and von Stroheim was depressed to be reenacting the same screen villainy he had portrayed in 1917.

Jack Warner and Darryl Zanuck saw the matter differently. Both were pleased with von Stroheim's performance in *Three Faces East*. They had both also liked his suggestions for the improvement of the script, and they now proposed that he accept a writing-directing-acting contract. He was contemplating this when Paul Kohner, an old friend and a producer at Universal, came to him with a more tempting offer.

Kohner had been employed in the New York office of Universal when von Stroheim went East to attend the première of *Foolish Wives*, and Carl Laemmle had asked him to act as the visiting director's temporary aide and companion. Born in Czechoslovakia and schooled in Vienna, Kohner had a deep appreciation of von Stroheim and a unique understanding of his work and his aims. It was he who had recommended Leo Perutz's novel *From Nine to Nine* to the director as possible material for a film. He was widely read, well-mannered, exceedingly intelligent, and amusing. Von Stroheim liked him at once, and had recommended Kohner to Laemmle as a man of outstanding qualities who should be in the West Coast studios contributing his valuable knowledge to filmmaking.

Though not a relative of the Laemmle clan, Kohner had

another strong ally in Carl Laemmle, Jr., the precocious son of the Universal president. The elder Laemmle had an almost superstitious faith in his offspring's judgment of films and whenever possible had him view the rushes of films in progress. Clarence Brown remembers an occasion when his film *The Signal Tower* was submitted in the projection room for the verdict of Laemmle father and son. Brown, endeavoring to inject some originality into the final fade-out kiss of the young couple, had an express train rush past them so that the spectator caught only glimpses of them in the gaps between the cars. The elder Laemmle waved this innovation away as mere foolishness, but Junior disagreed and Senior quickly gave his approval. The warm recommendations of von Stroheim and Carl, Jr., moved Laemmle to transfer Kohner to Universal City, where he was assigned to production. He was an assistant on *Merry-Go-Round* and his knowledge of Imperial Vienna was so invaluable that he was retained on the film after von Stroheim had been dismissed and Rupert Julian took charge. Promotion followed promotion, and in 1927 his first production was a film version of Victor Hugo's *The Man Who Laughs*. Paul Leni, imported at Kohner's request from Berlin, directed, and Conrad Veidt enacted the grinning Gwynplaine. Mary Philbin, by then a star, played the blind girl who loves him, unable to see his mutilated face.

Many Universal executives regarded von Stroheim as anathema. When he had held such absolute power at the studio, his behavior, they felt, had been wildly irresponsible and his fabled extravagances were a financial hazard. They forgot that all his films had been box-office successes which had enriched them, despite his unorthodox methods of picture-making.

It had been largely due to the example set by von Stroheim that Universal branched out to gain a reputation as a major studio. Before his coming, Universal had relied principally on a routine output of Westerns and program comedies, with an occasional exception like *The Virgin of Stambul*, an early film of Tod Browning. With *Blind Husbands*, *The Devil's Passkey*, *Foolish Wives*, and *Merry-Go-Round*, Universal took rank as a formidable rival of Metro, Paramount, and United Artists. The studio continued to manufacture cowboy pictures—Hoot Gibson was one of their standard stars—and breezy, light comedies. But, after *Merry-Go-Round*, Universal turned increasingly to spectacle roadshows.

The Hunchback of Notre Dame, *The Phantom of the Opera*, *The Man Who Laughs*, *Show Boat*, *Broadway*, *The King of Jazz* (with Paul Whiteman as its star), and *All Quiet on the Western Front* were all productions that took their cue from von Stroheim's earlier successes, and all of them scored artistic and financial gains that earned for Universal the status of a "big" studio.

In 1930, Carl Laemmle announced his retirement from the presidency of Universal, placing his son, Carl, Jr., in charge. The younger Laemmle was twenty-one and hardly equipped by temperament for this important position. Nervous and shy of strangers, he reserved his outspoken opinions for his conversations with his father. Elmer Rice, John Huston, and others who had professional business with him at this time, found that he was reluctant to make decisions. When the elder Laemmle bought the screen rights to *All Quiet on the Western Front*, he considered summoning von Stroheim as its director. But his associates raised such strenuous objections that he withdrew the suggestion. Now Kohner proposed to both Laemmles that von Stroheim be brought back to the studio. This was a startling notion, but after much discussion the retiring president agreed, this time overriding the protest of other advisers. The senior Laemmle retained an affection for his "discovery," and was proud of having given him his first opportunity as a director. John Drinkwater, the well-known British dramatist, had come to Hollywood to write an official biography of Laemmle. He included among Laemmle's heroic achievements his unprecedented decision to allow a movie actor without major directorial experience to write, act, and direct his first film at Universal.

Kohner hurried to von Stroheim's home and excitedly related the good news. The next morning they were to motor out to Universal City and sign the contract. But when Kohner arrived to pick up von Stroheim, a black cat ran across their path as they walked to Kohner's automobile. Von Stroheim stood aghast.

"That means bad luck!" he exclaimed. "I can't go to see Laemmle today. Postpone the signing of the contract until tomorrow." And he went back into his house and refused to come out, despite Kohner's protestations. Kohner, finding it useless to try to reason with von Stroheim, telephoned Laemmle that von Stroheim was ill and postponed the interview for twenty-four hours. The following morning when Kohner called for von Stroheim, he rushed his omen-obsessed friend to the car before another black cat showed up.

It was remake time in Hollywood. All the studios were engaged in refilming their silent successes as talkies. Cecil B. DeMille was remaking *The Squaw Man* with spoken dialogue. *Anna Christie*, the O'Neill play, which Blanche Sweet had played so well on the silent screen, was to be Greta Garbo's first talking picture. Warner Brothers brought George Arliss back to star in talking versions of *Disraeli* and *The Green Goddess*. Ruth Chatterton came from the Broadway stage to appear in a talkie of *Madame X*. Paramount was busy with the manufacture of *The Virginian* and many other Westerns in talkie form.

It was first proposed that von Stroheim remake *Merry-Go-Round* at Universal, again with Mary Philbin as its heroine. But this project—perhaps because it had led to von Stroheim's dismissal—was rejected. Next, a second edition of *Foolish Wives* was considered—to bear a new title, *Riviera*. The Monte Carlo set, built in 1920, was still standing on the lot. Finally Laemmle, remembering that it was the first von Stroheim film that had earned the highest returns, suggested a talkie of *Blind Husbands*.

Von Stroheim, after his ghastly servitude under Roy del Ruth, found it reassuring to be under contract in the triple capacity of actor-director-author. He settled down to adapt his initial scenario for the talkies. The title would be retained —it was famous and would remind millions of the excellent old film. But, now eleven years older, he could no longer essay the part of a young lieutenant. He rewrote this role as well as those of the American husband and wife visiting the Tyrol on their honeymoon. Even Americans were no longer as naïve and ignorant of the ways of the European world as they had been in 1919. The script's dialogue was as complete as that of a published play, something of an innovation in this period when dialogue was often written at the last moment on the set. Both Laemmle and Kohner were pleased with this efficient screenplay, which denoted that von Stroheim had risen to the challenge of the talking pictures. Payment for it was immediately made, and as the filming was scheduled for September, von Stroheim was at leave to take a holiday. He decided to spend the summer abroad, visiting Austria on his travels, to purchase Tyrolean furniture and other accessories for his film.

Return trips to Europe had by 1930 become status symbols in the film colony. Adolph Zukor made a pilgrimage to the tiny village on the Hungarian puszta where he was born, and the festivities that attended the return of this native were reported in newspapers from Budapest to Los Angeles. Charlie Chaplin was smothered with official honors when he first returned to London; crowds blocked his limousine wherever he went, as he recalled the bitter poverty he had once suffered in that city. Mary Pickford and Douglas Fairbanks were the guests of royalty when they made a tour of the world as the most famous couple on the planet; even von Hindenburg was thrilled to meet Mary Pickford.

Business affairs also drew the American film leaders across the Atlantic. Universal and Paramount now had common interests with U.F.A. in Berlin; Lasky came to Paris to sign a contract with the Soviet director Eisenstein; Alexander Korda, failing as a producer-director in California, was in England preparing to establish London as a new motion-picture center.

The making of American films in Europe had begun in the twenties. Rex Ingram went to Tunis to shoot *The Arab* in 1923; much of *Ben Hur* had been made in Rome; Lillian Gish, forming her own company, produced *The White Sister* and *Romola* under Henry King's direction on locations in Italy; Gloria Swanson had made the Paramount special, *Madame Sans-Gêne* in Paris; and Rex Ingram had his own studios, the Vittorine, in Nice.

Von Stroheim had not been to Europe since he landed with a hundred dollars in his pocket in New York in 1909. As he explained to a reporter, when he had had the time to go to Europe he had not had the money, and when he had had the money he had not had the time. Now a few months of leisure were his and he decided to show the Continent to his wife and young son, Josef Erich, then eight years old.

First they visited Rome, where the von Stroheims had a private audience with Pope Pius XI. "I don't remember a

273

great deal about our special audience with the pope," he later told Sterling North. "Something about the preliminary pomp sweeps one away. You scarcely notice a thing about the actual audience. We spoke in German and the pope was magnificently dressed, all in white. Then he pinned the decoration of St. Theresa on my son, and we were courteously ushered out."

In Vienna, von Stroheim gave no interviews and the local Universal bureau was instructed to make no mention of his visit. He wanted principally to see his mother, who, though she had complained in her letters of failing health, seemed cured of the nervous attacks that had troubled their family life when her son was a boy. The local press—confusing von Stroheim with von Sternberg—had suggested that he was romantically involved with Marlene Dietrich, whose film, *The Blue Angel*, was running in Vienna. The elder Mrs. von Stroheim scolded her son about his alleged affair, but he cut short this reprimand by telling his mother that he had never met Miss Dietrich.

The von Stroheims went to the Austrian Tyrol, where the director arranged for a large shipment of peasant furniture and costumes to be sent to Hollywood. *Blind Husbands* was ready for immediate production when the director arrived home from his summer holiday. The efficient Paul Kohner had performed many useful tasks. His enthusiasm kept executive hopes high, and he had stirred much curiosity about the film with his press releases. He was to supervise its making. Von Stroheim had decided to film it in color. He had long been an advocate of the color film and had included color sequences in both *The Merry Widow* and *The Wedding March*. But suddenly there was an ominous snag.

The opening sequence of *Blind Husbands* was to take place at a mountain lake supposedly in the Tyrol, at a location site selected by Kohner. When the expedition was about to set off, von Stroheim inspected some church bells which were to be used. Kohner informed him that it would be wasteful to haul the real bells to the scene of the shooting, as the sound of the chimes would later be dubbed in at the studio.

"But the sound of bells across lake water is not the same as the tingling of bells in a sound room," objected von Stroheim.

Rather than argue, Kohner gave orders that the huge bells be placed in trucks and dragged up the mountain side, a major engineering feat. This news was soon all over the studio. Von Stroheim's enemies passed the word along to reporters. Soon newspapers published accounts of this latest von Stroheim extravagance, citing it as another example of his well-known mania for realism. Universal executives, unfriendly to the director, rushed to the inexperienced young Laemmle.

"This man almost brought your studio to bankruptcy some years ago. This time he is going to accomplish that objective," one executive warned the bewildered president, who summoned von Stroheim from the mountain top to explain the matter. When he entered Laemmle's office, he found the young man nervously toying with objects on his presidential desk.

"Sit down, Von," he muttered in what at first seemed acute embarrassment. The preliminaries of this conversation did not touch on films or the expense of making them. "Do you remember years ago, when I was a little boy, we were in the garden of Dad's house?" the young man asked.

Von Stroheim said he recalled many such occasions.

"Well, my nose was running and you took out your handkerchief and blew my nose. Then you threw the handkerchief behind the bushes." After this introduction, he changed the subject abruptly. "I'm stopping production on the picture, Von. We won't do it."

That was all. It was the end of von Stroheim's return engagement at Universal City. Kohner pleaded, but the matter was closed.

15

The Dark Years

THE year 1931 dawned bleak for von Stroheim. There were no prospects of any sort on the horizon, and to remind him of his recent defeat, crates of Tyrolean furniture stood about in the hallway and living room of his Brentwood home. He had spent the Christmas holiday solving this space problem by converting the cellar into an Austrian country-style room for this furniture.

On New Year's Eve he was a guest at the Cocoanut Grove of the Hotel Ambassador. The party reminded him of a former celebration in the same room over his signing a contract with Goldwyn in 1922. He superstitiously hoped that history would repeat itself and that some wonderful opportunity was again awaiting him. Instead, Myron Selznick, a producer who had turned actors' agent, came up to his table and delivered some insulting remarks. Blows were exchanged while the other guests looked on, scandalized. In the morning the proud Austrian who loathed notoriety found his picture on the front page with the accusation that he had provoked a drunken brawl. It is not surprising that von Stroheim sought even more desperately to avoid all Hollywood social gatherings.

The depression that followed in the wake of the Wall Street stock crash of 1929 had deepened into a financial crisis that now threatened the movies. To reduce expenses, producers were dispensing with directors who had established themselves in the silent era, and were importing stage directors from New York. These directors could not demand high wages, at least at first. This cunning business stratagem, however, did not prove successful. Few of the Broadway-trained directors were to have long screen careers, though there were exceptions—Rouben Mamoulian and George Cukor were two. Once the novelty of merely hearing voices had worn off, the public wanted the movies to move again. Soon Cecil B. DeMille, Henry King, Allan Dwan, Raoul Walsh, Sidney Franklin, Robert Z. Leonard, King Vidor, and other veterans of the silents were in high favor once more, as producers reluctantly decided that they were more reliable filmmakers than stage directors were.

But no Hollywood producer at this time would employ von Stroheim as a director. His extravagant ways were judged wasteful, and he was reputed to be a most difficult and unreasonable genius. He had, of course, made some great successes and his name was a magnet, but his first attempt at making a talkie had now been abandoned. It would be a double risk to entrust him with a talkie.

"The parade has passed him by," Laemmle Junior dourly

commented when questioned about the sudden termination of the remake of *Blind Husbands*.

But von Stroheim the actor was still a valuable property. Early in 1931, RKO announced a film to be directed by Victor Schertzinger, *The Sphinx Has Spoken*, an adaptation of a Maurice Dekobra novel. Schertzinger, though a program-picture director, was a versatile man. Later he made several major musicals, notably *One Night of Love*, with Grace Moore, in 1934, which critics voted one of that year's best films. He himself was a musician and lived in a Beverly Hills mansion which contained a grand organ. He had composed many popular songs, among them "Ramona." He was a von Stroheim fan and approached him, promising him a good role, rewarding payment, and proper billing. The cast was to be an exceptional one, including Lili Damita; Adolphe Menjou, one of von Stroheim's close friends; and a promising young English actor, Laurence Olivier.

Despite Schertzinger's promise, the role was less than interesting. Von Stroheim was again to impersonate an evil German agent who extracts military secrets from British officers in India through his seductive wife, Lili Damita.

Olivier remembers the shooting of this, his first Hollywood film, as a comic-tragic experience: "Von Stroheim was preoccupied with a bit of business throughout the rehearsals. To appear ultra-sinister, he was to wear a black patch over one eye and a monocle over the other. But which ornament for which eye? He kept reversing black patch and monocle for Schertzinger's approval. He was a hard worker, but off the set he seemed to me distracted, worried, lost. Years later when I saw him in *Sunset Boulevard*, it occurred to me that he was very much like that in real life, even in 1931, the fallen giant of the silent era, dazed by his fall."

Friends and Lovers (the release title given *The Sphinx*

Has Spoken), though only a program picture trading on big names, had moderate box-office success. Von Stroheim received favorable notices and it was regretted that he was killed so early in the film. The critics inquired why he was not directing as well as acting.

Discovering that he was still a popular favorite, RKO at once signed him to act in a second film, which contained a role especially tailored for him. This second film, *Lost Squadron*, had been written by Dick Grace, an American ace flyer during the First World War. The scenario concerned a trio of demobilized wartime aviators who work as stunt flyers in the motion pictures. A megalomaniac German director is preparing an aviation epic and engages them, but he hates them bitterly as former enemies. His madness leads him to pour acid on the wires of the planes just before he sends the pilots up. The ensuing crashes not only will avenge their bombing of German towns but will furnish him with a spectacular sequence for his film.

Dick Grace modeled the director after the credulous moviegoers' notions of von Stroheim. It was suggested that he simply be billed as himself, but he balked at this absurd proposal which would place him on the screen under his own name as a murderous lunatic.

News of the strong anti-German nature of the new film spread fast. Walter Winchell, in a national broadcast, informed his listeners that *Lost Squadron* would be the most violently anti-German movie to be made since the war. When this broadcast was repeated in Europe the following week, it was heard by von Stroheim's mother in Vienna, and she fell from her chair in a faint. The German consul in San Francisco, alerted by the Winchell broadcast, hurried to Los Angeles to confer with von Stroheim. United States relations with Germany were friendly (this was two years before

Von Stroheim as the mad film director in *The Lost Squadron*, 1932

Hitler came to power) and such a film would only stir up the embers of dying hatred, he argued. Von Stroheim replied that he was Austrian-born, he had not written the scenario, and the Germans had never accorded him any favors. In fact, they had waged a campaign against his films and against him. He was an American citizen, and an actor engaged to be a villain, and a villain he would be.

Lost Squadron was scarcely worth a diplomatic incident, and the German government made no further protests, though the name von Stroheim, already on the Nazi blacklist, was now underlined. George Archainbaud and Paul Sloane directed the controversial melodrama competently, and the cast included Richard Dix, Mary Astor, and Joel McCrea. Von Stroheim, caricaturing his public image, pleased the press and public. In his impeccable clothes, with his haughty, neatly shaven head held high, his gold bracelet tingling, and his white kid gloves immaculate, he moved with military precision, an ebony walking stick in his hands. His scarred forehead winked ominously when he encountered the ex-A.E.F. flyers. In his final scene the ruthless director is shot and falls to his death down a flight of stairs. Von Stroheim, a stunt man in his early movie days, took the fall himself so realistically that he broke three ribs and had to be taken to the hospital.

Greta Garbo, fresh from her leap from silent films to talkies, was *the* reigning star at Metro-Goldwyn-Mayer in 1932, and deservedly so. Under the guidance of Clarence Brown, who had made one of her early successes, *Flesh and the Devil*, in 1926, she had dared to face the sound film's microphones. Brown had carefully selected Eugene O'Neill's *Anna Christie* for her talking debut in 1930, because her marked Swedish accent and deep voice would be suited to the role. *Anna Christie* proved a box-office triumph. It was followed by *Romance* and *Inspiration* (after Daudet's novel, *Sappho*), both directed by Brown. Her position was now more secure than ever. In 1932 she played the ballerina in *Grand Hotel*, an all-star film that had tremendous success despite a decline in picture-going caused by the depression.

Garbo's next film was to be a screen version of Pirandello's play *As You Desire Me*. Its heroine, suffering amnesia as a result of shock during the war, lives in Budapest, the prisoner of a sadistic writer. She does not know who she is, and becomes a star performer in cabarets. A man claiming to be her Italian husband discovers her whereabouts and takes her back to Florence so that, in the surroundings of her youth, she will regain her memory. But it is never certain that she *is* his lost wife. She can become so only if she believes that she is.

Thalberg assigned George Fitzmaurice, well known for his silent films, to direct. Melvyn Douglas was cast as the husband searching for his wife; Owen Moore as his friend; and Hedda Hopper, Rafaela Ottiano, and Albert Conti had supporting parts. There remained the sinister role of the novelist who stands between the heroine and her happiness. Discussing this problem with her friend and adviser, Salka Viertel, Greta Garbo suddenly thought of von Stroheim.

When she first came to the United States in 1925 as the protégée of Maurice Stiller, Greta Garbo remembered Stiller's remark that von Stroheim was the most important man in the American movies. During their stay in New York, before entraining for Hollywood, she and Stiller saw *The Merry Widow*, then playing its initial engagement on Broadway. Garbo had been impressed with the film and with John Gilbert, with whom she was later to star in *Flesh and the Devil*. She had made a point of seeing all the subsequent von Stroheim films, much taken by his unusual work. But they had never met, as neither she nor he frequented Hollywood gatherings. He had already departed from M-G-M when she arrived.

Salka Viertel knew von Stroheim through her husband-director, Bernard Viertel, and invited him to her Santa Monica home to meet Greta Garbo. The role interested him because Benjamin Glazer informed him that it was a caricature of the Hungarian playwright Ferenc Molnár. But there was a stumbling block, he told Miss Garbo. Mayer and Thalberg had vowed that the rebellious von Stroheim would never be permitted to pass through the gates of M-G-M again. Garbo laughed at this, saying she would tell Thalberg that von Stroheim must have the part or she would go on strike. She had done this successfully some years before, when Mayer tried to hold her to her original salary when her films were M-G-M's biggest successes. Garbo was as good as her promise, and a few days later von Stroheim entered the long-forbidden portals. Mayer and Thalberg, making the best of the situation, were outwardly friendly. The rest of the company seemed to resent his friendship with Garbo, who sat at his feet between scenes, listening to his talk.

George Fitzmaurice, though not resorting to the tactics of Roy del Ruth, just tolerated him. Melvyn Douglas remembers his association with von Stroheim on this film as a great disappointment: "I had looked forward to meeting him, regarding him as a true genius for his *Foolish Wives* and *Greed* in particular. But he was rude and common, and had such a hopeless stutter that his scenes had to be shot over and over again—angle by angle, phrase by phrase. I was very surprised that a man who had shown such gifts had no subtlety, no savoir-faire, and was what is called today a square."

Hedda Hopper in her memoirs claimed that von Stroheim

Greta Garbo with von Stroheim in *As You Desire Me*, 1932

A close-up from *As You Desire Me*

caused such confusion by blowing up in his lines that he gave a champagne party on the final day of shooting to make amends. When von Stroheim read this he was furious, declaring that he had never muffed a line and that on *Sunset Boulevard* a brief scene with Hedda Hopper had to be shot many times because she read her lines so badly. The truth is that von Stroheim was very uncomfortable on his return to M-G-M. He distrusted everyone, he was recuperating from a painful operation caused by a fall, and on several occasions he was so ill that he was unable to work. His repeated absences might ordinarily have ended in his being dismissed. Yet Greta Garbo was so protective of him that she did an unusual thing: she told him to telephone her when he felt he could not report for shooting, so that she could then inform the studio that *she* was indisposed. This extraordinary gesture saved him from being discharged.

In the advertising of *As You Desire Me*, von Stroheim was starred with Garbo. This brought him considerable prestige and suggested to Winfield Sheehan, a leading producer at Fox, that von Stroheim should be offered another directorial chance.

Sheehan, like two former von Stroheim producers, Pat Powers and Joseph Kennedy, was Irish-American; like them too, he had no respect for the Hollywood hierarchy. He was opposed to the kind of tyranny that Louis B. Mayer and his imitators were seeking to impose on the industry. The fact that von Stroheim had bucked the system and fought back bravely appealed to him. Even Mayer and Thalberg had been forced to retract on their vow that von Stroheim would never work at their studio again.

Sheehan, a man of taste, had little in common with his rivals. He had married Maria Jeritza, the famous soprano of the Vienna Opera and the Metropolitan. The talk at the

Sheehan table was not of percentages, salaries, and package deals but of books, plays, and music, as the British impresario, Charles B. Cochran, has recorded in his memoirs.

The new current of the times was against elaborate productions. Sheehan told von Stroheim that he wanted nothing in the spectacular vein; rather he hoped to get extraordinary direction, and a gripping story told by a master of the cinema. The producer and the director agreed on an adaptation of a play by the talented novelist Dawn Powell, *Walking Down Broadway*. It was the story of two girls rooming together in uptown New York. It would be done in the true-to-life von Stroheim style, and its only spectacular scene would be a fire in an apartment house caused by the heroine's attempt to commit suicide by turning on the gas.

In the von Stroheim reworking of the original, on which Leonard Spiegelgass collaborated, the two girls who come to live in New York were accorded deep psychological study. ZaSu Pitts, von Stroheim's favorite screen actress, was given the lead, and in the film this character also bore the given name of ZaSu.

"ZaSu is a very complicated and interesting character, in love with death. She goes to funeral parlors on Saturday afternoon to have a good cry at some stranger's last rites. In short, a psychopathic case," von Stroheim announced when he was writing the screenplay. Thwarted in love, ZaSu develops an insane jealousy of her attractive roommate's success with men. Lonely and neglected, with a pet turtle as her only consolation, she tries to break up her friend's affair with an ordinary young man who is constantly proposing marriage. ZaSu's intrigues finally separate the lovers, but they are reunited at her deathbed after she attempts suicide.

As usual, von Stroheim brought out the supporting figures

of the story; in particular, a prostitute, played by Minna Gombell, who lives in their apartment house. Her professional interlude with a commonplace traveling salesman was rather bold. It showed the prostitute's customer studying obscene photographs with her as a prelude to their love-making. James Dunn, an actor Fox had brought from Broadway, was cast as the pretty roommate's beau, and Boots Mallory played the country girl who arouses ZaSu's envy. The relationship of the two women was given overtones of incipient lesbianism.

Von Stroheim worked quickly and efficiently on the shooting. Once it was underway, he told a journalist that the legends of his extravagance were exaggerated inventions of press agents, as were the stories of his violent temper. As evidence he called attention to the harmonious and friendly atmosphere that prevailed on his set. Sheehan was proud of having brought von Stroheim to Fox and he was pleased at the smooth course of the film. When Mrs. Roosevelt, whose husband had just taken office, visited Hollywood, he conducted her with pride to the set. "I want you to meet the greatest director in the world," he said, presenting his prize acquisition. Von Stroheim bowed and clicked his heels, while Mrs. Roosevelt smiled her toothy smile and murmured appreciatively, "Yes, I know."

Von Stroheim had completed another scenario prior to embarking on *Walking Down Broadway*. His attorney, Kornblum, a gifted musician, had composed a score for it. Sheehan was anxious to read it, but von Stroheim said he had a better plan. He came to the Sheehan mansion one evening and gave a reading for the producer and his friends. He brought with him a twenty-five-piece orchestra; they played

289

The principals of *Walking Down Broadway*: James Dunn, ZaSu
Pitts, Terrance Ray, and Boots Mallory

James Dunn, Boots Mallory, and dog in a scene unmistakably directed by von Stroheim for *Walking Down Broadway*

Kornblum's score as accompaniment. The scenario's title was *Her Highness* and Sheehan purchased it as von Stroheim's next Fox film. It appears still to be a property of the studio, but it has never been filmed.

Unfortunately, Sheehan was called abroad on business before *Walking Down Broadway* was completed. In his absence, Sol Wurtzel was in charge of the studio's production.

"Wurtzel," von Stroheim has recalled, "was a producer who consistently made cheap films which showed profits. We disliked each other. I thought he was stupid and destructive. He thought I was crazy."

Wurtzel was shocked by *Walking Down Broadway*. He found it strange and unpleasant, and he was unable to understand its psychological subtleties. Not such a fool as to trust his own opinion, he told von Stroheim that he would leave the decision to the general public. Von Stroheim at first thought this meant that the film would be released, or in any case presented at a public preview, but not at all. Wurtzel summoned the secretaries and other employees of the Fox studios to come to a private screening and give their opinions. Since the word had already gone forth that Wurtzel disliked the film, most of his underlings wrote on the opinion cards that the film was muddled and morbid and certainly not good, clean entertainment.

This was the end of von Stroheim's directorial career. He was dismissed from Fox. *Variety* reviewed his quarrels with the major studios, reporting that, as a result of his unorthodox behavior and temperament, he was out at Universal, at Paramount, at M-G-M, at United Artists, and now at Fox. He was through as a director, the weekly said. There was dismal truth in this harsh estimate. Von Stroheim *was* through in Hollywood. No producer, however eccentric or daring, was ever to entrust him with the direction of another film.

The texts of two cables to Sergei Eisenstein that have recently come to light reveal the seriousness with which von Stroheim regarded his Hollywood plight or, as he described it in the first cable, the "crisis of my life." The original cable sent to Eisenstein in Moscow (presumably in December 1934) reads:

REMEMBERING YOUR APPRECIATION OF MY WORK, I BEG YOU TO TRY TO SECURE WORK FOR ME, PRIVATE OR GOVERNMENT. CONSIDER ME ALSO AS ACTOR AND WRITER. YOU KNOW MY ABILITY AND EXPERIENCE. AM GOING THROUGH CRISIS OF MY LIFE. PLEASE ANSWER SOON. MERRY CHRISTMAS AND HAPPY NEW YEAR.

ERICH VON STROHEIM

The Soviet filmmaker's reply appears to have been a brief acknowledgment, with the promise of further information. At this period Eisenstein was having troubles of his own in Russia. Since his return from abroad in 1932, he had not been in the good graces of the Soviet film executives. Though he was teaching at the Government Institute of Cinematography (GIK), all his projects for new films were being vetoed on one pretext or another. It was not until 1935 that Eisenstein was allowed to start a new film, *Bezhin Meadow*, but after nearly a year's work the authorities halted the film and the director was forced to apologize publicly for his "mistakes."

Von Stroheim's second cable to Eisenstein, which followed within a week, contains the memorable words, "am not as bad as Hollywood says." The full text is as follows:

RECEIVED YOUR CABLE PROMISING FURTHER INFORMATION BUT NOTHING ARRIVED. AM PREPAYING FIVE DOLLARS FOR NIGHT LETTER. PLEASE DO YOUR BEST TO GET ME JOB DIRECTING, WRITING OR ACTING. AM NOT AS BAD AS HOLLYWOOD SAYS. WOULD LOVE TO WORK UNDER YOUR SUPERVISION.

THINK THAT FILMED RUSSIAN TRAFFIC WOULD MAKE TRE-
MENDOUS HIT IN AMERICA NOW.

Since there was little traffic in the streets of Moscow and
Leningrad in 1934, the meaning of "filmed Russian traffic"
is hard to fathom; perhaps it refers to the new Moscow subway. Eisenstein's reply to the second cable is not extant, but
by some means or other he appears to have put von Stroheim
in touch with Soviet film representatives in Hollywood. I
recall von Stroheim, many years later, recounting a meeting
in Hollywood to discuss possible film work in the Soviet
Union with some Russian officials, who explained to him that
if he went abroad he could not send any money out of Russia
to his family. The officials then suggested that he might be
paid in part in exportable furs. "I told them I had not gone
into the movies to become a furrier," von Stroheim remarked,
a reference to early Hollywood producers, like William Fox,
who gave up the fur trade for the film trade. Characteristic-
ally, von Stroheim seems to have ended this whole episode
with a quip.

Quickly his financial state worsened, and he was forced to
seek employment in the productions of "Poverty Row,"
where quickies were turned out after two or three weeks'
shooting. These films traded on his name and fame in the
past. *Crimson Romance*, the first step in this descent, has
been happily forgotten. Even von Stroheim could never recall what it was about. *Fugitive Road*, which followed, was
somewhat better, with von Stroheim impersonating a military commander of some Balkan frontier post. One can detect
his touch in a scene in which the bored, brutal officer attempts to seduce a fair fugitive over a supper in his tawdry
frontier quarters. He cranks up an old-time phonograph to
play a Viennese waltz as his stupid orderly, played by Hank

Mann from the Mack Sennett slapstick comedies of old, is so rapt at the sight of the pretty dinner guest that he continues to pour champagne into the overflowing wineglasses.

After these two quickies, von Stroheim was summoned to New York to appear in another low-budget production, a sorry adaptation of an Edgar Allan Poe story, *The Crime of Dr. Crespi*, which was shot in only one week before the cameras. It may occasionally be seen on television, where it has had a run of almost twenty years.

Returning to Hollywood after this depressing experience, von Stroheim began writing a novel, *Paprika*, based in part on his memories of gypsy life as he had observed it as a lieutenant in the Bosnian campaign. It is the story of a gypsy girl who scorns the love of a young, handsome youth of her tribe, who rises to become a celebrated violin virtuoso. The girl, Paprika, is used by a vicious Austrian prince, whose misconduct comes to the ears of Franz-Josef, who commands him to marry the gypsy maid. The violinist lover reappears on the wedding night and, after slitting the bridegroom's throat, abducts the bride. The gypsy couple are shot down while trying to escape.

Paprika must be judged as a scenario rather than a novel, since it was written in the hopes of capturing the attention of film producers. Most of its scenes are so detailed that they could go at once before the cameras. Budapest is pictured vividly in its pages, down to the color of its streetcars, and with the city's geography accurately related, though von Stroheim never visited the Hungarian capital. *Paprika* might possibly have been transformed into a striking motion picture by its author. It was published by the Macaulay Company in 1935, and also appeared in England, in a slightly censored edition with the lesbian relationship of a jaded woman of the world with her serving maid eliminated. There have also been translations of the book into French, Italian, and Dutch.

After its publication, Samuel Goldwyn, vaguely interested in purchasing it, invited von Stroheim to his home. "Are you a gypsy now, in addition to everything else?" Goldwyn jokingly inquired when his guest arrived. They laughed and talked together of the twenties, already so far away, when Goldwyn had engaged opera stars for silent films and von Stroheim's extravagances had scandalized even that extravagant era. But Goldwyn's interest in *Paprika* was fleeting. It would, he said, have been better suited to the silent screen.

Clarence Brown, realizing von Stoheim's financial plight, invited him to come to M-G-M again, this time as adviser on the military uniforms for *Anna Karenina,* in which Greta Garbo was to star. The chief costumer, a department head, disapproved of most of von Stroheim's suggestions and sketches of military regalia. "He's trying to turn Russians into Prussian officers," she objected to Clarence Brown. But Fredric March, who was to play the elegant Vronsky, found the von Stroheim uniforms very becoming and approved them.

The von Stroheim fortunes were nevertheless at a very low ebb. Just before Christmas, friends and admirers at the studio took up a discreet collection to present him with a Yuletide gift. Louis B. Mayer contributed fifty dollars, and others were more generous. A list of all the contributors was sent to von Stroheim and no one thought of the matter again, believing it an act of charity. But two years later, when he was a star in France, he returned to everyone who had helped him the sums they had contributed, accompanying each reimbursement with a charming note of gratitude.

It was during this difficult period that the handsome Mrs. von Stroheim suffered a terrible accident at a hairdresser's.

While Mrs. von Stroheim was being given a dry shampoo with a highly volatile product, an attendant in the neighboring booth lighted a curling iron over a gas flame. This ignited the fumes of the shampoo lotion, and Mrs. von Stroheim's hair caught fire. She was in great danger, but she hid her eyes with her hands and thereby escaped blindness. To smother the flames, a hairdresser reached for a fur coat on a clothes rack in the hallway. A firm hand seized his arm. It was a client from another booth who, alarmed by the shrieks and the smell of smoke, had emerged. "Not with my coat!" she cried out in rage, but the hairdresser wrenched the garment from her grasp to fling it over the head and shoulders of the woman on fire. The client who valued her fur coat above the life of another woman was, it must regrettably be reported, a film actress of some repute.

The flames were at last quenched, an ambulance was summoned, and Mrs. von Stroheim was transported to the Queen of Angels Hospital. There for some weeks she lay near death, so seriously burned that she was hardly recognizable, her face and torso blackened by the fire. The von Stroheim son, Josef, now twelve, fell ill with what was diagnosed as infantile paralysis. He was placed in the same hospital, where von Stroheim decided to take a room to be near his wife and child.

While residing in the hospital, he received a telephone call from Irving Thalberg. *The Merry Widow* was being remade as a musical spectacle, directed by Lubitsch, with Maurice Chevalier as Danilo and Jeanette MacDonald as the widow. Marcel Achard had been brought from Paris to write an *opéra-bouffe* treatment of the old plot. Von Stroheim had been so preoccupied with his family troubles that he was ignorant of these plans.

"How are you, Von?" Thalberg asked jauntily, ignorant of

the plague of troubles that had descended upon von Stroheim. When he heard all the bad news, he was genuinely sympathetic. He had always admired the director's talents, but in Thalberg the anxious businessman overshadowed the artistic appreciator. (He, too, was soon to suffer an unexpected blow from his employer; Mayer suddenly promoted his son-in-law, David O. Selznick, to a post above that of his faithful production chief.) The purpose of Thalberg's call had been to forestall von Stroheim's bringing a suit against M-G-M over the similarities between the two scenarios. In such cases, film executives avoided possible legal action by settling in advance a threatening nuisance claim. Von Stroheim would probably not have sued even if his old scenario had been used, for he had sold it outright to M-G-M in 1924, but Thalberg offered him $10,000 and this money was a welcome windfall.

Thalberg, a sense of guilt perhaps troubling him, was touched by von Stroheim's plight and directed the literary department of the studio to engage him as a writer. During the next few months von Stroheim labored in a cubbyhole office at the studio where he had once been a feared tyrant. At the request of Hunt Stromberg, one of the many M-G-M producers, he wrote a story of the younger generation in Soviet Russia, predicting a return to the old bourgeois family life, despite the official Communist religion. But neither Mayer nor Hearst, who had a financial interest in the company, wanted any film dealing with Soviet Russia. His other chores were writing dialogue and doctoring scripts. He collaborated on *San Francisco*, a screenplay by his old friend, Anita Loos; on *The Devil's Doll*, a weird fantasy about a man who disguises himself as an old woman and by black magic reduces his enemies to the size of insects, which Tod Browning was preparing; and on *The Emperor's Candlesticks*, which had a

Viennese setting and in which Luise Rainer was to star. He wrote an original screenplay, *General Hospital*, inspired by his observation of hospital life during the three months he had lived in the Queen of Angels Hospital. A year or two later, after he was famous again as a star of the French cinema, this scenario was filmed at M-G-M as *Between Two Women*.

One night at home he received a telephone call from Paris. Would he consider coming to France to star in a screen version of Pierre Benoît's novel *Königsmark*? He was bewildered by the suddenness of this demand and asked a day or two to think it over. He went at once to consult with his favorite clairvoyante, for he had an indestructible faith in fortune-tellers. She advised him against accepting the offer and foresaw that he would soon receive a better proposal to work abroad. The forthcoming proposal must be accepted, as it would lead to a profitable career overseas. In any case, a week later another proposal arrived from France. Would von Stroheim come to Paris to play the chief of the German Secret Service in a film about Marthe Richard, the patriotic French spy of the Great War? Edwige Feuillère had been engaged to portray the national heroine; Steve Passeur, the distinguished French dramatist, had written the screenplay; and Raymond Bernard would direct. Von Stroheim hurried to see his clairvoyante, who of course advised him to leave immediately for France.

Just before his departure, he had another serious fall from a horse. He was forced to make the transatlantic journey with his head wrapped in turbanlike bandages. He arrived in Paris looking like a haughty maharaja. Some of the journalists who came to interview him at Cherbourg may have vaguely wondered whether this striking headdress was not a publicity stunt. If so, they were too polite or considerate to say so in their front-page news stories next day.

16

Paris and Maurepas

THE Germans have a strange image of contentment, *Gott
im Frankreich*, as happy as God in France. The basis of
this metaphor is unknown, but few mortals have ever been
as happy in France as von Stroheim was. The ovation that
awaited him in Paris seemed to be a sort of miracle, the resurrection of his career. He was suddenly "a personality" in
France. Almost daily the newspapers carried items about
him. After a short stay at Claridge's, he decided to make the
Hotel Bas-Breau in Barbizon his residence. But he was kept
so busy at the studios that he often had to spend the night in
town.

He was soon a familiar figure in the restaurants and night-
clubs, at which he was always accompanied by the trained
nurse he had engaged to treat his head wounds. She herself

was an imposing figure. Swiss-born, she had served as a Red Cross nurse at the front, and she had been decorated by both the German and the French governments for bravery under fire. It was impossible for the clients of restaurants and cabarets to keep their eyes off this unusual pair.

There had always been a von Stroheim cult in France. In Jean Cocteau's opinion, *Greed* was the greatest of all films; and in the early thirties *The Wedding March*, as well as its sequel, *The Honeymoon,* and the unfinished *Queen Kelly* (which had been released abroad), were great popular successes. The French cinema in 1937 was in the midst of a happy renaissance, and was gaining international acclaim. The first signs of this had been seen a few years earlier, when René Clair's initial sound film, *Sous les Toits de Paris*, had attracted a following for French films in foreign lands. Clair had followed with *Le Million* and *A Nous La Liberté,* and now important French theater personalities were eager to try the movies. Louis Jouvet, Raimu, Jean-Louis Barrault, Fernandel, Harry Baur, Sacha Guitry, Marie Bell, Edwige Feuillère, Viviane Romance, and Max Dearly were only a few of them. In the train of the René Clair successes came Sacha Guitry's *Le Roman d'un Tricheur* and *Les Perles de la Couronne*; Jean Renoir's *Les Bas Fonds,* Duvivier's *Poil de Carotte* and *Pepe le Moko,* Marcel Carné's *Quai des Brumes,* and Pagnol's *The Baker's Wife*. There was most definitely a new wave of French films, a cinematic springtime.

Von Stroheim was the latest attraction. He received a shower of offers from a horde of get-rich-quick producers who made fantastic proposals. Few of them were to be trusted and von Stroheim insured himself against fraudulence by demanding his salary in advance. It became known that his salary was one thousand dollars a day, to be paid before shooting started. He also demanded that a fresh bottle of

Scotch be delivered to his dressing room each morning, for during the dry era he had been converted into a heavy drinker and consumed more than one bottle of spirits each day.

An able French journalist, Georges Fronval, wrote a biography of von Stroheim in magazine form that had a great sale at newsstands and railroad-station kiosks. Everyone wanted to interview the famous visitor from Hollywood. Such authors as Joseph Kessel and Marcel Achard came to discuss film notions with him. In his initial French film, *Marthe Richard*, he again impersonated the Prussian heavy of old, diabolically intelligent, a crack shot, an able amateur pianist, who gave himself a fatal injection of morphine when the jig was up.

Foolish Wives had had a powerful influence on the artistic destiny of Jean Renoir, the son of the Impressionist painter. Renoir, who happened to see the film in 1923 when it was first released in Paris, said that he sat before it enthralled. He studied it frame by frame and saw it, he claims, thirty-four times. It convinced him that the cinema was a medium for his own artistic expression and he decided to become a film director. Renoir was thrilled to learn that von Stroheim was in Paris and hurried to make his acquaintance. The recently arrived celebrity was somewhat taken aback when a heavily built man with vivid blue eyes rushed into his hotel room and, embracing him, planted kisses on both his cheeks. Though by nature undemonstrative, he felt impelled to return this greeting of loving admiration. Renoir launched into an enthusiastic address of welcome. Finally, he came to the point.

Charles Spaak had written a screenplay for Renoir called *La Grande Illusion*, the noble illusion being that men could live together in peace and brotherhood. It was based on Spaak's experiences during the First World War. Serving at the front in 1915, he had been captured and held prisoner by the Germans for many months. In his script there were two German parts of importance, that of a warrior invalided out of combat and appointed commander of a prisoner-of-war camp, and that of a German aviator who brings down French planes. Which role did von Stroheim want?

"Both," he told Renoir.

In the end, von Stroheim took over both roles, compressing them, somewhat to Spaak's uneasiness, into one. Von Stroheim suggested that the pilot, having suffered injury, might have been retired to the behind-the-lines post. Since Spaak was opposed to explanatory scenes, an idea occurred to von Stroheim. He decided that the invalided officer's injuries should be visually apparent. He thought, at first, of having a cane or a crutch to support him or of moving around in a wheel chair. At last he struck on the idea of a neck brace. He searched the telephone directory for a shop that specialized in medical appliances in the nearby town of Colmar. The proprietor demanded that von Stroheim present a doctor's order. The actor, a persuasive talker, finally obtained the gruesome accessory and next morning arrived on the set wearing it. Both Renoir and Spaak were delighted with this innovation, which made explanatory scenes unnecessary.

In the revised scenario, von Stroheim invites some French pilots, who have been taken prisoner after their planes are shot down, to a meal in his outpost headquarters. As he chats with them in a friendly manner, the funeral wreaths that are to decorate the graves of their slain fellow soldiers are brought through the mess. He leaps to his feet to salute, exclaiming the military farewell: "May the earth rest lightly on our brave fallen enemies!" The men with the wreaths file out and the host barks out for music, this command being answered by the sound of a waltz. The French flyers—two

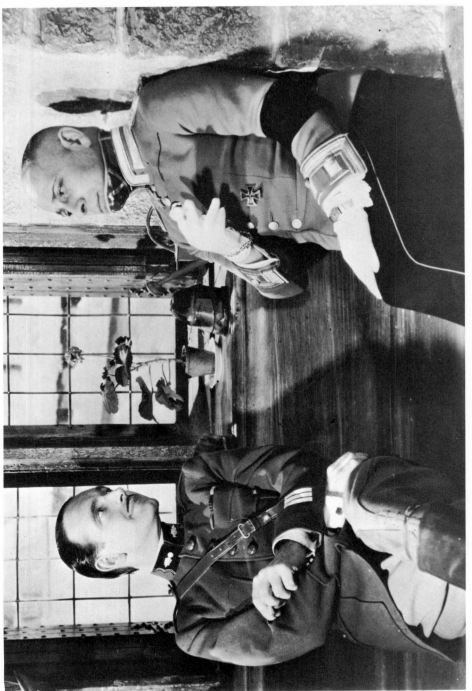

Pierre Fresnay with von Stroheim in *La Grande Illusion*, 1936

non-coms (Jean Gabin and Dalio) and their captain (Pierre Fresnay)—are sent to various prison camps, until they end up at the one where von Rauffenstein (von Stroheim) is in charge.

The solidarity that existed in the First World War among the officer class is ironically treated in *La Grande Illusion*. Von Rauffenstein must shoot his French colleague (Pierre Fresnay), wounding him fatally, when he attempts to escape. The German's affection for his victim is revealed when he places the last flower in the fortress on the bier of the man he has killed.

La Grande Illusion remains a major French film and is still playing all over the world. Its appearance during the Paris Exposition in 1937 was an important event. Even the Nazi press, though objecting to the anti-German von Stroheim, praised it. When it was shown at the Venice film festival in 1937, Dr. Goebbels, who was present as a guest, commented: "Von Stroheim's impersonation of a German officer is a caricature. There are no German officers like that." To which a French journalist replied: "Too bad for them!" The underlying pacifism of the film met a wide response in those pre-Munich days. At the Venice festival it was the logical candidate for the Golden Lion prize, but Italy's political alliance with Germany and the fact that Goebbels was a guest caused the jurors to award the first prize to Luis Trenker's film, *Der Kaiser von California*. A special jury prize was created and bestowed on *La Grande Illusion*, but the film was banned from Germany and Italy until after the fall of Fascism.

Pierre Chenal wanted to co-star von Stroheim and Louis Jouvet in a thriller and called upon Marcel Achard to write the scenario. Achard consulted with von Stroheim and was mys-

Louis Jouvet with von Stroheim in *L'Alibi*, 1936

tified by his strange requests. There must be one scene in which he would luxuriously relax in a bathtub while an Oriental cut his toenails. In addition to this exotic pedicure, the star insisted on a second scene in which he would wear a monk's cowl, and a third in which he would be clad in eighteenth-century white breeches. Achard, though bewildered, incorporated these passages in a detective story about an American vaudeville mind-reader on a European tour who becomes involved in a murder case and is hounded by a cunning sleuth (Louis Jouvet). It was called *L'Alibi*.

"Von Stroheim with his cinema sense was absolutely right in demanding the unusual costume changes," Achard told me recently. "I wrote them with many doubts, but they proved effective on the screen, giving the character extra dimension by accenting his eccentricities." The first scene was a difficult one, and after an initial take or two, there was a break in the shooting.

"Mr. Jouvet," said von Stroheim, nervously offering his co-star a cigarette from a gold case, "the idea of playing opposite you has nearly scared me to death."

"You know, I have been just as frightened at the prospect of doing a scene with you," replied Jouvet, with his charming smile. The two actors were mutual admirers and soon became friends. They intended to collaborate on other films, but they were never to play together again.

Roger Blin, a pale young man with catlike eyes and feline grace, played von Stroheim's dresser in *L'Alibi*. His jet-black uniform, contrasting with his chalk-white face, gave him a sinister appearance. Blin was later to become a celebrated director, introducing Samuel Beckett's plays in Paris with the first performance of *Waiting for Godot*. Later he staged the dramas of Jean Genet to a chorus of critical praise.

Blin, a student and disciple of Antonin Artaud, the creator

307

of the "Theater of Cruelty," was one of Artaud's favorite actors. Blin believed that von Stroheim had founded the "Cinema of Cruelty," and that his directorial technique was surrealistic in concept. In a long discussion with his idol, he was amazed that von Stroheim rejected his theory.

"No, no. I'm not a surrealist. I'm a realist," said von Stroheim. "At least, I tried to be a realist. But perhaps you are right. One begins with dedication to an idea and believes one is working towards a certain goal. Then one reaches— who knows why?—another goal."

Of the other films that von Stroheim made in France at this time, *Les Disparus de Saint-Agil* was of particular interest. Directed by Christian Jaque, it accorded the visiting star the role of a kindly professor of English at a lycée, a boys' school, where the pupils mysteriously disappear. It was an opportunity for von Stroheim to demonstrate his range. Liberated from his usual role of the "heavy," he took advantage of the change and contributed a warm and humorous characterization.

During his first professional stay in France—a period covering only three years—he appeared in some sixteen films. He also took a brief leave to act in another, in England, *Mlle Docteur.* But though the von Stroheim name was box office and any motion picture bearing it was assured of some success, at least a dozen of these ventures were low-grade. It became the policy to engage von Stroheim at his thousand-dollar-a-day salary and shoot a few scenes with him, while economizing on scenarios, supporting players, and direction. A continuation of this scheme would eventually have led to a devaluation of his name on a marquee. He understood the danger and set to writing a scenario that he hoped he would be allowed to direct and act.

This was *La Dame Blanche,* another story of Vienna, in

which the son of the Master of the Royal Hunt falls in love with a baker's daughter and is prevented from marrying her by his father. The white lady of the title was a symbolic figure of doom, a ghost who allegedly was seen in the Imperial Palace prior to some terrible disaster. Von Stroheim himself intended to play Hubertius, the hunt master, and created important roles for Louis Jouvet and Jean-Louis Barrault. By 1939 the producer Max Cassvan agreed to finance the project and a contract was actually signed, but in September war was declared and the film was postponed indefinitely.

Some time after von Stroheim arrived in France, a pretty, young journalist, Denise Vernac, who had also started a budding career as an actress, had come to interview him. He was first struck by her beauty and then by her extraordinary knowledge of his films and his career. She told him she had run away from school one afternoon to see *The Merry Widow*. Mlle Vernac, at his request, abandoned her newspaper work to become his collaborator and an actress in some of his films. They traveled together to make a film aboard the French liner *Normandie* on a round-trip voyage. This film, *Paris–New York*, written and directed by the witty Yves Mirande, was inconsequential in motion-picture history. But for von Stroheim the sea voyage with its companionable all-star cast—Gaby Morlay, Michel Simon, Gisele Preville, André Lefaur, Simone Berriau, and Claude Dauphin—was in the nature of a vacation. Von Stroheim's hopes were high when the *Normandie* reached New York Harbor on a spring day in 1939. He informed reporters that he was returning to France to direct again.

When war came in September, von Stroheim volunteered for service in the French Army, despite his age—fifty-four. His age and his American nationality—as the United States remained technically neutral until the Japanese attack on

Pearl Harbor in December 1941—caused the French government to reject his offer. According to his friend Claude Dauphin, his application struck French officials as odd: he had offered his services with the stipulation that he serve in the *cavalry*.

As the "phony war" dragged through the winter and the prospect of directing again became more and more remote, an offer arrived from Hollywood, where his stock had risen due to *La Grande Illusion*, which was being widely shown in America. The offer came from Darryl F. Zanuck, a long-time admirer, who was now the dynamic production chief at Twentieth Century-Fox. In March, von Stroheim, with Denise Vernac as his companion, left France on what they believed was a temporary visit. But after Paris fell to the Nazis in June 1940, return to France was impossible.

The assignment that awaited von Stroheim in California was a routine one. He was to play an elegant impostor, a rather comic villain, in *I Was an Adventuress*, which Gregory Ratoff directed in broad, almost slapstick style. The beautiful ballerina Vera Zorina was the leading lady, and Peter Lorre was the henchman of the polished but insolvent bad man. Von Stroheim's salary was high, but he felt it had hardly been worth crossing the Atlantic to find himself again on the scene of so many defeats. Yet this undistinguished comedy may have saved his life. If he had been in Paris when the Nazis marched down the Champs-Elysées, there is no question that he would have been arrested and probably executed.

Albert Lewin, who had been Irving Thalberg's assistant when *Greed* and *The Merry Widow* were being made, had become an independent producer and proposed that von Stroheim play his first Nazi role, that of a relentless Gestapo chief, in a film version of Erich Maria Remarque's novel *So Ends Our Night*. John Cromwell directed and he proved so

Vera Zorina and Peter Lorre with von Stroheim in *I Was an Adventuress*, 1940

nagging that the screen Gestapo commander wished he really had the power to put Cromwell behind bars.

"Now, now, Von, come on," Cromwell would urge. "Faster, faster. You know Hollywood has nothing against you except that you take so long to do anything."

Von Stroheim had brought with him the outline of a play he intended to write, set in an air-raid shelter in Paris before the fall of France. He had a title, *Abri—50 Personnes*. After *So Ends Our Night*, he went to New York hoping to find an established playwright who would collaborate with him on his drama. Unfortunately, the setting of *Abri—50 Personnes* had become passé. Ben Hecht and Clare Boothe Luce, who had tried to obtain von Stroheim to play the Nazi consul in her play, *Margin for Error*, the previous season, suggested that he change the scene of his play to London, but he felt he knew too little of this city.

Various vague hopes held him in New York. There was an announcement that the city authorities intended to set up a motion-picture center, backed partially by municipal funds and partially by private enterprise, for the making of films. Of course, von Stroheim, whose rare New York visit was much in the news, was to be consulted. He discussed this promised development with Pat Powers, his old backer. After the showing of Powers's uncut print of *The Wedding March* (described in the Introduction), Thomas Mann talked with von Stroheim about filming *The Magic Mountain*. Dr. Mann said he had often thought that sections of his novel, especially the Mediterranean dream chapter, would have been ideally suited to the silent film.

The actor-director made his debut on the American stage in *Arsenic and Old Lace* in Baltimore in February 1941. Henry Irving once explained his technique briefly: "There are two ways of portraying a character on the stage. Either you can try to turn yourself into that person—which is impossible—or, and this is the way to act, you can take that person and turn him into yourself. This is how I do it." Without altering a line of *Arsenic and Old Lace,* von Stroheim transformed the evil ghoul into himself. Indeed, this had always been his approach as an actor on the screen. *Arsenic and Old Lace* toured the country for almost a year. When von Stroheim arrived for an engagement in Chicago, the well-known writer and Civil War historian, Lloyd Lewis, came to his hotel to interview him.

"In the Chicago company of *Arsenic and Old Lace,* Erich von Stroheim, once famous for a sartorial splendor that was practically sinful, is now playing Jonathan Brewster, murderer and fugitive, in a suit that makes him look like a baseball umpire. Although this annoys him, knowing as he does that the public prefers him in a magnificent Austrian uniform, he wears the Brooklyn hand-me-down with fortitude, since he needs the thousand dollars a week which he is receiving. What he describes as the 'Hollywood boycott' of his directorial talent reduced him financially, in recent years, and he is glad to play grimy Mr. Brewster. But after the show is over and he is in his hotel apartment, he is the old von Stroheim—all but that insolent monocle. He lights his cigarette with an antique horse-pistol that flames from the firing-pin; he serves elaborate lobster salad *à la buffet* to his guests; he decorates little cigarette tables with silver spurs. As he strides about his suite talking, his back is like a ramrod, and his head, with its jagged duelling scars, is held high. All is just as it was when he was billboarded as 'The Man You Love to Hate,' the film symbol of Prussian military caste-snobbery."

He told Lewis that he had made *Greed* in forty-two reels and been called a lunatic. Now, he reminded his listener,

Gone with the Wind, which was no shorter, was proving that no one objects to a long film if the story is sufficiently interesting.

"He sits down in a chair," Lewis concluded, "but his back is still as straight as a cavalry-man's in the saddle. He told me that if he should die tomorrow, there would be sorrow only in one group in Hollywood, the workmen, the laborers, the artisans. 'I had no trouble with them; never! I got on well with them for the plain reason that I was one of them. I have always stood with them better than I have with the wealthy and the powerful. I could *never* get on with vice-presidents.' "

Von Stroheim returned to New York to replace Boris Karloff in *Arsenic and Old Lace* in December 1941, after the United States had entered the Second World War. Hollywood had also entered the conflict and was turning out propaganda films that almost equalled those of 1917–18 in nonsense. The actor who impersonated the fearful Hun better than anyone else was soon receiving wires and telephone calls from the Coast urging him to take up his patriotic duties. But he preferred to go on acting on the stage until something exceptionally intriguing came along. It came along in the spring, when Billy Wilder and Charles Brackett sent him the script of *Five Graves to Cairo.* It was about Rommel in North Africa, and they wanted von Stroheim to play Rommel. Wilder, a hero-worshiper of the fallen idol, had never met him and hurried to do so after his arrival in the Paramount costuming department, where he was trying on uniforms.

"This is a true honor," said Wilder by way of introduction. "In my opinion, you were twenty years ahead of your time."

"Thirty," replied von Stroheim without smiling.

When *Five Graves to Cairo* was released, he received

Franchot Tone and Peter Van Eyck with von Stroheim in *Five Graves to Cairo*, 1943

special billing in a separate credit line at the end: "AND MR. VON STROHEIM AS ROMMEL."

Lewis Milestone was making an all-star epic of the Nazi invasion of the Ukraine for Samuel Goldwyn. Written by Lillian Hellman, it was to be called *North Star*. Both Milestone and Miss Hellman informed Goldwyn that von Stroheim was the only actor who could convincingly interpret the part of a Nazi medical officer intent on employing Ukrainian women and children for his scientific experiments. Though the role was a brief one, he was rewarded with lengthier critical consideration than his co-performers.

The fall of France had brought many of the French film celebrities to Hollywood for the war's duration. Among these were Jean Renoir, Michele Morgan, and Jean Gabin. Renoir gave a dinner for D. W. Griffith one evening, at which Lillian and Dorothy Gish, Rex Ingram and his wife Alice Terry, and the host's French colleagues were guests. It was a nostalgic occasion for von Stroheim to find himself reunited with important figures he had known during his long career. Rex Ingram, retired and living in semi-seclusion on the outskirts of the movie colony, was devoting himself to writing, sculpting, and philosophical meditation. He had been converted to the Moslem faith on his last stay in North Africa, after giving up his film studios in Nice. He spoke bitterly of the men who had debased the motion pictures for quick profits and who had driven them all from the commanding positions they had occupied twenty years before. Griffith, older and more aloof than ever, seemed to accept his defeat with serene resignation.

Suddenly Renoir leaned over the table and asked von Stroheim what film he would most like to make, if he were given carte blanche as a director.

"Octave Mirbeau's *Diary of a Chambermaid*," replied the

ex-director without hesitation, going on to outline his screen concept of the book. He considered Myrna Loy an ideal choice for the chambermaid. He himself would play the brutal servant Joseph, to whom the young, attractive girl is sexually drawn despite her loathing. Tully Marshall, of course, would act the degenerate country gentleman obsessed with a fetish for women's shoes. Renoir agreed that the Mirbeau novel was indeed an intriguing subject for a film. Two years later he directed a film version of the book, and Luis Buñuel later directed another version.

As the production of war films increased, there were many roles of the sort that von Stroheim had played in *Five Graves to Cairo* and *North Star*. George Cukor, who was to direct Ingrid Bergman in *Gaslight*, fancied von Stroheim for the sinister villain of the Victorian melodrama, but he was over-ruled by M-G-M.

Serious illness now struck von Stroheim for the first time. He was taken to the Queen of Angels Hospital and under-went a major operation. In the opinion of his physicians he had little chance of surviving, and his sons, Erich Jr. and Josef, serving in the army, were given emergency furloughs to hurry to his bedside. To the amazement of the medical staff, the patient rallied and was soon allowed to sit up and walk about. The drastic surgery left him weakened, how-ever, and though he had been a heavy drinker for many years, he took alcohol only sparingly thereafter.

Once he was recovered, he informed his agent, Paul Kohner, that he was in need of work to settle his medical bills. Work was quickly found, but it was of a hack nature. Again he appeared in a string of Poverty Row productions: *Storm over Lisbon, The Lady and the Monster, Scotland Yard Investigator, The Great Flammarion,* and *The Mask of Dijon,* all of them quickies.

Denise Vernac with von Stroheim in *The Mask of Dijon*, 1946

Shortly after the liberation of Paris in 1944, French producers and directors began to correspond with him, urging him to return to France. Even before the war was officially over, many of his prewar films were being revived on the Continent. In November 1945 he was on his long-postponed return trip across the Atlantic, tempted officially by a script that Pierre Chenal had sent him, but in fact eager to quit a Hollywood that seemed to him even more of a cultural desert than it had been before the war.

The original story by Jacques Companeez and Ernst Neubach that Pierre Chenal had posted to him seemed a promising cinematic subject, but its realization transformed it into trash. It bore the title *La Foire aux Chimères*. The next film he made in France, *On Ne Meurt Pas Comme Ça!*, was not much better, neither of them superior to those of Poverty Row. Yet in 1947 he found himself on the list of the ten favorite players in France. This so amazed the editors of *Time* magazine that they dispatched a reporter to Paris to talk to him. The interview was muddled. As quoted, von Stroheim spoke with admiration of the officer-gentleman class and of his first alliance with the workers. He denounced "the bosses," remembering Louis B. Mayer, but forgetting Carl Laemmle, who had opened the door to his directorial career.

At that time he was preparing to act with Denise Vernac in a film based on Strindberg's *The Dance of Death*, under the direction of Marcel Cravenne. Von Stroheim worked on the adaptation and the dialogue with Michel Arnaud and Jacques-Laurent Bost. The setting was shifted at the star's request from a Swedish island to one off the Dalmatian coast during the Austrian occupation. This enabled von Stroheim to play an Austrian officer again. *The Dance of Death* required an interminable time to film and its erratic work schedule is reflected in the finished product. Some of it was made in the Paris studios; other scenes were shot in Rome and on locations on the Italian seacoast. Though the original play never stirs from one room during its six acts, the film company that transferred it to the screen traveled widely and not to great purpose. The performance of von Stroheim is perhaps one of his most memorable, but it is obscured by its mediocre production and diffuse direction. It enjoyed box-office success, as did all films with von Stroheim in France, and after its release he was engaged to go to Austria for the filming of another French production, *Signal Rouge*, again with Denise Vernac as co-star.

Much of *Signal Rouge* was filmed at the Tobis-Sacha studios at Rosenhugel, outside Vienna, and von Stroheim's return to his native city was now greeted with official honors. He was given the keys of the city by the mayor and belatedly recognized by his former countrymen.

In 1949 Billy Wilder summoned von Stroheim back to Hollywood at a handsome salary to appear in *Sunset Boulevard*. This melodrama about a forgotten silent star living in isolated and dusty grandeur reveals that she is insane, making believe that time has stood still since her retirement. Gloria Swanson was signed to play the star and von Stroheim was to enact her butler, who turns out to be her former husband and director. The shooting of *Sunset Boulevard* took six months, and Wilder succeeded in obtaining several memorable figures of the silent era for his cast. Cecil B. DeMille appeared in one sequence, and Buster Keaton, H. B. Warner, and Anna Q. Nilsson were brought back to stir the memories of veteran filmgoers.

Gloria Swanson and von Stroheim had not met since the abrupt and enigmatic halting of *Queen Kelly* twenty years before. Their reunion was friendly, for they had not parted in anger, as it was generally believed. Miss Swanson offered her one-time director the use of her New York apartment on his return trip to France. Both regretted the unhappy fate of *Queen Kelly*, and the star talked of having von Stroheim re-edit the footage and add a prologue in which Kitty Kelly would look back on her past. Nothing came of this, but in 1957 Miss Swanson did re-release the version that Irving Thalberg had edited for her. It played a successful run in Paris and was favorably reviewed. Copies of it are now in the film library of the Museum of Modern Art, New York, and in that of the Cinémathèque Française.

When *Sunset Boulevard* was released in the summer of 1950, Gloria Swanson was nominated for an Academy Award for her portrait of the silent star desperately and pathetically trying to recapture her glorious past. Von Stroheim was the recipient of enthusiastic reviews for his characterization of the loyal servant who writes the movie queen fan mail to sustain her morale. But he never liked the role, referring to it often as "that lousy butler part." He felt it capitalized on his own downfall, and indeed the whole film was a mockery of the old-time Hollywood in which he had accomplished his best work.

Von Stroheim was happy to return to France once more. There he was not considered a has-been, or exhibited as a prehistoric monster making a comeback. He was treated as an honored artist who, if he were never to work again, would still hold rank for his accomplishments. He found postwar Hollywood tired and frightened by the growing threat of television. D. W. Griffith had died in 1948, unhonored by the town he had literally put on the map, and Rex Ingram was dead by the time *Sunset Boulevard* opened. Only a few contemporaries, principally Cecil B. DeMille and Clarence Brown, were still directing films. The long reign of Louis B. Mayer at M-G-M was virtually at an end and he was to be unseated from his throne by a stockholders' fight in 1951.

Von Stroheim, shortly after his postwar return to France, made his permanent residence in a country mansion belonging to Denise Vernac at Maurepas, Seine-et-Oise. This secluded spot, in the heart of the lovely Corot country, was only thirty miles from Paris. The century-old house, walled off from the town's road, stood in the midst of a large garden with tall elms shading the drive from the entrance gate. As the district's most imposing home, it was known as the Château Maurepas. Its drawing room might have been taken for the set of a von Stroheim film. Austrian and Hungarian sabers hung on its walls. Army pistols, transformed into giant cigarette lighters, and spurs, serving as ashtrays, decorated the tables. The desk chair was a military saddle. In the library, phalluses of molded lead stood at attention as bookends. These would have been banished from the screen by Will Hays, and it amused von Stroheim to observe the shock they produced on visitors.

Here he spent the time between film commitments in writing, with Denise Vernac as his companion and collaborator. The French translation of his novel *Paprika* had sold so well that his publishers were clamoring for more fiction from his pen. He complied by turning a scenario on which he was working into a two-volume novel, *Les Feux de la St. Jean*. This scenario was being designed as an active vehicle for Denise Vernac, for whom he wrote a dual role. If a producer could be found, von Stroheim hoped to direct it himself. *Les Feux de la St. Jean* had a Tyrolean setting and is the story of two sisters. The first, Veronica, is the embodiment of all virtues, while the second, Constanzia, is the incarnation of every evil known to woman, a destructive fury.

Von Stroheim spent many months converting the scenario into a novel. Zola, it must be noted again, was the strongest literary influence on the director-actor when he turned to fiction. The writing of *Les Feux de la St. Jean* (volume one was published in 1951 and volume two in 1954) interrupted his plan to write his autobiography. Later he sold the rights to all his literary works to Denise Vernac, trusting her judgment, which he had come to appreciate during the eighteen years of their life together. Miss Vernac intends one day to write of these years.

Les Feux de la St. Jean enjoyed a good sale, and its publisher called for another novel to follow. Von Stroheim dug into his files and proceeded to transform a scenario that he had written in Hollywood, *Poto-Poto*, into a novel. This was his last literary work.

There were constant calls for von Stroheim to act. His popularity remained strong despite the poor quality of most of the films in which he now appeared. Aside from his brief bit as Beethoven in Sacha Guitry's all-star film, *Napoleon*, these last performances were unmarked by any startling innovations.

Von Stroheim's instinctive showmanship overflowed from his screen self to his off-screen appearances. The two often seemed one, but beneath the arrogant surface there was a very different inner man, kind and generous to his colleagues and associates. He was uncommonly sympathetic to the troubles of others, perhaps because he had overcome so many of his own.

He guarded his public image with care, even exaggerating its strong lines. When on his last visit to London an interviewer inquired whether he was as brutal in real life as on the screen, he replied at once, "Much more so." Another journalist, seeing him looking for an ashtray to squash out a cigarette, extended his palm and said, "If this was a film, you would put the cigarette out on my hand."

"If you were a woman, I would," he replied.

Yet the truth is that his compassion for people was deep and sincere. He had in a high degree what the French call "politeness of heart." He did not make friends quickly, being by nature distrustful, and he was not a good mixer. To conceal his acute embarrassment among strangers, he resorted to an iron reserve. He had a morbid fear of being mocked.

As his films dealt freely and boldly with sex, often touching on its pathological aspects, the legend grew that he was himself a Freudian case. "Any man who made *The Merry Widow* and *Queen Kelly* and wrote *Paprika* must be a sex maniac," an otherwise intelligent critic once said to me. But such a view rules out the imagination. Similar charges were brought against Zola for his open treatment of sexual matters. It was thought that he must be a sadist, a sex-obsessed fiend. On those grounds, every author of detective stories ought to be taken for a murderer.

Gossip about von Stroheim's other eccentricities was widespread. A woman once asked me if at home von Stroheim often dressed himself in medieval armor, as she had heard. Thinking this might amuse him, I repeated the story. He flushed with anger and began stalking about.

"Imagine that!" he stormed. "I suppose people think that I throw babies out of windows and shoot hostages in my cellar. Idiots!" Then, appreciating the comic aspect of these delusions, he threw himself into a chair and laughed uproariously.

Though a strong irony marked both his directorial work and his performances, it was generally believed that von

Von Stroheim with Denise Vernac, Thomas Quinn Curtiss, Albert Lewin, and an unknown guest

Stroheim had little if any humor. Actually, he had a lively sense of the absurd and a rich appreciation of comedy, as his use of three Mack Sennett clowns—Hughie Mack, Chester Conklin, and Frank R. Hayes—has indicated. Von Stroheim also greatly admired Chaplin and Buster Keaton.

More curious was his admiration for Danny Kaye, whom he first saw in *Lady in the Dark* in New York in 1941. He wrote two scripts designed for Kaye, for he detected in this knock-about comedian an actor of rare potential. During the Second World War, A. J. Liebling published several stories, set at the African front, in *The New Yorker*. One was an account of a soldier in the American Army who was ridiculed by his comrades for being obsessed with the Russian victories over the Nazis; this taunted private, who was nicknamed "Molotov" or "Molly," pinned maps of the Soviet drive against the Germans over his camp cot and lectured all who would listen on Russian military strategy. "Molly" died a hero in combat and was posthumously awarded the Congressional Medal. Von Stroheim saw a film for Danny Kaye in this tale and tried to obtain an option from Liebling while outlining a screen script. Liebling was pleased at the ex-director's interest, but was advised by his agents to deal directly with the studios. Liebling's agents, however, were unable to arrange such a sale.

After settling at Maurepas in 1948, von Stroheim wrote another script with Kaye in mind. This was entitled *I'll Be Seeing You*, a fantasy with wartime New York as its setting. Kaye was under contract to Samuel Goldwyn. When Goldwyn visited Paris in 1950, von Stroheim telephoned him and told him about his screenplay. Goldwyn said he was preparing an elaborate film about Hans Christian Andersen for Kaye, and *I'll Be Seeing You* would not be possible for the star.

Throughout his sixties, until illness disabled him after his seventieth birthday, von Stroheim led a crowded, active life, working hopefully on film projects that might restore him as a film director. He talked of the past as he prepared the writing of his memoirs, but he did not dwell on past events unless questioned. About future plans he was always full of enthusiasm. He became more sociable than he had been in Hollywood, finding congenial company among the French artists. He attended theatrical premières—always those of Louis Jouvet and Pierre Fresnay—and frequented the Parisian restaurants and cabarets. At the Maurepas château, he entertained old friends and some new ones: Anita Loos, Clarence Brown, Albert Lewin, William Wyler, Charles MacArthur, Jed Harris, and many others. On New Year's Eve he kept open house, and the house was thronged with his Parisian theater and cinema associates. In 1954 he made his only visit to South America, flying to São Paulo, Brazil, to attend the winter film festival. Location work on *Alerte au Sud* took him to North Africa and he decided to motor through Spain on the way down. He spent summers on the Riviera and was often a guest at the spring film festival at Cannes. The shooting of *Alraune* brought him to Munich for a three-month stay.

In 1955 he was invited to be guest of honor at the British Film Institute for the opening of a season of his films in London. A snowstorm prevented his arrival for the première, and Peter Ustinov read the address von Stroheim had prepared. As Ustinov was acting in an M-G-M film (*Beau Brummel*) in London at the time, he was slightly embarrassed to deliver some of the caustic comments that von Stroheim made about that studio. In the same year, von Stroheim was in Brussels to speak before a showing of *The Merry Widow* at a gala project at which royalty was present.

327

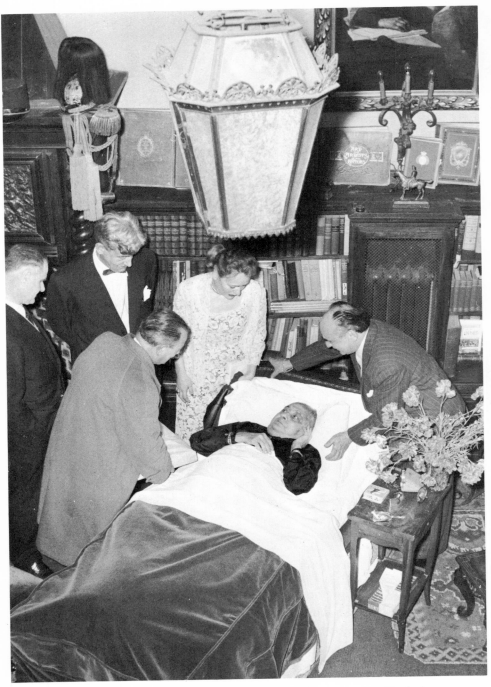

At Maurepas a French official arrives to decorate von Stroheim with the order of the Legion of Honor

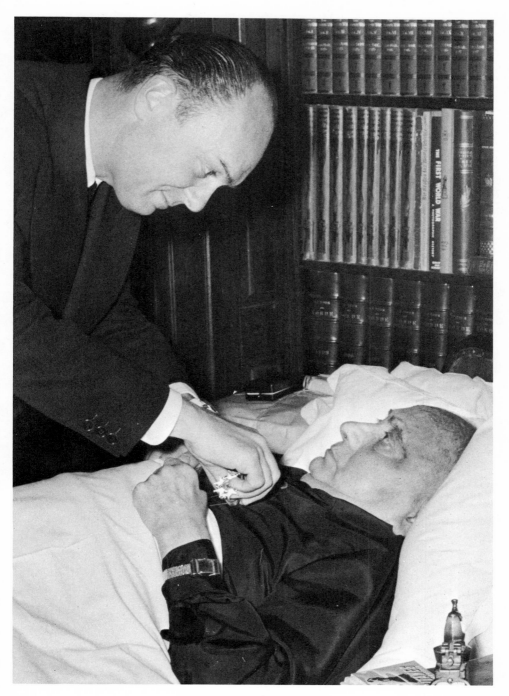

The order is pinned on

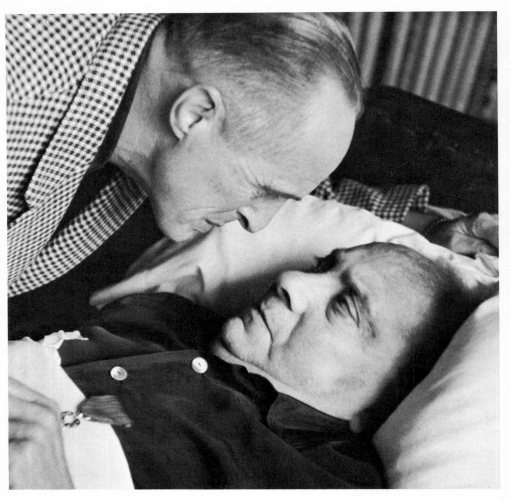

The French director, René Clair, congratulates von Stroheim

(OPPOSITE) A portrait of Denise Vernac and von Stroheim at Maurepas

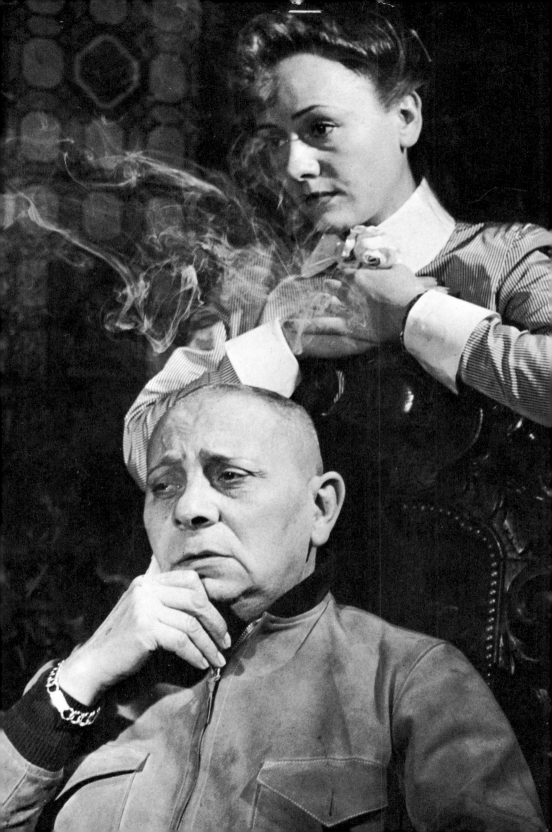

Von Stroheim at Maurepas writing his memoirs

At Maurepas he often spent ten to twelve hours at his desk writing; until his very last years, he remained an inexhaustible worker. To relieve monotony, he would leave his worktable for a quick meal or a tonic walk with his two dogs, a small mongrel dachshund he had found while motoring in the south, and a beautiful Irish setter. These animals would lie at his feet, regarding him affectionately as he wrote.

He continued to read widely, and with a "film sense." Lajos Zilahy's novel *The Dukays*, and its sequel, *The Angry Angel*, a study of an aristocratic Hungarian family, struck him as an inviting subject for a film, as did Merezhkovsky's *The Romance of Leonardo da Vinci*, in which he pictured Jean Marais in the title role. One day I gave him an English translation from the Portuguese, *Cousin Brazilo*, by Eça de Queiroz. He fell in love with this novel, a gripping tale of an ugly, abused old servant who blackmails her young mistress (the latter has committed adultery with her cousin from Brazil while her husband is away). He prepared a screenplay outline, shifting the scene from mid-nineteenth-century Lisbon to provincial Austria at the turn of the century; and he wrote the novel's American publishers, inquiring about the motion-picture rights. When Clarence Brown came to Europe on a summer holiday and talked about investing in film production, von Stroheim read him his treatment, but Brown thought the time was ripe for comedies, not tragedies.

In the summer of 1956 von Stroheim was stricken with cramping pains in his spine. He found it an effort to take the stairs. By late autumn he was confined to his bed. He was not told, but undoubtedly realized, that he was suffering from cancer. It was cancer that had necessitated the operation performed thirteen years earlier. Soon he could no longer move his body freely and was forced to hold his head in a rigid position, as he had when he played von Rauffenstein in

La Grande Illusion. But his mind remained alert, and he enjoyed reading and conversing with visitors.

In March 1957 he was made a member of the Legion of Honor. He was brought into the drawing room of the house to lie on a sofa for the ceremony, surrounded by friends. When the medal was pinned to his pajamas, by the representative of President Coty, he replied with a military salute. During the weeks that followed, he went into a swift decline. The drugs administered to ease his pain sometimes clouded his thought, but he had long, lucid intervals, even on the afternoon of the day he died. One morning as I sat by his bedside he remarked suddenly: "This isn't the worst. The worst is that they stole twenty-five years of my life."

When death appeared inevitable, a priest who was a chaplain at SHAPE headquarters came to hear his confession and administer the last rites of his religion. He died peacefully in his sleep in the early evening of May 12, 1957.

In a curious fashion, strong personalities seem to stamp their mark on the events of their destinies. The funeral of von Stroheim might have been a sequence in one of his films. A throng of 150 mourners followed on foot along a dusty country road the hearse that bore his remains to the tiny church of Maurepas. A priest spoke from the pulpit on the emptiness of worldly fame and commended the soul of the departed to God. It had been the long-standing request of the dead artist that at his funeral services an orchestra of gypsy violinists play a Hungarian melody that he loved. Permission for them to do so was granted. It was strange to hear suddenly in a country chapel the throbbing, passionate lament on the violin strings.

The cortege then continued its sad march along the rustic road to the cemetery. Cows at pasture in the fields, startled by the sight of a crowd, came to fences to gaze at the procession. The muggy May morning was oppressive, the low sky threatening a downpour. After the coffin was lowered into the ground and the last mourner had cast a flower into the grave, a storm broke, catching everyone unprepared for the return journey. The mourners made an effort to maintain an appropriately dignified pace, but instinctively hastened their steps as the rain lashed at them.

APPENDIX

THE FIRST SCREENING OF "GREED"

(This is the only extant account of the nine-hour screening of the uncut 42-reel version of *Greed* at MGM on January 12, 1924. It took place almost a year before the film's release to the public, in the 10-reel version, the following December. Idwal Jones, who was the drama critic of the San Francisco *Daily News* and a friend of von Stroheim's, printed this account in the drama section of his paper on the Saturday following the first screening.)

by IDWAL JONES

Every time I meet a movie fan on the street and he grabs my lapel, like the Ancient Mariner, I know he's going to ask about von Stroheim's screen version of *McTeague*. Last year I witnessed a little of its filming here [in San Francisco], at the corner of Hayes and Laguna, a bit of thoroughfare which old-timers tell me is the dead ringer for Polk Street in the pre-fire days.

Early Saturday morning I found myself bowling through that town of architectural models, Hollywood, and through a forest of oil derricks, until I arrived at the studios in Culver City. There was a pretty lawn, a stucco building, and at the door Erich von Stroheim received us, with military bows. Like a diplomatic attaché, he is always surrounded.

In the group were two San Francisco actresses, Carmel Myers and Aileen Pringle, in costume and with teeth painted a heavy white; Joseph Jackson, the urbane young president of the Wampas, thereby kingpin of publicity men, and Fritz Tidden, the director's shadow and courier.

"Better put on a wig and disguise," whispered Tidden to us. "The gatekeeper's dog bites dramatic critics."

339

"Ten o'clock," announced von Stroheim. An unholy hour to see a picture. Through an iron door back of us we were admitted into a cosy little theater. The door clanged. In the darkness all snuggled into deep armchairs. Attendants passed cigarettes. A projector whirred like a wind machine in a blizzard melodrama. On the screen was flashed: *Greed,* made from Frank Norris' novel, *Mc-Teague.*

Next to us sat the only other newspaperman there, Jack Jungmeyer. We recalled faintly having seen the title on the screen before. Years ago it was, and a lurid thing, rather comical now, named *Life's Whirlpool,* with the Russian actress, Fania Marinoff, and Holbrook Blinn.

"When the picture's over," said Jungmeyer, "which will be about seven, we'll have dinner and compare notes."

On the screen a 20-stamp mill raised, dropped and pounded its iron shoes rhythmically, fading out to reveal the immense Mc-Teague pushing his car of ore through the murk of the tunnel. That's the Big Dipper mine, described in the book. It was closed down for a generation, almost, but revived for picture purposes.

Then was depicted the home of McTeague, with his worn mother slaving for a score of hungry miners in the kitchen. Then father McTeague, a roystering old sinner, boozing himself with harridans in the saloon, and his end, which comes suddenly, would have elated a temperance lecturer.

Then came a panorama of life in an old California mining camp, its types drawn from the uttermost ends of the earth; all very realistic, yet somehow with a glamour, that quality with which art and time invests everything.

Can art, even in the motion picture, come within a million miles of depicting actual life? Perhaps never. But the creative artist, and a director can be that, may create the illusion of life, and do well, if he does nothing else.

So far the picture was like the book, not a single detail omitted. It is evident that von Stroheim, sitting motionless in a straight chair, cane in hand and staring right ahead, as if boring through the screen, worships realism like an abstract ideal; worships it more, and suffers more in its achievement, than other men do for wealth or fame.

Twelve o'clock now, and McTeague is pulling teeth down in Howard Street. He yanks ivories from the jaws of derelicts and big sailors, with fine aplomb. Then a slangy dame guys him, and he wilts, to the uproar of the crowd, echoed by everyone in the little theater. Gibson Gowland plays McTeague with great naturalness.

Every episode is developed to the full, every comma of the book put in, as it were. Before our eyes was enacted the tale of McTeague's blundering courtship of Trina, the thrifty little toymaker. The scenes are Shell Mound Park, where the cool breeze snaps the flags; the Orpheum lobby, where little Owgoost makes an uproar and gets yanked; the Sieppe home, where a decent Swiss family eats enormous quantities of frankfurters and sauerkraut and children are brought up by a martinet of a papa, whose pomposity is comical even to the youngsters. If we mistake not, Chester Conklin makes Papa Sieppe one of the greatest humoristic studies of the screen.

One o'clock. Frank Norris was a great writer. Never took off his hat to truckle for pennies, not he; nor turn out bunkum to masquerade as art. This tale of his ranks with the modern masterpieces. Good as anything of Zola's, and better than most. The realism is getting relentless, but the humor is a good foil, and is full-bodied.

We wonder if pictures will ever be shown on the installment plan. Von Stroheim's *Foolish Wives* is shown in South America in 24 reels. You buy a pair of tickets and go two nights running. In the movie palaces there the films are shown with the house in total darkness, and two minutes before the lights are turned on, a warning bell is rung. That, you see, gives the ladies a chance to powder their noses, a very thoughtful idea, we think.

Now comes the romance of Maria Macapa and Zerkow, the junk man. Dale Fuller plays the cracked woman, and Caesar

Gravina, the greatest of screen clowns, a master of simple panto-
mime, the nearest we have today to Grimaldi, is the miser. The
man acts with his great brown eyes, like a dog's.

Two o'clock, and he marries her. The courtship and its aftermath are rare fantasy. Much as *Dr. Mabuse*. Few pictures are sound
enough in psychological hypothesis to warrant a moment's consideration. Off-hand, one can name but two, *Caligari*, with its
study of a diseased imagination, and this, showing the working
of a mind seized with avarice, that of a miser who marries solely to
hear a woman tell of riches that never existed outside of her own
head.

We cannot find a trace of the conventional in the narrative. All
is original. Drama is vigorously expounded.

The fault in motion pictures is obviousness, the stressing of the
trite. Time was when Buchowetzki, Seastrom, Lubitsch and others
in Europe, challenged American directors to incessant advance.
Now all three are in Hollywood, and properly Americanized, or
very nearly. Let us hope they will retain their magic, fight for a
degree of independence. The gifts they bring over with them are
not paper marks, but the native gold of genius.

Three o'clock. The murder of Maria is shown by shadow panto-
mime. Old Zerkow, having gone quite mad, is fished out of the bay.
Now begins the slow degradation of Trina, the loss of dignity, the
descent to ignoble poverty, though she has won thousands in a
lottery game.

Marcus Schouler, played by Jean Hersholt, with a gay and sinister
vividness, has wrought his evil, and McTeague, deprived of his
dental practice, sinks into the gutter. Step by step his fall is
depicted, much as that of the unhappy man in Dreiser's *Sister
Carrie*. Old Grannis works out his autumnal romance with the
little old lady of the next room. Frank Hayes is the actor; now
dead, he will live again in the shadows on the screen.

It is nearly five. All is immensely interesting, and laughter greets
the comedy touches, but we have to change chairs. German pro-
fessors sit for years before they develop "sitzfleisch." The Greeks

sat for hours on marble benches in their theaters. And so we tell von Stroheim.

He listened with his head thrust forward in alert politeness, and nodded.

"A great people, the Greeks," he said. "Their audiences were immense in the amphitheaters, sometimes 6,000, like football crowds today. A great audience deserves great drama. The great spectacular drama will be revived in America, and it will be taken in by the eye, not the ear." He nodded with earnest conviction. He believes in the motion picture.

Five-thirty, and McTeague draws near to his catastrophe. The psychoanalyst will perceive in ZaSu Pitts' delineation of Trina a laboratory study of masochism. She loves her husband, but stronger than her love is her passion for gold, though it scourges her broken body as with lacerating thongs.

Her end comes with the inevitableness of a Greek tragedy. Mc-Teague is drawn back to the haunts of his boyhood; an instinct known to the police. His conscience, like a will-o'-the-wisp, leads him a devious route to Death Valley, Trina's fortune in his saddle-bag, with Schouler, his Nemesis, riding hard on his trail.

It is almost seven. And we go through Emigant Canyon, past mountains of snowy porphyry, crowned with red diurite, a wilderness of incredible horror. This portion of *Greed* is already in the records of the Smithsonian. You consort with tarantulas, trading rats, chuckawallas, rattlers and such-like fauna. The sun beats brazenly on the sink of arsenical muck in the floor of the valley. McTeague meets his pursuer.

Schouler captures him. There is no water. McTeague slays his enemy, but seats himself on the sand, for he is enchained by the wrist to a dead man. In the sky a premonitory vulture hovers. . . .

Seven o'clock. The entire novel has been depicted.

Silence, then applause. The doors swing open and out we go into darkness.

"Pretty hard-boiled lot of picture fans, I'll say," muttered the gatekeeper with the ferocious dog which somehow failed to bite us, perhaps because we were so appreciative in our comments.

"We'll never have such a chance again," said Jungmeyer. "A chance to hear a show crowd departing without any complaints. Regular film gluttons. Too bad mortal clay demands it be compressed into 12 reels. The trick will be done nicely in a week. Now, about supper—"

We dined at the Writers' Club, with Rob Wagner, Jim Tully, the prizefighter novelist, and other interesting humans. Over coffee we philosophized over the art of the motion picture, of which we had enough for a day, a week, even. Then at a far table uprose that urbane young president of the Wampas, Joseph Jackson.

"Ladies and gentlemen," he said, "for dessert, so to speak, we will have on the screen a previewing of a picture in nine reels by Victor Seastrom."

But that, as Kipling would say, is another story.

FILMOGRAPHY

The nine major films directed by von Stroheim, including the unfinished ones, are starred. His contributions to the other films were those of an actor, technical or military advisor, art consultant, assistant director, or—as in the earliest group—an extra.

1914

1. **THE BIRTH OF A NATION.** Reliance-Majestic. Directed by D. W. Griffith. During its filming in 1914, von Stroheim got his first movie job as an extra; see pp. 37–39. The film was released in March, 1915.

1915

2. **CAPTAIN MACLEAN.** Griffith-Triangle. Directed by Jack Conway; assistant director, Emmet Flynn. Adapted from a novel by Richard Harding Davis. *Cast:* Lillian Gish, Jack Dillon, von Stroheim as an extra.

3. **GHOSTS.** Griffith-Mutual. Directed by George Nichols. Adapted by John Emerson from Ibsen's play. George Siegman and von Stroheim were assistant directors. *Cast:* Mary Alden, Henry Walthall and Nigel de Brulier, with von Stroheim in a bit part.

4. **OLD HEIDELBERG.** Griffith-Triangle. Directed by John Emerson. Assistant director and technical consultant, von Stroheim. *Cast:*
Wallace Reid, Dorothy Gish, Raymond Wells, von Stroheim playing his first real part, Lutz.

1916

5. **THE SOCIAL SECRETARY.** Griffith-Fine Arts. Directed by John Emerson. Scenario by Anita Loos. Assistant director, von Stroheim. *Cast:* Douglas Fairbanks, Norma Talmadge, Herbert Frank, von Stroheim as a "yellow journalist."

6. **INTOLERANCE.** Directed by D. W. Griffith, assisted by Tod Browning, Jack Conway, Christy Cabanne, Lloyd Ingram and George Nichols. Chief cameraman: G. W. Bitzer. Assistant directors: George Siegman, John Henaberry, W. S. Van Dyke, Bert Sutch and von Stroheim. In the large and historic cast (see page 65) of this four-part epic, von Stroheim played the Second Pharisee in the Judean story.

7. **MACBETH.** D. W. Griffith-Fine Arts Films. Directed by John Emerson. Assistant director, von Stroheim (his first screen credit

as such). *Cast:* Sir Herbert Beerbohm Tree, Constance Collier, Wilfred Lucas.

8. **HIS PICTURE IN THE PAPERS.** D. W. Griffith-Fine Arts. Directed by John Emerson. Scenario by Anita Loos. Assistant directors, von Stroheim, Emmet Flynn. *Cast:* Douglas Fairbanks, Loretta Blake, Nick Thompson, with von Stroheim as the villain.

9. **LESS THAN THE DUST.** Famous-Players-Lasky. Directed by John Emerson. Assistant directors, von Stroheim, Emmet Flynn. *Cast:* Mary Pickford, David Powell.

1917

10. **PANATHEA.** Joseph Schenck. Directed by Alan Dwan. Assistant directors, von Stroheim, Arthur Rosson. *Cast:* Norma Talmadge, George Fawcett, Earle Fox, with von Stroheim as a Russian police official.

11. **SYLVIA OF THE SECRET SERVICE.** Pathé. Directed by George Fitzmaurice. Assistant director and consultant, von Stroheim. *Cast:* Irene Castle, Elliot Dexter, von Stroheim.

12. **FOR FRANCE.** Vitagraph. Directed by Wesley Ruggles. *Cast:* Betty Howe, Edward Earle, with von Stroheim as a Prussian officer, his first important acting part.

1918

13. **THE UNBELIEVER.** Edison. Directed by Alan Crosland. Adapted from a novel by Mary Andrews. *Cast:* Marguerite Courtot, Raymond McKee, von Stroheim as the Hun.

14. **THE HUN WITHIN.** Famous-Players-Lasky. Directed by Christy Cabanne. *Cast:* George Fawcett, Douglas McLean, von Stroheim as the Hun.

15. **IN AGAIN, OUT AGAIN.** Fine Arts-Aircraft. Directed by John Emerson from a scenario by Anita Loos. Assistant director and consultant, von Stroheim. *Cast:* Douglas Fairbanks, Arline Pretty, Bull Montana, von Stroheim as a Russian officer.

16. **HEARTS OF THE WORLD.** A D. W. Griffith Production. Camera, G. W. Bitzer. Military advisor, von Stroheim. *Cast:* Lillian and Dorothy Gish, Robert Harron, George Fawcett, Josephine Crowell, George Nichols, Kate Bruce, Noel Coward, and von Stroheim as a Prussian officer.

17. **THE HEART OF HUMANITY.** Universal. Directed by Allen Jolubar. Military consultant, von Stroheim. *Cast:* Dorothy Phillips, William Stowell, von Stroheim as the Hun.

*18. **BLIND HUSBANDS.** Universal. 8 reels. Directed by von Stroheim. Scenario by von Stroheim, based on his own story, *The Pinnacle.* Camera, Ben Reynolds. Settings designed by von Stroheim. Shooting time, 7 weeks. Cutting by the director, with the assistance of Frank Lawrence and Viola Mailory.

Lieutenant von Steuben	Erich von Stroheim
Doctor Armstrong	Sam de Grasse
Mrs. Armstrong	Francela Billington
Sepp, the Mountain Guide	Gibson Gowland
Waitress	Fay Holderness
Newlyweds	Valerie Germonprez, Jack Perrin

Also Ruby Kendrick, Richard Cummings, Louis Fitzroy, William Duvalle, Percy Challenger, Jacques Mathes.

1919–1920

*19. THE DEVIL'S PASSKEY. Universal. 12 reels. Directed by von Stroheim. Scenario by von Stroheim, from a story by Baroness de Meyer. Camera, Ben Reynolds. Assistant director, Eddy Sowders. Settings designed by von Stroheim. Shooting time, 12 weeks.

Warren Goodwright	Sam de Grasse
Mrs. Goodwright	Una Trevelyan
La Belle Odera	Mae Busch
Rex Strong	Clyde Fillmore
Madame Malot	Maude George
Monsieur Malot	Leo White

1921

*20. FOOLISH WIVES. Universal. 32 reels filmed; 14 reels released. Directed from his own screenplay by von Stroheim. Camera, Ben Reynolds and William Daniels. Settings designed by von Stroheim and Captain Richard Day. Assistant directors, Eddy Sowders and Louis Germonprez. Musical score by Sigmund Romberg. Shooting time, 11 months.

"Count" Karamazin	Erich von Stroheim
"Princess" Olga	Maude George
"Princess" Vera	Mae Busch
U.S. Ambassador Hughes	George Christians
Mrs. Hughes	Miss Dupont (Armstrong)
Ventucci, the counterfeiter	Cesare Gravina
His daughter	Malvine Polo
Lady's maid	Dale Fuller

347

1922

*21. **MERRY-GO-ROUND.** Universal. 12 reels. Direction started by von Stroheim and completed by Rupert Julian. Produced by Irving Thalberg. Original story and screenplay by von Stroheim. Camera, Ben Reynolds and William Daniels. Assistant directors, Eddy Sowders and Louis Germonprez. Settings designed by von Stroheim and Captain Richard Day.

The Count	Norman Kerry
His fiancée	Dorothy Wallace
Mitzi	Mary Philbin
Her father	Cesare Gravina
Carousel owner	George Siegman (replacing Wallace Beery)
His wife	Dale Fuller
The hunchback	George Hackathorn
Count's valet	Albert Conti
Emperor Franz-Josef	Anton Wawerka
The groom	Sidney Bracey
The madam	Maude George

1923–1924

*22. **GREED.** Metro-Goldwyn-Mayer. Filmed in 42 reels; released in 10 reels. Screenplay by von Stroheim based on Frank Norris' novel, *McTeague.* Camera, Ben Reynolds, William Daniels, Ernest B. Schoedsack. Assistant directors, Eddy Sowders and Louis Germonprez. Settings designed by Captain Richard Day. Cut to 24 reels by von Stroheim; 18 reels by Rex Ingram; 10 reels by Joe W. Farnham. Shooting time, 9 months.

McTeague	Gibson Gowland
Trina Sieppe	ZaSu Pitts
Marcus Schouler	Jean Hersholt
Maria Macapa	Dale Fuller
Zerkow	Cesare Gravina
Papa Sieppe	Chester Conklin
Mama Sieppe	Sylvia Ashton
August Sieppe	Austen Jewel
Sieppe Twins	Oscar & Otto Gottel
Old Grannis	Frank Hayes
Miss Baker	Fannie Midgley
Uncle Oelberman	Max Tyron

Cousin Selina	Joan Standing
Heise	Hughie Mack
Mrs. Heise	Tiny Jones
Traveling dentist	Erik von Ritzau
McTeague's father	Jack Curtis
His mother	Tempe Pigott
Cribbons	Jack McDonald
Sheriff	James Fulton
Lottery agent	Lon Poff
Mrs. Ryer	Reta Revela
Old hag	Florence Gibson
Deputy sheriff	James Gibson

1925

*23. THE MERRY WIDOW. Metro-Goldwyn-Mayer. Filmed in 14 reels; released in 12. Screenplay by von Stroheim and Benjamin Glazer, based on the Victor Leon-Leo Stein operetta. Camera, Ben Reynolds and William Daniels; color sequences by Oliver T. Marsh. Settings designed by Captain Richard Day and Cedric Gibbons. Assistant directors, Eddy Sowders and Louis Germonprez. Arrangement of Franz Lehar score by Mendoza and Axt. Shooting time, 12 weeks.

Prince Danilo	John Gilbert
Sally O'Hara	Mae Murray
Crown Prince Mirko	Roy d'Arcy
Baron Sixtus Sadoja	Tully Marshall
King Nikita	George Fawcett
Queen Milena	Josephine Crowell
Adjutant to Danilo	Albert Conti
Adjutant to Mirko	Don Ryan
Innkeeper	Hughie Mack
Danilo's footman	Sidney Bracey
Sadoja's maid	Dale Fuller
Janitor	George Nichols

1926–1928

*24. THE WEDDING MARCH. Paramount. Directed by von Stroheim. Screenplay by von Stroheim. Camera, Ben Reynolds and Hal Mohr. Settings designed by Captain Richard Day. Musical score by L. Zamecnik. Filmed in 24 reels in two parts, intended as a single film with intermission. Part one, *The Wedding March*, 14 reels, was released in America; part two, *The Honeymoon*, 10 reels, was released only in Europe, von Stroheim having refused permission for American release because it was not cut by him. The definitive editing of the film was done in 1954 for the Cinémathèque Française by von Stroheim, Denise Vernac, and Renée Lichtig.

Prince Nicki	Erich von Stroheim
His father, Prince Ottokar	George Fawcett
His mother, Princess Maria	Maude George
Mitzi	Fay Wray
Mitzi's father, a violinist	Cesare Gravina
His wife, Katherina	Dale Fuller
Wine-garden keeper	Hughie Mack
His son, the butcher, Schani	Matthew Betz
The Magnate, Schweisser	George Nichols
His daughter, Cecilia	ZaSu Pitts
Emperor Franz-Josef	Anton Wawerka
Valet	Sidney Bracey
Mountain idiot	Danny Hoy
Servant	Lulee Wilse

Officers of the Imperial Guard: Captain Peters, von Hartman, Carey Harrison, Schuman Heink, Harry Rinehardt, Don Ryan, Albert Conti, William von Brincken.

1928

*25. QUEEN KELLY. Joseph Kennedy-Gloria Swanson-United Artists. Directed by von Stroheim. Based on his story, *The Swamp*. Unfinished; only 10 reels of the 25 or so planned by von Stroheim were completed before work was halted by the producers. Camera, Gordon Pollock and Paul Ivano. Assistant directors, Eddy Sowders and Louis Germonprez. Settings designed by Harold Miles. Musical score by Adolf Tandler. In the 8-reel version released by Miss Swanson, an ending was filmed for her by Irving Thalberg.

Kitty Kelly	Gloria Swanson
Prince Wolfram	Walter Byron
Queen	Seena Owen
Prince's valet	Sidney Bracey
Prince's aide	William von Brincken
Kelly's aunt	Sylvia Ashton
Old planter Vooyheid	Tully Marshall

1929

26. **THE GREAT GABBO.** Cruze-Sono Arts. Directed by James Cruze. Screenplay by Ben Hecht. Von Stroheim played the title role, with a cast including Betty Compson, Donald Douglas, Margie King and Helen Kane.

1931

27. **THREE FACES EAST.** Warner Bros. Directed by Roy del Ruth. Von Stroheim played the part of Valdar. The cast included Constance Bennett, Crawford Kent, Anthony Bushell, William Courtney and Charlotte Walker.

28. **FRIENDS AND LOVERS.** RKO. Directed by Victor Schertzinger.

Besides von Stroheim, the cast included Lily Damita, Laurence Olivier, Adolphe Menjou and Hugh Herbert.

1932

29. **THE LOST SQUADRON.** RKO. Directed by George Archainbaud and Paul Sloane. Von Stroheim played the mad film director. In the cast, Richard Dix, Mary Astor and Joel McCrea.

30. **AS YOU DESIRE ME.** MGM. Directed by George Fitzmaurice. Screenplay adapted from Pirandello. Greta Garbo starred, von Stroheim was featured; Hedda Hopper, Melvyn Douglas, Owen Moore in the cast.

1932–1933

*31. **WALKING DOWN BROADWAY.** 20th Century-Fox. Produced by Winfield Sheehan. Screenplay by von Stroheim and Leonard Spiegelgass after a novel by Dawn Powell. Camera, James Wong Howe.

Millie	Boots Mallory
Peggy	ZaSu Pitts
Jimmy	James Dunn
Mac	Terrance Ray
Prostitute	Minna Gombell

This, his first sound film, was left unfinished and unedited by von Stroheim. In Sheehan's absence, producer Sol Wurtzel fired von Stroheim. New scenes were directed by Alfred Werker and Edwin Burke. The version released in May 1933 was edited by Frank E. Hull and was called *Hello, Sister!*

1934

32. **CRIMSON ROMANCE.** Mascot-Nat Levine. Directed by David Howard. Von Stroheim played a German aviator with Ben Lyon,

and Sari Maritza, William von Brincken.

33. **FUGITIVE ROAD.** Invincible. Directed by Frank Strayer. Von

Stroheim was consultant, worked on the script, and acted the part of Captain von Traunsee.

1935

34. **THE CRIME OF DR. CRESPI.** Republic. Directed by John Auer. Based on a Poe story. Von Stroheim played the title role.

1936

35. **THE EMPEROR'S CANDLESTICKS.** MGM. Directed by George Fitzmaurice. Von Stroheim collaborated on the screenplay.

36. **SAN FRANCISCO.** MGM. Directed by W. S. Van Dyke. Von Stroheim collaborated on the dialogue.

37. **THE DEVIL DOLL.** Directed by Tod Browning. Von Stroheim collaborated on the screenplay.

38. **BETWEEN TWO WOMEN.** MGM. Directed by George Seitz. Original screenplay, *General Hospital*, by von Stroheim.

39. **MARTHE RICHARD, AU SERVICE DE LA FRANCE.** Paris-Film. Directed by Raymond Bernard. Music by Arthur Honegger. Screenplay by Steve Passeur, from original story by Commandant Ladoux. VS as von Ludlow; with Edwige Feuillère, Jean Galland, Délia Col, Marcel Dalio.

40. **LA GRANDE ILLUSION.** R.A.C. Directed by Jean Renoir. Screenplay by Charles Spaak. Art director, Jean Lourie. VS as von Rauffenstein; with Jean Gabin, Pierre Fresnay, Marcel Dalio, Carette, Dita Parlo, Gaston Modot, Georges Peclet, Jean Daste, Sylvain Itkine.

41. **L'ALIBI.** Eclair-Journal. Directed by Pierre Chenal. Screenplay by Jacques Companeez, from the play by Marcel Achard. Music by Georges Auric. VS as Professor Winkler; with Albert Préjean, Jany Holt, Louis Jouvet, Margo Lion, Phillipe Richard, Roger Blin, Foun Sen, Florence Marly.

42. **MADEMOISELLE DOCTEUR.** Trafalgar. Filmed in England. Directed by Edmond Greville. Produced by Max Schach. Screenplay by Ernest Betts and Rudolph Bernauer. Photography by Otto Heller. Music by Hans May. VS as Colonel Mathesius; with Dita Parlo, Claire Luce, John Loder, Clifford Evans, Gyles Isham, John Abbott, Raymond Lovell, Edward Lexy.

43. **L'AFFAIRE LAFARGE.** Osso-Trianon. Directed by Pierre Chenal. Screenplay by Ernest Fornairon. Music by Georges Auric. VS as Denis; with Marcelle Chantal, Pierre Renoir, Raymond Rouleau, Margo Lion, Sylvie, Florence Marly, Sylvette Fillacier, René Bergeron, Boverio, Palau.

1938

44. **LES PIRATES DU RAIL.** Osso. Directed by Christian-Jaque. Screenplay by O. P. Gilbert. VS as Tchou Kin; with Charles Vanel, Suzy Prim, Simone Re-

nant, Marcel Dalio, Lucas Gridoux.

45. **LES DISPARUS DE SAINT-AGIL.** Vog-Dimeco. Directed by Christian Jaque. Screenplay by Leo Lania with dialogue by Jacques Prevert. Camera, Marcel Lucien. Music by Henri Verdun. VS, Michel Simon, Aime Clariond, Robert Le Vigan, Jean Claudio.

46. **ULTIMATUM.** Pan Films. Directed by Robert Wiene. With VS, Dita Parlo.

47. **GIBRALTAR.** Osso-Safor. Directed by Fedor Ozep. With VS, Viviane Romance.

1939
48. **DERRIERE LA FAÇADE.** Regina Francinex. Directed by Yves Mirande and Georges Lacombe. VS, Jules Berry, Michel Simon.

49. **RAPPEL IMMEDIAT.** *Milo*-Sirius. Directed by Léon Mathot. VS, Mireille Balin, Denise Vernac.

50. **MENACES.** G.E.C.E. Directed by Edmond T. Gréville. With VS, Mireille Balin, John Loder, Denise Vernac.

51. **PIEGES.** Speva Discina. Directed by Robert Siodmak. VS, Maurice Chevalier, Marie Dea, Pierre Renoir.

52. **LE MONDE TREMBLERA OI LA REVOLTE DES VIVANTS.** C.S.C.S. Directed by Richard Pottier. VS, Claude Dauphin, Madeleine Sologne, Julien Carette.

53. **TEMPETE SUR PARIS.** Discina. Directed by Bernard Deschamps. VS, Arletty, Annie Ducaux, Marcel Dalio.

54. **MACAO, L'ENFER DU JEU.** Paris-Films. Directed by Jean Delannoy. VS, Mireille Balin, Sessue Hayakawa.

55. **PARIS-NEW YORK.** Regina-Film. Directed by Yves Mirande and Claude Heymann. Filmed on the *Normandie*. VS, Gaby Morley, Michel Simon, Claude Dauphin.

1940
56. **I WAS AN ADVENTURESS.** 20th Century-Fox. Directed by Gregory Ratoff. VS, Peter Lorre, Richard Greene, Vera Zorina, Sig Rumann.

1941
57. **SO ENDS OUR NIGHT.** United Artists. Directed by John Cromwell. VS, Fredric March, Glenn Ford, Frances Dee, Margaret Sullavan, Anna Sten.

1943
58. **FIVE GRAVES TO CAIRO.** Paramount-Charles Brackett. Directed by Billy Wilder. VS, Franchot Tone, Anne Baxter, Akim Tamiroff.

59. **NORTH STAR.** Produced by Sam Goldwyn for RKO. Directed by Lewis Milestone. Screenplay by Lillian Hellman. VS, Anne Baxter, Dana Andrews, Walter Huston, Walter Brennan, Farley Granger.

1944

60. **THE LADY AND THE MONSTER.** Republic. Directed by George Sherman. VS, Richard Arlen, Vera Ralston.

61. **STORM OVER LISBON.** Republic. Directed by George Sherman. VS, Vera Ralston, Richard Arlen, Otto Kruger.

1945

62. **THE GREAT FLAMMARION.** Republic. Directed by Anthony Mann. VS, Dan Duryea, Mary Beth Hughes.

63. **SCOTLAND YARD INVESTIGATOR.** Republic. Directed by George Blair. VS, C. Aubrey Smith.

1946

64. **THE MASK OF DIJON.** P.R.C.V. Directed by Lew Landers. VS, Denise Vernac, Jeanne Bates.

65. **LA FOIRE AUX CHIMERES.** Cinéma National. Directed by Pierre Chenal. VS, Madeleine Sologne.

66. **ON NE MEURT PAS COMME ÇA.** Neubach-Tarcali. Directed by Jean Boyer. VS, Denise Vernac.

1947

67. **LA DANSE DE MORT.** Alcina. Directed by Marcel Cravenne. From Strindberg's play *The Dance of Death*. Von Stroheim collaborated on adaptation and dialogue. VS, Denise Vernac, Jean Servais.

1948

68. **LE SIGNAL ROUGE.** Neubach-Pen Film. Directed by Ernest Neubach. VS, Denise Vernac.

1949

69. **PORTRAIT D'UN ASSASSIN.** P.S.-E.C.A. Paris. Directed by Bernard Roland. VS, Arletty, Pierre Brasseur, Marcel Dalio, Jules Berry, Maria Montez.

1950

70. **SUNSET BOULEVARD.** Paramount-Charles Brackett. Directed by Billy Wilder. Screenplay by Billy Wilder, Charles Brackett and D. M. Marshman. Photographed by John Seitz. VS, William Holden, Gloria Swanson, Jack Webb, Fred Clark, Cecil B. DeMille, Hedda Hopper, Buster Keaton, Anna Q. Nilsson, H. B. Warner.

1951

71. **MINUIT, QUAI DE BERCY.** E.T.-P.C. Directed by Christian Stengel. VS, Madeleine Robinson.

1952

72. **L'ENVERS DU PARADIS.** Pafico. Directed and written by Edmond T. Gréville. VS, Denise Vernac.

1953

73. **ALERTE AU SUD.** Neptune-Sirius. Directed and written by Jean Devaivre. Filmed in Morocco. Jean-Claude Pascal, VS, Lia Amonda.

74. **ALRAUNE.** Styria-Carlton. Filmed in West Germany. Di-

rected by Arthur Maria Rabenalt. VS, Hildegard Neff, Denise Vernac.

1954

75. NAPOLEON. Directed and written by Sacha Guitry. With Sacha Guitry, and 102 other leading actors, including VS as Beethoven.

76. SERIE NOIRE. Pathé. Directed by Pierre Foucaud. VS, Henri Vidal, Monique van Vooren, Robert Hossein.

1955

77. L'HOMME AUX CENT VISAGES (MAN OF A HUNDRED FACES). Nasht Film. Directed by Robert Spafford. A twenty-minute pilot film for a projected TV series. VS, Denise Vernac, Pascale Roberts.

78. LA MADONE DES SLEEPINGS. Le Film d'Art. Directed by Henri Diamant-Berger. VS, Gisèle Pascal, Denise Vernac.

BIBLIOGRAPHY

Barna, Jon. *Stroheim*. Osterreichisches Film-museum, Vienna, 1966.

Bergut, Bob. *Erich von Stroheim*. Le Terrain Vague, Paris, 1960.

Bianco e Nero. Special issue on von Stroheim. Nos. 2 and 3 (February-March) Rome, 1959.

Bondy, François, "Erich von Stroheim: Zwischen zwei Legenden," in *Der Monat*, Berlin, February, 1967.

Costello, G. C. and Buache, F. *Erich von Stroheim*. Premier Plan (29), Paris, 1963.

Curtiss, Thomas Quinn, *Erich von Stroheim*, préfaces par René Clair et Jean Renoir, Editions France-Empire, 1970.

Etudes Cinématographiques. *Erich von Stroheim*. Nos. 48-50. Paris, 1966.

Finler, Joel W. *Stroheim*. University of California Press, Berkeley, California, 1968.

Gobeil, Charlotte, editor. *Hommage à von Stroheim: A Tribute*. Canadian Film Institute, Ottawa, 1966.

Guttinger, Fritz, "Frank Norris," in *Neue Zurcher Zeitung*, Zurich, July, 1964.

Koszarski, Richard, "Hello, Sister!" in *Sight and Sound*, London, Autumn, 1970.

Lambert, Gavin, "Stroheim Revisited," in *Sight and Sound*, London, Spring, 1953.

Marion, Denis, "Stroheim, the Legend and the Fact," in *Sight and Sound*, London, Winter, 1961–62.

Noble, Peter, *Hollywood Scapegoat*, Fortune Press, London, 1951.

von Stroheim, Erich. *Greed*, the screenplay, Cinémathèque de Belgique, 1958. Also see final entry under Herman G. Weinberg. *Les Feux de la Saint-Jean*, volume 1, "Veronica"; volume 2, "Constanzia," André Martel, Paris, 1954. *Paprika*, Macauley, New York, 1935; Butterworth, London, 1936; André Martel, Paris, 1949. *Poto-Poto*, Editions de la Fontaine, Paris, 1956.

Weinberg, Herman G. "Another Film Carnage," *Cinema Quarterly*, London, Summer, 1933; "Erich von Stroheim," *Film Art*, London, Spring, 1937; "An Index to the Creative Work of Erich von Stroheim," Supplement to *Sight & Sound*, British Film Institute,

London, June, 1943; "The Work of Stroheim" in *The Work of the Great Film Directors*, Dennis Dobson, London, 1950; "Stroheim's Place in Film History," in *Hollywood Scapegoat* by Peter Noble, 1951; "Greed," *Cinemages*, New York, Spring, 1955; "Two Synopses: 'Queen Kelly' and 'Walking Down Broadway,'" *Film Culture*, No. 1, New York, Spring, 1955; "A Footnote to Foolish Wives," *Film Culture* No. 18, New York, April, 1958; "Erich von Stroheim," *Introduction to the Art of the Movies* by Lewis Jacobs, Farrar, Straus and Giroux, New York, 1960; "The Legion of Lost Films," *Sight & Sound*, London, Autumn, 1962; "A Note on 'The Wedding March,'" *Montreal Film Festival Souvenir Program*, Montreal, Summer, 1964; Interview, *Objectif*, No. 29-30, Montreal, 1964; "A Note on 'The Wedding March,'" "The True Films Maudits of the Cinema," "Greed," "Two Synopses: 'Queen Kelly' and 'Walking Down Broadway,'" "Coffee, Brandy & Cigars XXX," *Hommage à Erich von Stroheim*, Canadian Film Institute, Ottawa, February, 1966; "Erich von Stroheim," *Interviews with Film Directors*, edited by Andrew Sarris, Bobbs-Merrill, New York, 1967 and Avon Books, New York, 1967; "A Footnote to 'Foolish Wives'" and "Coffee, Brandy & Cigars XXX," *Film Culture Reader*, Praeger, New York, 1970; "Erich von Stroheim," "Greed," "Merry-Go-Round," "Queen Kelly" in *Saint Cinema*, DBS Publications, New York, 1970.